Discourse and Social Media

Discourse and Social Media is a unique and timely collection that breaks ground on how discourse scholars, coming from a range of disciplinary perspectives, can critically analyse different social media, including YouTube, Facebook, Twitter and news content. The book fills a gap in the market for a multi-disciplinary collection for analysing the discourse of social media.

In providing a thorough review of the field to date, the opening chapter considers some of the common and divergent interests and priorities that exist in social media discourse analysis. It also discusses the wider methodological and theoretical implications that social media analysis brings to the process of discourse analysis, as new forms of connections and communication call us to re-think the static models that we have been using. The rest of the collection draws on different traditions in discourse studies, including Critical Discourse Analysis, Sociolinguistics, Pragmatics, Foucaultian analysis and Multimodality, to bring several unique approaches to critically analysing social media from a discourse perspective. Each ground-breaking chapter shows how different forms of social media data can best be selected, analysed and dealt with critically.

As a whole, *Discourse and Social Media* provides a go-to resource for social media scholars, as well as graduate students. The book is a significant contribution to the development of the field at this present shifting time.

This book was originally published as a special issue of the *Journal of Multicultural Discourses*.

Gwen Bouvier is Assistant Professor in New Media at Zayed University, Abu Dhabi, UAE. Her main areas of research interest are social media, the Middle East region and news representation. Her recent publications have focused on 9/11 and representation, discourse analysis, social media and the visual (mis)representation of crises in news.

Discourse and Social Media

Edited by
Gwen Bouvier

LONDON AND NEW YORK

First published 2016
by Routledge
2 Park Square, Milton Park, Abingdon, Oxon, OX14 4RN, UK

and by Routledge
711 Third Avenue, New York, NY 10017, USA

Routledge is an imprint of the Taylor & Francis Group, an informa business

© 2016 Taylor & Francis

All rights reserved. No part of this book may be reprinted or reproduced
or utilised in any form or by any electronic, mechanical, or other means,
now known or hereafter invented, including photocopying and recording,
or in any information storage or retrieval system, without permission in
writing from the publishers.

Trademark notice: Product or corporate names may be trademarks or
registered trademarks, and are used only for identification and
explanation without intent to infringe.

British Library Cataloguing in Publication Data
A catalogue record for this book is available from the British Library

ISBN 13: 978-1-138-19155-6

Typeset in Times New Roman
by RefineCatch Limited, Bungay, Suffolk

Publisher's Note
The publisher accepts responsibility for any inconsistencies that may have
arisen during the conversion of this book from journal articles to book chapters,
namely the possible inclusion of journal terminology.

Disclaimer
Every effort has been made to contact copyright holders for their permission to
reprint material in this book. The publishers would be grateful to hear from any
copyright holder who is not here acknowledged and will undertake to rectify
any errors or omissions in future editions of this book.

Contents

Citation Information	vii

1. What is a discourse approach to Twitter, Facebook, YouTube and other social media: connecting with other academic fields   1
Gwen Bouvier

2. The pursuit of power in Iraqi political discourse: unpacking the construction of sociopolitical communities on Facebook   15
Thulfiqar H. Al-Tahmazi

3. YouTube as a site of debate through populist politics: the case of a Turkish protest pop video   32
Lyndon C.S. Way

4. 'Should each of us take over the role as watcher?' Attitudes on Twitter towards the 2014 Norwegian terror alert   49
Joel Rasmussen

5. Radicalist discourse: a study of the stances of Nigeria's *Boko Haram* and Somalia's *Al Shabaab* on Twitter   66
Innocent Chiluwa

6. Visual forms of address in social media discourse: the case of a science communication website   88
Yiqiong Zhang, David Machin and Tao Song

7. Food fight: conflicting language ideologies in English and French news and social media   105
Rachelle Vessey

Index	125

Citation Information

The chapters in this book were originally published in the *Journal of Multicultural Discourses*, volume 10, issue 2 (July 2015). When citing this material, please use the original page numbering for each article, as follows:

Chapter 1
What is a discourse approach to Twitter, Facebook, YouTube and other social media: connecting with other academic fields?
Gwen Bouvier
Journal of Multicultural Discourses, volume 10, issue 2 (July 2015) pp. 149–162

Chapter 2
The pursuit of power in Iraqi political discourse: unpacking the construction of sociopolitical communities on Facebook
Thulfiqar H. Al-Tahmazi
Journal of Multicultural Discourses, volume 10, issue 2 (July 2015) pp. 163–179

Chapter 3
YouTube as a site of debate through populist politics: the case of a Turkish protest pop video
Lyndon C.S. Way
Journal of Multicultural Discourses, volume 10, issue 2 (July 2015) pp. 180–196

Chapter 4
'Should each of us take over the role as watcher?' Attitudes on Twitter towards the 2014 Norwegian terror alert
Joel Rasmussen
Journal of Multicultural Discourses, volume 10, issue 2 (July 2015) pp. 197–213

Chapter 5
Radicalist discourse: a study of the stances of Nigeria's Boko Haram *and Somalia's* Al Shabaab *on Twitter*
Innocent Chiluwa
Journal of Multicultural Discourses, volume 10, issue 2 (July 2015) pp. 214–235

CITATION INFORMATION

Chapter 6
Visual forms of address in social media discourse: the case of a science communication website
Yiqiong Zhang, David Machin and Tao Song
Journal of Multicultural Discourses, volume 10, issue 2 (July 2015) pp. 236–252

Chapter 7
Food fight: conflicting language ideologies in English and French news and social media
Rachelle Vessey
Journal of Multicultural Discourses, volume 10, issue 2 (July 2015) pp. 253–271

For any permission-related enquiries please visit:
http://www.tandfonline.com/page/help/permissions

What is a discourse approach to Twitter, Facebook, YouTube and other social media: connecting with other academic fields

Gwen Bouvier

College of Communication and Media Studies and Zayed University

> The wider field of discourse studies is still only beginning to turn its attention to social media despite a number of notable scholarly works. But as yet there has been little that has dealt specifically with issues of multicultural discourse – how language, identity, cross-cultural social relations and power play out in the rapidly evolving landscape of social media. In this paper, I show why discourse studies must engage with theories and empirical work on social media across academic fields beyond discourse studies and linguistics, at how these can help best frame the kinds of research that needs to be done, how to best formulate some of the basic questions of critical discourse analysis for this new communicative environment. I use this as a platform to point to the areas where multicultural discourse studies can work – where all the ambiguities of former studies of 'identity' and 'culture' are present, but realised in new ways. Yet these new forms of communication are fused into wider patterns of changing cultural values about forms of social structure, knowledge itself and the kinds of issues that tend to form our individually civic spheres.

Introduction

This special edition of *Journal of Multicultural Discourses* brings together a set of papers that take different approaches to the study of discourse and social media, with an emphasis on issues of culture and identity. Social media offer new challenges and new possibilities, and create new requirements for the study of multicultural discourses, for which, I want to show, we would be wise to engage across the scholarly work in a number of academic fields in order to help gauge priorities and to place our work well in the landscape of social media research.

The *Journal of Multicultural Discourses* can play an important role in promoting the role of culture in discourse studies, where social media now provide a site of fundamental shifts in communicative practices, genres and modalities. Such a contribution is important to offset the emphasis on work that tends to focus on the 'global centres', driven partly by the way that networks have tended to be driven by Anglo-American and English language academic publishing (Larsson 2009) with the consequent definitions of theories, concepts and prioritised topics (Shi 2013). The journal has aimed to foreground studies which help us to understand the ways in which different cultural communities interact differently, in terms of worldviews, concepts, values, rules, strategies, means, channels, purposes and consequences. And in this introduction I want to make the case for why social media provide one central site where we can, and should, carry out this important work. Discourse studies should certainly have more to say about this, especially given the pace of processes of globalisation, where it is important to understand not only these worldviews in themselves but also the ways in which these interact and are in transformation. Social media are part of this, now fused into the fabric of everyday life, providing new possibilities for intercontinental communication, new ways of maintaining, creating, or imagining cultural communities and identities, and new ways of combining more locally nuanced ideas, values and identities (Shi 2014).

Social media, globalisation and culture

Blommaert (2010, 1) pointed out that globalisation does not lead to a 'global village' but to a complex web of parts, interconnected in different ways and to different degrees. And with new forms of connections and communication possible through social media, this transformation calls us also to re-think the static models that we have been using. For Blommaert, it calls for a whole new vocabulary and new kinds of arguments to explain what we are seeing. Multicultural discourse studies needs to study social media to look at these more or less interconnected parts, at the way that ideas and values are shared or not shared, and consider the linguistic tools and modes deployed to do so. And importantly, it needs to engage with the wider issue of power. We live in a world dominated by some key kinds of power relations, specifically with the continued dominance and global spread of free-market capitalism. What may not be so important is how and if people are different, but the nature of the wider power relations that they inhabit and how these may be influenced by shifts in the communications landscape. In this world where social media are fused into everyday lives, this is a crucial part of this study, but which demands new ways of thinking. Later in this introduction I want to return to the kinds of power interests scholars identify as driving social media platforms.

Globalisation has also brought population shifts and migration, although it is often the migrant wage labourers who are the least rewarded by these shifts. These too involve issues of intercultural communication, as migrants use social media to link with more established migrants and foster new ties, which can aid and make the whole process much easier (Dekker & Engbersen 2014) and faster, while at the same time providing an 'ambient' sense of home (Komito 2011, 1075). Charmarkeh (2013) shows how Somali refugees used Facebook in cybercafes to maintain contacts with other refugees met while in transit countries, and also to seek out contacts and romantic connections once in Europe. It has also been shown how diasporic social media groups can become highly radicalised and xenophobic (Conversi 2012). But migration can also create a situation in which existing citizens feel there is need to compete for material and symbolic resources (van Dijk 1996), sometimes leading to surges in interest in far right parties. But overall, these too involve interplays of worldviews, values and concepts, yet are played out under the dominant system of the ideology of neoliberalism, where concerns and fears are 'shared' and 'liked' through the social media embedded in the lives of the participants (Correa et al. 2010).

Castells (2000, 3) once argued that in a world of cross-national media flows, where former institutions break down, the search for identity becomes a key source of social meaning. And it seems that for many, as Livingstone (2008) suggests, creating and networking online content is becoming an integral means of managing one's identity, lifestyle and social relations. Some theorise the very use of sites as fundamentally performative acts (Cover 2012). Social media are one place where we can study just how this plays out. Particularly, as some scholars have argued, this has been accompanied with massive shifts in what people present about themselves for public knowledge (Nussbaum 2007). And certainly what is clear from studies of social media is that it is used for a combination of identity construction, the maintenance of social relationships and also to engage with more socially relevant matters. All of the papers in this special edition, despite their wide range of interests and theoretical approaches, point to such combinations.

Social media and cross-cultural sharing

De Zuniga et al. (2012) argue that the growing popularity of social media has created a debate: Do these Internet services contribute to society by allowing people to become informed, find common causes and participate in public life more often (e.g. Bennett 2008)? In this sense, is there a place for greater cross-cultural sharing? Or do they foster shallower relationships, distract people from public affairs and deepen their political and civic disengagement (e.g. Hodgkinson 2008)? As such, do social media lead to increasingly disengaged and insular forms of ideas, values, concepts, worldviews and means of realising these? Social media are social, but only in an immediate sense. The works of Lindgren (2010) and Georgakopoulou (2014) suggest that discussions of socio-political issues online do not deal with actual details but rather seek to frame events into pre-existing personal interests and alignments. Some scholars are more optimistic. Hilbert (2009) argues that people may well use social media for personal identity construction, but they may still use, contribute and share information that has civic relevance. It is to this kind of debate that two papers in this collection, by Way, in his study of YouTube posts about political protests in Turkey, and by Thulfiqar, about political views on Facebook in Iraq, make less than optimistic contributions.

Social theorists make some important observations about the wider shifts that online interactions may both be part of and a symptom of. Žižek (1997) pointed to his concerns that language in forums and blogs ceases to be 'subjectivized'. Simply by this he meant that users of a forum do not have to stand by what they say. They can intervene and then disappear, and can simply unhook if they do not like a response or want to escape the consequences of what they have said. An exit from social media is always just a click away. Users can leave a harsh comment and then come back several days later to see its effects. Dean (2010) points to the way that this can lead to discussion threads quickly disintegrating. Members unsubscribe, feeling attacked and embarrassed. The imbalance between participants and lurkers, who may appear suddenly, in threaded discussions can also add to this problem. In fact, Johnson (2001, 143) argues that when you consider the proportions of lurkers to discussants in a particular forum it is in fact less interactive than a face-to-face lecture and much less so than a conversation around a dinner table. In the light of Blommaert's (2010) comments about the need for discourse studies to adapt, are new approaches and tools needed to deal with these changes?

Dean (2010) adds a further point as regards this tendency to find snark comments on social media forums. She suggests that the Internet, the culture of engagement, of participation and of scan-and-go, has generated scepticism. This can be traced to the collapse of a sense of the 'big other', as Žižek (1997) would describe it, in other words a waning of the force of a central, forceful and institutional body of knowledge and is commonly agreed upon, or at least enforced, ideas, values and identities. Hardt and Negri (2000) saw this decline as resulting in a shift from a culture defined by the role of the citizen subject with more determined identifications to a culture that continually offers new ways to imagine ourselves. Dean (2010, 5) refers to this new situation as the culture of 'communicative capitalism'. In sum, a decline of 'the symbolic', or 'the decline of symbolic efficiency', to use Žižek's exact words, leaves a gap into which the images and effects of social media can be poured (Dean 2010, 5). On the one hand, this leads to a shift of more specialist kinds of forums and online spaces, often with their own more specialist language and terms that can easily exclude, annoy and confuse the outsider. On the other hand, Myers (2010) shows that successful blogs simply *should* have such specialist language as part of signalling a community of shared interest. Downey and Fenton (2003) point to a trend whereby political activist sites on social media can easily become radical, inhospitable ghettos. In this sense, much is to be established in a discursive sense as regards social media groupings, where more localised identities, ideas and values are celebrated as regards how esoteric there are. I will consider the research implications for such issues shortly. But clearly, this marks a requirement for the new kinds of approaches and tools, to which Blommaert refers, as we shift away from either highly personalised or mass media-based texts. And it also raises the question as to whether such shifts so adequately apply cross-culturally. Do the arguments of Žižek and others apply so well in cultures with very different histories, ideas and values? Are these 'symbolic gaps' of the same order?

For Dean (2010), the decline of the symbolic has a further consequence which may have great relevance for intercultural communication through social media. She suggests that along with the demise of central authoritative ideas and identities that the Internet with its culture of engagement, of participation and of scan-and-go has generated scepticism. This scepticism means that users tend to regard comments always as opinion and not as information, which in turn means that we tend not to engage in receptive discussion but fall back on what is comfortable. All else is just opinion. And this too chimes with the kinds of wider changes observed by sociologists where there has been a shift to placing emphasis on the personal-as-political and where this is realised in a world where everything is supposed to be rewarding (Chaney 1996). Studies of the discourses in forum posts about important civic issues such as shootings in schools (Lindgren 2012) or pressing political events such as the economic crisis in Greece (Georgakopoulou 2014) become, rather, launch pads for existing views on gun control or xenophobic ideas about Germans. There was little evidence of receptivity. In this collection, the papers by Way and by Rasmussen both allow us to think a little more about these processes in very different contexts and on different social media platforms.

Understanding multicultural discourse now means, in part, acknowledging that acts of communication take place in these broader changes. Coupland (2010) pointed out that it was time for linguistics to engage with such wider forces sweeping the planet. Globalisations, shifts in technologies and forms of communication are all interlinked. While discourse analysts have skills specialist for closer analysis, the details found at this level will be shaped by the macro. And, crucially, this whole is driven by the forces of global consumer capitalism. I say a little more about this that follows, and why social media may tie into this in quite specific ways. It has been the case that discourse analysts have been less strong in connecting to these larger matters, such as the political economy of the media.

The political economy of social media

Early studies of the Internet were extremely optimistic, associating it with the liberation of the voice of the public taking power back from the arrogant big media (Bolter 1996) and how the structural features of online spaces facilitated self-presentation and expression (Papacharissi 2002, 2007). At least social media offer people an opportunity to share mostly unfiltered opinions and allow a greater variety of ideas and opinions to be available in the public sphere (Gillmor 2006). But more recently, scholars have turned their attention to the ways in which social media platforms directly profit from the activities of users, which in turn can provide information favourable to the interests of the state (Fuchs 2014), and have questioned how this is shaping their nature.

Social media are driven by the need to produce profits. As we use social media, such as Facebook or YouTube, scholars such as Van Dijck (2013) have shown, algorithms continually compute not only who our family, friends and former school friends are likely to be but also our consumer patterns and preferences. In fact, as Dean (2010) notes, it is no longer necessary to spy on activist groups as all the information is online.

And while social media present themselves in terms of connectivity and are always presumed a good thing, many platforms are in competition and lock each other out (Van Dijck 2013). Bigger platforms may include the buttons of other bigger platforms, but the aim is ultimately to lock users into their own chain of platforms (2013, 156). This is important to channel users from networking into consumer activity. Google aims to lock users into their own algorithmic flow of buttons.

This is a world of algorithms where our contacts and relationships with friends become the engine for commercial activities (Fuchs 2011). All our past behaviours will be converted to likely future behaviours. It is a world where we are continually being told what is already the most successful comment, idea, picture or story. Algorithms themselves become realisers of discourse, of forms of social relations, signalling up what your user community values, and signalling what kinds of ideas and attitudes are common across the section of connectivity. Things that get liked more get higher rankings and then will get more interest. They can then become high-profile, attracting further discussions and bringing into focus other similar content. The early optimistic view of social media may still carry as regards the flourishing of different points of view and the facilitation of unique specialised shared interest groups, but these remain largely hidden unless specific search terms are used (Dean 2010). What we find at the top is something else. In some ways, this is not unlike older big media. But again these processes are part of the ways in which media corporations seek to shape behaviours towards acts of consumption. What is different here is the micro way that personal and cultural tastes can be identified, fed back and used, as 'you may also like' fuses content, promotions, adverts and connections with other people and groups. Doctor (2010) has looked at the way the news industry is meeting this shift. Here, the decline of the symbolic is also evident at a practical and commercial level where news is selected and shaped, not for a citizen but through algorithms worked out through your patterns of connectivity. And as product information and ranking websites with their own consumer review link, using algorithms to Facebook and YouTube, users too become part of this chain of endorsement, which itself figures as an act of citizenship. Dean (2010, 31) suggests that these networks of communications circulate 'less as potential for freedom than as affective intensities produced through and amplifying our capture'. Niche communities that have more clearly established consumer patterns, or who perform the role of reviewer better, may even float to the surface more easily.

Scholars write of wider cultural shifts fostered by the Internet and particularly by Web 2.0. This shift is from big media that transmitted formal, more distant authoritative information to a relatively powerless receiver, to a new kind of cultural characterised by 'scan and go' (Dean 2012). As Yiqiong et al., in this collection, point out, this marks a shift in social relations from where big media can assume users will accept the position of the informed to one where they expect to be engaged, addressed and treated as 'knowers'.

In one of the earlier examinations of the potential of cyberspace, Gunkel and Gunkel (1997) argued that new worlds are invented with principles transcribed from old worlds and concluded that: 'naming is always an exercise in power ... The future of cyberspace, therefore, will be determined not only through the invention of new hardware, but also through the names we employ to describe it.' (1997, 133). Couldry (2012) introduced the idea of 'media practice' to think about the way that media become incorporated into everyday lives in unremarkable and socially learned ways, such as 'searching', 'sharing', 'showing', 'being shown', 'community', the value of the 'latest update' and the 'new'. In critical discourse analysis, given the assumption of the clear relationships between language and concepts and social practices (Fairclough 2000), this would indeed have massive consequences as regards how we go on to organise our societies and the institutions we build (Kress 2010).

What Couldry (2012) wonders is how these media practices inform us about wider senses of our relationships with people, with the social and civic world. Concepts such as 'network' and 'making connections' have themselves become highly valued and are a common form of understanding the world, society and social relations. But are these the same as older terms like 'cooperation'? Pfeiffer (2004, 22) notes that the computer and social media are viewed as almost inventing things like interaction, communication and cooperation, as if they formerly did not exist. Nor is it true, Pfeiffer points out, that all computer and social media use are really interactive or communicative. Yet the rhetoric of the networked society, with its speed and connectivity, chimes with the values of innovation – the latest technology – and the value of communication, the value of speed. Žižek (1998), in fact, introduces the work 'interpassive' as a counter to 'interactive', to point to the casual and weakly engaged nature of many online relationships and activities. Dean (2010) too has pointed to the more passive nature of 'clickivism', as a form of replacing political activism, where platforms like Facebook allow users to click 'likes' in support of movements against major injustices – such as for the end of global capitalism.

Again, what is clear is that all this implies a challenge for the study of discourse and for multicultural discourse. In the 1990s and around the turn of the century, it was in vogue in the field of media studies to investigate the ways in which global media genres and formats disseminated more 'Western' or at least 'consumer capitalist' ideas, values and identities around the planet, asking how local cultures took these up and negotiated them (Featherstone et al. 2001). Social media provide a whole new set of resources to follow these processes and of course the demand that we develop the tools and concepts to do so.

So, in Couldry's (2012) sense, have these media practices helped to generate scepticism of, and a scan-and-go attitude to, information, a retreat into the comfort of being with those who share our existing opinions, un-receptiveness to new ideas online, a culture of not standing by our words? And in terms of the core questions of multicultural discourse studies, how does this influence and feed into the way people express cultural identities and engage with those of others?

In order to engage with multicultural discourse online, we need to be open to the challenge played by these shifts, or at least open to the fact that there may be such shifts that shape the nature of the deployment of language and other semiotic resources that we seek to study. Van Dijck (2013) reminds us that social media, structured by powerful platforms such as Facebook and Google +, have shifted in the last decade from a culture of connectedness to one of 'connectivity'. This connectivity is the culture characterised by the colonisation of terms associated with 'the social', 'sharing', and 'community'. This is done so in the direct cause of increasing the quantity of traffic that can be converted into packeted information.

For discourse studies, all of this is crucial to take on board for a number of reasons. Van Leeuwen and Wodak (1999) described discourses made up of kinds of 'scripts' that are the 'doings' of social practices. These are comprised of identities, ideas, values, actions, sequences of events, settings and times. To what extent can these 'media practices' of social media be found incorporated into the wider multicultural discourses that become realised on social media platforms like Facebook, Instagram and Twitter? What does acting in a network of social contacts actually mean in terms of scripts? Just as scholars call on more detailed empirical study of the ways in which the ideas, values and identities of international media interact with local contexts and local cultures (Aiello and Pauwels 2014), so too we need more work on the way that these new media practices now infuse, are transformed by or transform existing diverse cultural discourses.

Identity, online performance and the relationship between the online and offline worlds

One question for the study of social media discourse, from what we have so far said, involves the question of how online discourse relates to offline. What is the relationship to what people do, say and show – the concepts, values and discourse – online, to their offline lives, or even across social media platforms? The need to acknowledge the social goings on that lie behind texts has been something that discourse analysts have more widely acknowledged (Fairclough 2000; Richardson 2007) in order to more fully understand the nature and origins of the ideologies that can be revealed in texts.

Of course, a simple distinction between offline and online does not capture the complex way that social media have become so thoroughly embedded in the routines of everyday life (Bakardjieva 2005) as we become reliant on the Internet to accomplish basic daily tasks, do shopping, find a playground for the children, learn how to play the piano and check out a diagnosis for a rash on a child's foot. The online/offline distinction greatly inhibits our ability to describe and understand these communication processes. (Ellison et al. 2011). But this does not mean that we simply ignore any such relationships. For Thurlow et al. (2004, 75), the task is rather to look at how these social media are embedded in our everyday lives and also how our lives are embedded in social media. For discourse analysts therefore, this has consequences for what data are required and also for the tools of analysis.

Empirical studies have pointed to the great value of understanding online behaviour as it interrelates with the offline. One such case is research on language use and minority language, where it is important to relate the vitality of language use both in everyday use and in social media as regards lessons that can be learned from this for helping endangered languages (Cunliffe et al. 2013). Minority language may be used online while majority language is used offline (Fleming and Debski 2007).

Some scholars have pointed to the importance of the role of anonymity and how this influences behaviour, also in the case of anticipated subsequent face-to-face encounters (Ellison et al. 2006, 416) allowing them to make comments on the discrepancy between 'actual selves' and 'ideal selves' in people's online self-presentation. Although it seems that to the present, most of the research on such discrepancies has been done on Internet dating sites. Here it has been suggested that users tend to 'stretch the truth a bit' (Yurchisin et al. 2005, 742) in their online self-presentations, and also that they can give faithful representations of their selves, in order to avoid disappointments in subsequent offline meetings (Ellison et al. 2006). What seemed clear in interactions was that the nature of the lag in responses gave users time to carefully craft an attractive persona (Gibbs et al. 2006), which we might say is true of most social media even though in Facebook and Twitter anonymity is less of an issue.

However, Zhao et al. (2008) made a slightly different argument. Users saw their constructions of online 'hoped-for possible selves' (Yurchisin et al. 2005) as indeed part of their overall identities. It appears that Facebook users, where of course there is no anonymity, 'predominantly claim their identities implicitly rather than explicitly; they "show rather than tell" and stress group and consumer identities over personally narrated ones' (Zhao et al. 2008, 1816). But what is certain is that such issues of idealised identities should be of interest to a study of multicultural discourses.

Researchers were calling for more research to unpack the ways in which identities play out in face-to-face and online contexts (Ellison et al. 2011). In the context of Facebook, much research orbited around the way that profiles were used to increase levels of social capital (Burke et al. 2010, 2011; Ellison et al. 2007; Valenzuela et al. 2009), a form of capital that describes resources embedded in social relationships and interactions within a network (Lim 2012). Such social capital can then transfer to face-to-face contexts (Hampton et al. 2011). But it was clear that this needed tying to specific kinds of instances, rather than dealing more abstractly with the issue of social capital. For the study of discourse and identity, for example, we would want to know more about what resources and what kinds of identity characteristics were legitimised or delegitimised, for example.

Work on Twitter has also placed identity and self-presentation at its heart. Murthy (2012), for example, has drawn on the likes of Goffman (1981) and Bourdieu (1984) to look at the way that Tweeting about the banal, even about what you had for breakfast, is about self-affirmation and signals of being an engaged user. This was a time when Twitter had high cultural capital, was able to signify 'debate' and was popular with professional middle classes. This was partly as Twitter was a social networked media sending messages out to be forwarded and responded to by anyone, whereas social networked media like Facebook tended to be more about an extension of face-to-face relationships (Murthy 2012). Page (2012) has also looked at Twitter in terms of it being a 'linguistic marketplace' where people carry out a process of self-branding – although she views this 'synthetic personalization' (Fairclough 1989) very much as the same thing found in mainstream media talk. From the point of view of critical discourse analysts, such identity construction and self-presentation are important not only in themselves, but rather as these serve to position people against others, as part of processes of evaluation and legitimisation of wider kinds of identities and social processes.

Murthy (2012, 1063) sees a further shift through social media drawing on Turner's (2010) idea that contemporary media forms have taken a 'demotic turn'. Ordinary people have become increasingly visible and have become a major part of media content. They are the topic of TV shows and, themselves, are able to break news or provide the mobile phone camera footage of an explosion. But Turner sees this not as a form of democratisation. In mainstream media, the symbolic representation of these people is highly controlled. Even in social media, debates can happen very close to existing frames of reference often laid out by traditional sources of information and by dominant discourses (Murthy 2012). For example, 'trending' topics on Twitter will be based around breaking news events, as defined by mainstream media, and often contain links to full articles. Commentaries on the production of citizen-generated images circulated in social

DISCOURSE AND SOCIAL MEDIA

media, of conflicts and major events, on the one hand point to the way alternative viewpoints can emerge from societies where they are normally suppressed, as in the Iranian revolution (Gillmor 2011). But, on the other hand, this stream of images tends to produce the dominant frames of reference, into which we have been tutored by mainstream news media. Political uprisings will show close-ups of shouting people and give a sense that we are being taken close to the raw events, but they will tell us nothing about the complexity of the events (Cottle 2009).

Murthy (2012) suggests that perhaps we see Twitter and Facebook as part of what Therborn (2000, 42) calls the 'event society' or what Huyssen (2000, 25) calls the 'society of experience': we appear to, need to, focus upon, privilege and base our debates around, a stream of transient or trivial events. To a large extent these can be considered to be 'pseudo events' (Katz and Dayan 1985), based around immediate yet trivial occurrences, consumption of goods, and cultural events along with generic news stories. To some extent, this appears reminiscent of the arguments of Adorno and Bernstein (2001). They noted that social media should be studied as regards the way they are linked into the wider consumer and culture industries. Murthy (2012, 1064) notes that trending topics on Twitter are usually things like the music people are listening to, hated celebrities or favourite book titles that never made it to the shelf. For Dean (2010), this sits alongside commentaries of what someone is doing or how they feel at any given moment – what she says is blogging stripped to its most banal and repetitive. Although from the point of view of the discourse analyst, it is in such apparently banal things that the political, that the signals of wider social relations, can be best located (Bourdieu 1984).

Scholars have also been critical of the basic effects of social media use on everyday linguistic skills, of our very vocabulary, and ability to use grammar and to spell (Tucker 2009). In response, it can be argued that these share the more truncated in informal characteristics of face-to-face conversations. And in sociolinguistics we are beginning to understand more about the novel ways in which language is used in social media and how users adapt (Herring 2008).

Of course, we can find more positive accounts of social media and its links with the offline world. Scholars have linked social media use and information gathering to civic and political participatory behaviours offline (De Zuniga et al. 2012). It may be that people surely use social media for social relationships or entertainment, but people who have an interest in social and political issues are highly likely to also contribute and share information that is public-oriented in nature (Hilbert 2009). A study of the 2008 US presidential election showed that Facebook users shared links to news organisations such as CNN, the *New York Times* and the *Huffington Post* as well as cross-posted comments on their own Facebook profiles and on the main candidates' Facebook profiles (Robertson et al. 2010).

The most impressive online–offline link made by scholars has been related to protest movements, with wild celebrations that social media can simply bring light to the democratic nature of people, and others pointing to the need for more careful and thorough study. And this too points to grasping the relationships between online and offline identities and discourses.

Scholars have discussed the use of social media to mobilise people in anti-capitalist movements and environmental rallies (Bennett and Segerberg 2012; Howard and Hussain 2011). Social media are described as the main force behind the popular movement against authoritarian regimes in the Middle East and North African region (Cohen 2011; Webster 2011). Twitter, in particular, has been pinpointed as the fastest and most critical campaign tool for reaching and mobilising people, for gathering data and responding to public reactions (Parker 2012; Vergeer and Hermans 2013). Twitter was used not only to foster revolution through activism but also to recruit, as well as radicalise protesters and militants (see Gonzalez-Bailon et al. 2012).

Others have been more sceptical about just how much revolutions have been related to Twitter and Facebook (Rich 2011; York 2011 as cited in Lim 2012), and these observations are important to the status that we attribute to online discourse. Harsher critics pointed to the ways in which Twitter, as regards the Egyptian conflict, as in Iran, was more influential in fostering support outside of the countries (see Cottle 2011).

Lim (2012) gives a highly useful analysis, showing the rewards of combing analysis of online activity and offline situations. Her argument is that it is not true that the Egyptian revolt was a 'social media revolution', but rather better said that social media was one important tool. Quite simply, the means of communication are not enough. To draw on two of Lim's (2012) points, in the first place, it is well know that 'biographical availability' is needed to mobilise individuals to such social upheaval (McAdam 1986; Tindall 1994; Tindall and Bates 1998, cited in Lim 2012, 234). In the case of Egypt, a third of its population was under 30, without family responsibilities, experiencing massive unemployment. Simply, a large section of the population had little to lose. In addition, there had been extensive use of the Internet in the form of blogging and online newspapers since around 2005. But there had been no strong common message to bring diverse interest groups together. This had later been achieved at the time of the revolution. Lots of it was done using different kinds of social media, but it needed much ground work, political know-how and the right kind of people (Lim 2012, 244).

The celebration of the Twitter revolution could partly be explained by the way journalists focused on Tweets in English available at the time (Rothkopf 2009), who were little connected to more grass-roots aspects of the upheaval. For the study of multicultural discourse on social media, what this means is simply that we really need to produce studies that do not treat the online in isolation. What we learn from the papers by Way, Chiluwa and Thulfiqar in this collection is that much identity work done on social media is a process of motivated persuasion, even though there are claims of being the voice of a community.

This special edition

The collection of articles in this special edition approach multicultural social media discourse in very different ways. They point to the vast areas where multicultural discourse studies can work, bringing skills of more detailed forms of documentation and analysis of complex and emerging communicative forms – in one sense all the ambiguities of former studies of 'identity' and 'culture' are present, but realised in new ways.

What we also see is that all the papers link into different bodies of literature. They use different models and point to how this project must be multimodal, and that we really must place analysis on the details of texts in broader contexts of production, of the political economy of the media and also into the everyday lives of users. We must also avoid working in a way which isolates single instances of social media use, or making generalisations about 'social media' from one specific type of platform which itself is always evolving. It would also be helpful to avoid highly generic and misleading terms like 'digital media', or 'digital discourse'. The papers by Way, Thulfiqar and Chiluwa use different approaches to look at the ways in which different political groups, or allegiances, use social media. Way offers a multimodal critical discourse analytical approach to analyse a Turkish YouTube protest pop video and the comments that are

DISCOURSE AND SOCIAL MEDIA

posted; Thulfiqar draws on the concept of delegitimisation from critical discourse analysis to look at how socio-political communities in Iraq manoeuvre for power online; and Chiluwa takes a sociolinguistic approach to how extremist groups present themselves and the wider community in Nigeria. All place their analyses with specific political situations. Rasmussen takes a discursive psychology approach to look at Twitter responses to a terror attack in Norway, and posts are characterised through suspicion of authorities and ethic labelling. Yiqiong et al. carry out a multimodal discourse analysis to look at how social media involve shifts in visual forms of address, embodying many of the kinds of shifts in identity and knowledge status discussed in this introduction. Vessey looks at social media as a 'barometer', gauging opinion against minority language ideologies in mainstream newspapers, and provides an interesting look at the way different discourses emerge and interrelate across media.

These papers also point to the fact that we must decentralise both what we study and the theories that we use to do so. What is meant by democracy, journalism, community and justice around the world may have much in common, especially as global capitalism expands. But they also will always have, at least, local accents and be characterised by transformations.

But the most salient point for me is that the changes we are seeing are not just about shifts in the use of grammar, an increase in the use of multimodal resources or new forms of collective mobilisation. Rather, these changes point to wider shifts in culture: globalisation, the demise of more centralised authoritative knowledge, shifts in a whole range of ideas and values of which concepts like 'networked' and 'innovation' are a part. Mumford (1934) warned against viewing such things in isolation from the greater sweep of historical change. Our culture may now prize social media and its connectivity because of other pathways of value change that lead us here, and not because they have value in themselves. Put simply, we will not find the answer to many of our question in texts alone. Coupland (2010) has made the point clear that sociolinguistics, for example, must engage with and have something to say about these wider forces. This is why here I wanted to take small steps in connecting with some of the wider ideas and theories of social media.

Disclosure statement
No potential conflict of interest was reported by the author.

Notes on contributors
GWEN BOUVIER (Ph.D.) lectures in New Media at Zayed University (UAE). Her research interests are social media, discourse and identity, news and representation. Her most cited paper is: 'How Facebook users select identity categories for self-presentation', in Multicultural Discourse (2012). Other recent papers are 'What is a discourse approach to Twitter, Facebook, YouTube and other social media: connecting with other academic fields?' in Multicultural Discourse (2015) and 'British press photographs and the misrepresentation of the 2011 "uprising" in Libya' in Visual Communication (2014). She is on the advisory board of a number of international peer reviewed journals, such as *Media, Conflict and Society*, and is editorial assistant at the journal *Social Semiotics*.

References
Adorno, T., and J.M. Bernstein. 2001. *The culture industry: Selected essays on mass culture.* London: Routledge.

DISCOURSE AND SOCIAL MEDIA

Aiello, G., and L. Pauwels. 2014. Special issue: Difference and globalization. *Visual Communication* 13, no.3: 275–285.

Bakardjieva, M. 2005. *Internet society: The Internet in everyday life*. London: Sage.

Bennett, W.L. 2008. Changing citizenship in the digital age. In *Civic life online: Learning how digital media can engage youth*, ed. E.L. Bennett, 1–24. Cambridge: MIT Press.

Bennett, W.L., and A. Segerberg. 2012. The logic of connective action. *Information, Communication & Society* 15, no.5: 739–768.

Blommaert, J. 2010. *The sociolinguistics of globalization*. Cambridge: Cambridge University Press.

Bolter, J.D. 1996. *Writing space: Computers, hypertext, and the remediation of print*. London: Routledge.

Bourdieu, P. 1984. *Distinction. A social critique of the judgment of taste*. Cambridge, MA: Harvard University Press.

Burke, M., R. Kraut, and C. Marlow. 2011. Social capital on Facebook: Differentiating uses and users. Paper presented at ACM CHI Conference on Human Factors in Computing Systems, May 7–12, in Vancouver, BC, Canada.

Burke, M., C. Marlow, and T. Lento. 2010. Social network activity and social well-being. Paper presented at ACM CHI Conference on Human Factors in Computing Systems, April 10–15, in Atlanta, GA, USA.

Castells, M. 2000. *The rise of the network society*. Malden, MA: Blackwell.

Chaney, D. 1996. *Lifestyles*. London: Routledge.

Charmarkeh, H. 2013. Social media usage, tahriib (migration), and settlement among Somali refugees in France. *Refugee* 29, no.1. http://pi.library.yorku.ca/ojs/index.php/refuge/article/view/37505.

Cohen, R. 2011. Facebook and Arab dignity. *New York Times*, January 24. http://www.nytimes.com/2011/01/25/opinion/25iht-edcohen25.html.

Conversi, D. 2012. Irresponsible radicalisation: Diasporas, globalisation and long-distance nationalism in the digital age. *Journal of Ethnic and Migration Studies* 38, no.9: 1357–1379.

Correa, T., A.W. Hinsley, and H.G. De Zuniga. 2010. Who interacts on the web?: The intersection of users' personality and social media use. *Computer in Human Behavior* 26, no.2: 247–253.

Cottle, S. 2009. *Global Crisis Reporting*. Maidenhead: OUP.

Cottle, S. 2011. Media and the Arab uprisings of 2011: Research notes. *Journalism* 12, no.5: 647–659.

Couldry, N. 2012. *Media, society, world: Social theory and digital media practice*. London: Polity.

Coupland, N. ed. 2010. *Handbook of language and globalization*. Malden, MA and Oxford: Wiley-Blackwell.

Cover, R. 2012. Performing and undoing identity online: Social networking, identity theories and the incompatibility of online profiles and friendship regimes. *Convergence* 18, no.2: 177–193.

Cunliffe, D., D. Morris, and C. Prys. 2013. 'Young bilinguals' language behaviour in social networking sites: The use of Welsh on Facebook. *Journal of Computer-Mediated Communication* 18, no.3: 339–361.

Dean, J. 2010. *Blog theory*. London: Polity.

Dean, J. 2012. *The communist horizon*. London: Verso.

Dekker, R., and G. Engbersen. 2014. How social media transform migrant networks and facilitate migration. *Global Networks* 14, no.4: 401–418.

De Zuniga, H.G., N. Jung, and S. Valenzuela. 2012. Social media use for news and individuals' social capital, civic engagement and political participation. *Journal of Computer-Mediated Communication* 17, no.3: 319–336.

Doctor, K. 2010. *Newsonomics: Twelve New Trends That Will Shape the News You Get*. London: St Martin's Press.

Downey, J., and N. Fenton. 2003. New media, counter publicity and the public sphere. *New Media and Society* 5, no.2: 185–202.

Ellison, N.B., R. Heino, and J. Gibbs. 2006. Managing impressions online: Self-presentation processes in the online dating environment. *Journal of Computer-Mediated Communication* 11, no.2: 415–441.

Ellison, N.B., C. Steinfield, and C. Lampe. 2007. The benefits of Facebook "friends": Social capital and college students' use of online social network sites. *Journal of Computer-Mediated Communication* 12, no.4: 1143–1168.

DISCOURSE AND SOCIAL MEDIA

Ellison, N.B., C. Steinfield, and C. Lampe. 2011. Connection strategies: Social capital implications of Facebook-enabled communication practices. *New Media & Society* 13, no.6: 873–892.

Fairclough, N. 1989. *Language and power*. London: Longman.

Fairclough, N. 2000. *New language, new labour*. London: Routledge.

Featherstone, M., S. Lash, and R. Robertson (eds.). 2001. *Global modernities*. London: Sage.

Fleming, A., and R. Debski. 2007. The use of Irish in networked communications: A study of schoolchildren in different language settings. *Journal of Multilingual and Multicultural Development* 28, no.2: 85–101.

Fuchs, C. 2011. The contemporary world wide web: Social medium or new space of accumulation? In *The political economies of media. The transformation of the global media industries*, eds. D. Winseck and D.Y. Jin, 201–220. London: Bloomsbury.

Fuchs, C. 2014. *Digital labour and Karl Marx*. London: Routledge.

Georgakopoulou, A. 2014. Small stories transposition and social media: A micro-perspective on the 'Greek crisis'. *Discourse Society* 25, no.4: 519–539.

Gibbs, J.L., N.B. Ellison, and R.D. Heino. 2006. Self-presentation in online personals: The role of anticipated future interaction, self-disclosure, and perceived success in Internet dating. *Communication Research* 33, no.2: 152–177.

Gillmor, D. 2006. *How to use Flickr: The digital photography revolution*. Boston, MA: Thomson Course Technology.

Gillmor, D. 2011. Rodney King and the rise of citizen photojournalism. *Mediactive*, March 15. http://mediactive.com/2011/03/02/rodney-king-and-the-rise-of-the-citizen-photojournalist/.

Goffman, E. 1981. *Forms of talk*. Philadelphia: University of Pennsylvania Press.

González-Bailón, S., N. Wang, A. Rivero, J. Borge-Holthoefer, and Y. Moreno. 2012. *Assessing the bias in samples of large online networks* (working paper) http://arxiv.org/ftp/arxiv/papers/1212/1212.1684.pdf.

Gunkel, D.J., and A.H. Gunkel. 1997. Virtual geographies: The new worlds of cyberspace. *Critical Studies in Media Communication* 14, no.2: 123–137.

Hampton, K.N., C. Lee, and E.J. Her. 2011. How new media affords network diversity: Direct and mediated access to social capital through participation in local social settings. *New Media & Society* 13, no.7: 1031–1049.

Hardt, M., and A. Negri. 2000. *Empire*. New York: Harvard University Press.

Herring, S.C. 2008. Computer-mediated discourse. In *The handbook of discourse analysis*, eds. D. Schiffrin, D. Tannen, and H.E. Hamilton, 612–34. London: Blackwell.

Hilbert, M. 2009. The maturing concept of e-democracy: From e-voting and online consultations to democratic value out of jumbled online chatter. *Journal of Information Technology & Politics* 6, no.2: 87–110.

Hodgkinson, T. 2008. With friends like these…. *The Guardian*. http://www.theguardian.com/technology/2008/jan/14/facebook.

Howard, P., and M. Hussain. 2011. The role of digital media. *Journal of Democracy* 22, no.3: 35–48.

Huyssen, A. 2000. Present pasts: Media, politics, amnesia. *Public Culture* 12, no.1: 21–38.

Johnson, S. 2001. *Emergence: The connected lives of ants, brains, cities, and software*. New York: Scribner.

Katz, E., and D. Dayan. 1985. Media events: On the experience of not being there. *Religion* 15: 305–314.

Komito, L. 2011. Social media and migration: Virtual community 2.0. *Journal of the American Society for Information Science and Technology* 62, no.6: 1075–1086.

Kress, G. 2010. *Multimodality*. London: Routledge.

Larsson, S. 2009. The emerging economy of publications and citations. *Nordisk Pedagogik* 29, no.1: 34–52.

Lim, M. 2012. Clicks, cabs, and coffee houses: Social media and oppositional movement in Egypt, 2004–2011. *Journal of Communication* 62, no.2: 231–248.

Lindgren, S. 2010. YouTube gunmen? Mapping participatory media discourse on school shooting videos. *Media, Culture & Society* 33, no.1: 123–136.

Lindgren, S. 2012. Collective coping through networked narratives: YouTube responses to the Virginia tech shooting. In *School shootings: Mediatized violence in a global age*, eds. G.W. Muschert and J. Sumiala, 279–298. (*Studies in Media and Communications* 7) Bingley: Emerald Group.

DISCOURSE AND SOCIAL MEDIA

Livingstone, S. 2008. Taking risky opportunities in youthful content creation: Teenagers' use of social networking sites for intimacy, privacy and self-expression. *New Media and Society* 10, no.3: 393–411.

Mumford, L. 1934. *Technics and civilization*. New York: Harper.

Murthy, D. 2012. Towards a sociological understanding of social media: Theorizing Twitter. *Sociology* 46, no.6: 1059–1073.

Myers, G. 2010. *The discourse of blogs and wikis*. London: Continuum.

Nussbaum, E. 2007. The kids, The Internet, and the end of privacy. Say everything. *New York Magazine*, February 12. http://nymag.com/news/features/27341/index7.html.

Page, R. 2012. The linguistics of self-branding and micro-celebrity in Twitter: The role of hashtags. *Discourse and Communication* 6, no.2: 181–201.

Papacharissi, Z. 2002. The virtual sphere: The Internet as a public sphere. *New Media and Society* 4, no.1: 9–27.

Papacharissi, Z. 2007. The blogger revolution? Audiences as media producers. In *Blogging, citizenship, and the future of media*, ed. M. Tremayne, 21–39. London: Routledge.

Parker, A. 2012. In nonstop whirlwind of campaigns, twitter is a critical tool. *New York Times*. http://www.nytimes.com/2012/01/29/us/politics/twitter-is-a-critical-tool-in-republican-campaigns.html.

Pfeiffer, S. 2004. *Arbeitsvermögen* [Working Capacity]. Wiesbaden: VS Verlag für Sozialwissenschaften.

Richardson, J. 2007. *Analysing newspapers*. London: Palgrave Macmillan.

Robertson, S., R. Vatrapu, and R. Medina. 2010. Off the wall political discourse: Facebook use in the 2008 U.S. presidential election. *Information Polity* 15: 11–31.

Rothkopf, D. 2009. There's no such thing as a virtual revolution. *Foreign Policy Magazine*, June 17. http://foreignpolicy.com/2009/06/17/theres-no-such-thing-as-a-virtual-revolution/.

Shi-xu. 2013. *Discourse and culture: From discourse analysis to cultural discourse studies*. Shanghai: Shanghai Foreign Languages Press.

Shi-xu. 2014. *Chinese discourse studies*. Basingstoke: Palgrave Macmillan.

Therborn, G. 2000. At the birth of second century sociology: Times of reflexivity, spaces of identity, and nodes of knowledge. *British Journal of Sociology* 51, no.1: 37–57.

Thurlow, C., L. Lengel, and A. Tomic. 2004. *Computer-mediated communication: Social interaction and the Internet*. London: Sage.

Tucker, P. 2009. The dawn of the postliterate age. *Futurist* 43, no.6: 41–45.

Turner, G. 2010. *Ordinary people and the media: The demotic turn*. London: Sage.

Valenzuela, S., N. Park, and K.F. Kee. 2009. Is there social capital in a social network site? Facebook use and college students' life satisfaction, trust and participation. *Journal of Comuter-Mediated Communication* 14, no.4: 875–901.

van Dijk, T.A. 1996. Discourse, power and access. In *Texts and Practices: Readings in Critical Discourse Analysis*, eds. C.R. Caldas-Coulthard and M. Coulthard, 84–104. London: Routledge

Van Dijck, J. 2013. *The culture of connectivity: A critical history of social media*. Oxford: OUP.

Van Leeuwen, T., and R. Wodak. 1999. Legitimizing immigration control: A discourse-historical analysis. *Discourse Studies* 1, no.1: 83–118.

Vergeer, M., and L. Hermans. 2013. Campaigning on Twitter: Microblogging and online social networking as campaign tools in the 2010 general elections in the Netherlands. *Journal of Computer-Mediated Communication* 18, no.4: 399–419.

Webster, S. 2011. Has social media revolutionized revolutions? *World News*, February 16, 87, 15. http://www.jcunews.com/2011/02/16/has-social-mediarevolutionized-revolutions/.

Yurchisin, J., K. Watchravesringkan, and D.B. McCabe. 2005. An exploration of identity re-creation in the context of Internet dating. *Social Behavior and Personality* 33, no.8: 735–750.

Zhao, S., S. Grasmuck, and J. Martin. 2008. Identity construction on Facebook: Digital empowerment in anchored relationships. *Computers in Human Behaviour* 24, no.5: 1816–1836.

Žižek, S. 1997. *The plague of fantasies*. London: Verso.

Žižek, S. 1998. *The interpassive subject*. Paris: Traversess.

The pursuit of power in Iraqi political discourse: unpacking the construction of sociopolitical communities on Facebook

Thulfiqar H. Al-Tahmazi

School of English, University of Leicester

> The paper aims to show how the pursuit of power polarizes political discussions on Facebook and consequently constructs online sociopolitical communities. Drawing on political discourse analysis and Bamberg's tripartite positioning analysis, the present paper investigates how the pursuit of power, by means of de/legitimization, is produced and perceived in the Iraqi political discourses produced in social media as discourses of ethno-sectarian and cultural contestations. The results show that recontextualizing political actions and actors to de/legitimize particular interpretations of political reality based on differentiation and exclusion polarizes the discussions on Facebook. The delegitimization process that is based on differentiation and exclusion emphasizes the distinction between in-groups and out-groups and motivates the commentators to categorize themselves in oppositional sociopolitical communities that are discursively constructed. These sociopolitical communities range from completely imagined communities to the online recreation of actual ethno-sectarian groups.

Introduction

This paper unpacks how the pursuit of interactional power by means of de/legitimizing particular interpretations of reality construct online sociopolitical communities in the under-investigated terrains of political Discourse in the multi-participant and asynchronous Facebook context. It aims to provide new insights to cultural discourse studies by highlighting the distinctiveness of the Iraqi political discourses produced in social media as discourses of ethno-sectarian and cultural contestations. Challenging the west centrism of Critical Discourse Analysis (CDA) as a disciplinary discourse, the paper, therefore, highlights the need to pay more attention to the cultural diversity of human discourses and to the ways these discourses can be approached and analyzed from culturally sensitive, but globally minded, perspectives (Shi-xu 2015).

Politically speaking, Iraq is a parliamentary consociational democracy, in which ethnic, religious and sectarian communities should be proportionately represented in the government. These communities mainly include Shiite Arabs, Sunni Arabs, and Kurds; each of these communities is represented politically by different ethno-sectarian parties and coalitions. Therefore, the paper focuses on how the current ethno-sectarian, and consequently cultural, divisions in Iraq are discursively (re)created, and perceived by wide range of marginalized actors whose voices are often overlooked in mainstream media. Analyzing political interactions on Facebook is compatible with the shift in political discourse analysis from 'macro-politics, and politics as a product, to the more recent focus on the investigation of the dynamics of politics and political process as it manifests in. e.g., the microanalysis of politics' (Fetzer 2013, 2). This is also entrenched in the Foucauldian view that the dynamics of power can be best felt and analyzed at the micro-level of analysis and practices where interactional power is negotiated (Thomas and Davies 2005, 684).

Earlier studies on de/legitimization have traditionally overlooked Computer Mediated Communication (CMC), focusing instead on highly formalized textual formats of political Discourse with capital 'D' (Gee 2005). But the popularity of social media as means of activism and political engagement has increased considerably since the political events of 2011–2012 in the Arab world[1]. Therefore, social media now function as an indispensable 'online public sphere' (Douai and Nofal 2012) for the traditionally marginalized political actors to produce counter-discourses (Dahlberg 2007, 837). Facebook is the most extensively used social media to discuss different political issues within the Iraqi context generating political discourses in which a wide spectrum of interlocutors can participate. This makes the investigation of the pursuit of power by means of de/legitimization in the context of Facebook a worthwhile and valuable academic endeavor, especially because the continuity and similarity between the virtual and the real can be 'fruitfully used to diagnose cultural change and societal conditions' of the real life (Bou-Franch and Garcés-Conejos Blitvich 2014, 22).

Theoretical framework

Power is an important analytical concept when dealing with political Discourse, because it is related to the goals each political actor attempts to secure. Politics is often defined a 'quest for power' (Bourdieu 2005, 39; Wodak 2011, 5). Power, as such, 'is not just the ability to coerce others or to get them to do something against their will, but rather, it is the ability to interpret events and reality, and have this interpretation accepted by those others (Diamond 1996, 13). The pursuit of this type of political power can be traced in political Discourse because 'the doing of politics is predominantly constituted in language' (Chilton and Schaffner 2002, 3). When discussing a political topic, political actors pursue power, at the micro-level, by discursively legitimizing or delegitimizing particular interpretations of political reality in accordance with their macro-level sociopolitical goals. For this reason, political discourse analysts principally investigate the teleological and strategic functions of political discourses rather than making claims about 'the strategic potential of certain linguistic expressions in general' (Chilton 2004, 45).

Power, as the ability to legitimize certain interpretation of political reality, may be maintained by 'arguments about voters' wants, general ideological principles, charismatic leadership projection, boasting about performance and positive self-presentation' (Chilton 2004, 46). Delegitimization is the 'essential counterpart' of legitimization by means of which the opponent is 'presented negatively, and [its] techniques include the use of ideas of difference and boundaries, and speech acts of blaming, accusing, insulting, etc' (Chilton 2004, 46). Emphasizing its relation to concepts of role and social identity, Cap (2008, 22) envisages legitimization as the discursive means to claim authority and deprive the opponent thereof. De/legitimization is, then, an argumentative strategy that may be achieved by empowering a political actor to take a course of action, or justifying the course of action taken itself via a 'claim to rightness' (Cap 2008, 22). De/legitimization, as such, is not only an argumentative strategy used for justification but it is in and by itself an exercise of power, because de/legitimization is primarily used to protect the political actors' interests. Chovanec (2010, 62) rightly argues that legitimization and delegitimization are the overarching goals of political discourse at 'the macro-level, and they are achieved through the use of several broad discursive strategies, realized by particular textual forms and structures as manifestations of the micro-level of discourse'.

From a discursive viewpoint, de/legitimization is achieved by virtue of recontextualization, because interlocutors tend to bring political actions and actors from other contexts of use and (re)characterize them in particular ways that better serve their interactional goals. Recontextualization, as it used here, refers to the process of transforming meaning from its original context to acquire different meaning in its new context (Linell 1998, 144). The transformed meaning may involve 'actual wordings, explicitly expressed meanings, or something only implicit or implied in the original text or genre' (Linell 1998, 148). Investigating de/legitimization process in terms of the action and actors recontextualized is compatible with Khosravinik's (2010, 63) heuristic to analyzing what the actors, actions and arguments are actually found in the text and how they are represented when investigating discourses on social and cultural categorization.

Broadly speaking, there seems to be two general orientations as to how de/legitimization is realized in discourse. The first orientation focuses on the presentation of actors as a justification process carried out by means of social categorization, i.e. in-group vs. out-group identity (e.g. Rojo and van Dijk 1997; Reisigl and Wodak 2001; Chovanec 2010; Sowińska and Dubrovskaya 2012). The ideological nature of this social and cultural categorization creates the justificatory function of de/legitimization (van Dijk 1998, 255). The second orientation, however, is more action-oriented as it views de/legitimization as the argumentation process that evaluates or ir/rationalizes politically significant actions based on the interlocutors' ideological preferences (e.g. Van Leeuwen 2007). It is important to note here that the distinction between these two trends is not stated explicitly, but is implied by the strategies described in the different frameworks of each author.

Employing insights, from both actor and action-oriented views, Reyes (2011) develops Van Leeuwen's (2007) typology, to account for political discourse. Reyes (2011, 781) states that de/legitimization can be discursively achieved through (1) appeal to emotions (particularly fear), (2) presenting a hypothetical future, (3) rationality, (4) voices of expertise, and (5) altruism. Reyes (2011, 785) argues that de/legitimization by means of an appeal to emotion is realized through social and cultural categorization that is motivated by representing out-group members negatively. While de/legitimization by projecting a hypothetical future, Reyes (2011, 786) maintains, is motivated by the interlocutor's authority to take an action that protects his/her group from expected detrimental force or action. This can be discursively presented in various ways including proximization, a 'strategy that relies upon the speaker's ability to present events on the discourse stage as directly affecting the addressee, usually in a negative or a threatening way' (Cap 2010, 119). Reyes's second legitimization strategy, i.e. presenting a hypothetical future, is included within van Leeuwen's (2007, 104) theoretical rationalization that takes the form of predication. Similar to Reyes's hypothetical future, prediction, according to van Leeuwen's (2007), requires an actor with a particular social position to take protective measures. Reyes's conceptualization of rationalization is similar to that of instrumental rationalization developed by van Leeuwen (2007), because it only includes instrumentality, which needs to be conceptualized as modus operandi (Reyes 2011, 786). The fourth de/legitimization strategy identified by Reyes, i.e. voices of expertise, is similar to van Leeuwen's (2007) authorization in terms of expertise. The last strategy identified by Reyes is altruism, which he defines in terms of positive representation of self (2011, 787).

Taking the typologies developed by van Leeuwen (2007) and Reyes (2011) as points of departure, de/legitimization will be defined as the argumentation process that aims to undermine/promote certain interpretation of reality as part of the pursuit for power in political discourses. This argumentation process can be action-oriented achieved by recontextualizing social actions to present them as il/legitimate and un/justified, and/or actor-oriented achieved by characterizing social actors as il/legitimate claimants of power. Therefore, the major discursive de/legitimization strategies can be classified as summarized in Table 1.

In practice, de/legitimization always comes in binary opposition, because legitimizing a political action or actor implicitly entails delegitimizing the opposing action and actor, and vice versa. Interlocutors involved in political interactions would expectedly legitimize their own or their in-group members' images as authorized, trustworthy, amiable, popular and the like, and/or their own or their in-group members' actions as legitimate justified, legal, beneficial and the like. Conversely, they would delegitimize their opponents' image as unauthorized, not trustworthy, and unpopular, or their actions as illegitimate, unjustified, illegal, and outrageous. Both action and actor-oriented de/legitimization may be employed simultaneously to reinforce effect.

In multi-participant interactions, like the ones analyzed in this paper, interlocutors' attempts to legitimize or delegitimize particular interpretations of political reality do not only engender political consequences but may also have social and cultural implications, because the abuse of power in terms of de/legitimization may involve a violation of the perceived rights of social actors or groups (cf. van Dijk 2008, 18–19). Therefore, de/legitimization tends to deepen the divisions between the interlocutors holding different political convictions.

Investigating the social and cultural implications of the pursuit of power necessitates micro-analytical approach that differs from the one used when analyzing the process of de/legitimization, which is traditionally analyzed by macro-level approaches. This paper argues that the methodological gap between the macro-analytical discourse approaches, e.g. the CDA-informed political discourse analysis, and micro-analytical approaches, e.g. the CA-styled analysis of the discursive construction of identity in interaction, can be bridged by appealing to the multi-tiered positioning theory, originally developed in narrative analysis (Bamberg 1997), to investigate the relational and interactional aspects of meso-level positioning. Bamberg's (1997) positioning analysis employs Davies and Harré's notion of positioning, which they (1990, 48) define as a 'discursive process whereby selves are located in conversations as observably and subjectively coherent

Table 1. De/legitimization strategies.

No.	Legitimization	Delegitimization	Type
1	Rationalization	Ir-rationalization	Action-oriented
2	Positive evaluation of action	Negative evaluation of action	
3	Authorization	De-authorization	
4	Positive representation of self/ in-group members	Negative representation of other/ out-group members	Actor-oriented

participants in jointly produced story lines.' Bamberg (1997, 337–338) views positioning as a discursive process that takes place at three different levels:

(1) Positioning level 1 is concerned about the ways characters, their actions and evaluations are positioned in relation to each other in the reported event.
(2) Positioning level 2 deals with the ways interlocutors are positioned to each other.
(3) Positioning level 3 is related to the ways interlocutors 'position themselves to themselves.' That is, how they want to be understood beyond the dominant discourses that frame the interaction 'in its temporal and spatial locality' (Moissinac 2007, 236).

Critical discourse analysts often argue that language is never politically neutral; this is perhaps brought to the fore most clearly by virtue of investigating the discursive construction of political identity. The process of de/legitimization, as defined above, is an inevitably positioning process (Davies and Harré 1990) by means of which interlocutors (re)position themselves relative to the political actors and/or actions reported in their Facebook comments, as well as to each other in the course of interaction, and by so doing they construct their political identities. Bamberg's (1997) positioning analysis captures meticulously how the recontextualization of political actions and actors from the there-and-then world to the now-and-here interaction, i.e. de/legitimization, is intimately related to and actively forms how interlocutors are related to each other in the interaction, and how interlocutors construct their own identities. This will help unpack the construction of sociopolitical communities on Facebook.

Data and methodology

The corpus analyzed in this paper represents three comment-threads consists of 396 individual comments (comprising 8322 words in total) selected from three publically available Facebook pages of leading Iraqi political commentators. Each comment-thread discusses different topics to ensure data triangulation. The selected topics include a purely political topic (the 2012 political impasse between multiple opposition parties and the ruling party), an ethno-political topic (the government policies that were perceived sectarianly biased by some Sunni opposition), and the election results in 2014. These comment-threads were selected based on several selection criteria. These criteria include: the relatively high level of comments which responded to the original post (minimum 100 comments), the original post-author's engagement with the commentators, and the topic discussed must be related to Iraqi politics. The three comment-threads compromising the dataset of this paper were posted originally in Iraqi Arabic. The examples provided are presented in semi-literal English translation in order to exhibit, as accurately as possible, how the positioning process at the three levels of analysis was done. As the selected pages are publically available to all Facebook users and part of the public domain, I consider it ethically acceptable to use the data for my analysis (cf. Markham and the AoIR ethics working committee, 2012). Nevertheless, I contacted the Facebook pages owners and I was given the approval to use the public discussions on their Facebook pages.

The analysis uses mixed methods that combine both quantitative and qualitative analyses to identify the patterns of discursive behaviors and in order to understand their underlying political, social, and cultural implications. The data were subjected to an in-depth qualitative analysis to identify the comments that have de/legitimizing functions.

These comments are coded for the types of the de/legitimization strategy used and analyzed quantitatively in order to see how interlocutors' characterized the targeted political actors and recontextualize the targeted political actions in the three comment-threads. As a result, the analysis helps unpack how de/legitimizing particular interpretations of political reality in specific way contributes in polarizing political discussions and consequently constructing online sociopolitical communities by interpreting which macro-social categories are used to position the participants within larger groups.

Analysis

Positioning level 1: de/legitimizing political actors and actions

De/legitimization takes place at the first level positioning, where the targeted political actors are positioned in relation to other political actors. This positioning process takes place in the there-and-then world of reported actions by characterizing those political actors, and recontextualizing their actions or action potentials in particular ways that better serves the commentators' interactional, and consequently, political interests (See De Fina and Georgakopoulou 2012, 163; De Fina 2013, 53).

The cases of actor-oriented de/legitimization can then be analyzed by identifying who the political actors are and how they are discursively represented in each of the comment-threads analyzed using van Leeuwen's (2008) models of representation of social actors and actions. In action-oriented de/legitimization, however, there must be an action involved; this action may include either a Material, Mental or Verbal process (cf. Halliday and Matthiessen 2004) for which the target of the de/legitimization is somehow responsible. The cases of action-oriented de/legitimization can be analyzed in terms of what the political actions and actors are actually found in the text and how they are discursively represented. Examples 1 and 2 show the difference between these two types of de/legitimization processes.

> Example 1: *Citizen (bloc) and Al-Ahrar (bloc) along with the small blocs become a half+1 and (they) nominate a Prime Minister Designate and bye bye Noori ... Allah's willing.*

In example 1, the commentator delegitimized a political actor and legitimized few others. He first attempted to legitimize the traditional Shiite rival of the ruling party, i.e. *Citizen (bloc) and Al-Ahrar (bloc)*, using the legitimization strategy of authorization by appealing their general public representativeness as indicated by their results in the elections and their ability to form the new government. The commentator discursively represented these political actors by means of association, which refers to 'groups formed by social actors and/or groups of social actors (either generically or specifically referred to) which are never labeled in the text (although the actors or groups who make up the association may of course themselves be named and/or categorized)' (van Leeuwen 2008, 38). Although, ruling party, individualized and nominated (see van Leeuwen 2008, 52) by using the first name of its leader, i.e. Noori, was the first winner in the parliamentary election; the commentator de-authorized it highlighting its inability to form a majority coalition that could form the government, i.e. *bye bye Noori ... Allah's willing.*

> Example 2: *Al-Maliki's enemies had raised his popularity to the utmost after they managed by their convulsive sectarian discourse to depict him as the greater danger to a certain sect. And this made the people from the other sect more attached to Al-Maliki as he (represented) them and their won sect's defender.*

In example 2, taken from the first comment-thread, the commentator, attempted to delegitimize the oppositions' practices using the delegitimization strategy of negative evaluation of an action. The commentator discursively represented the opposition in terms of possessivation (van Leeuwen 2008, 34) in relation to the former Prime Minister who was nominated (van Leeuwen 2008, 40), using a genitive construction, i.e. *Al-Maliki's enemies*. The delegitimized actions were first agentialized (van Leeuwen 2008, 66) to highlight the opposition's responsibility for them, i.e. *they managed to, they depicted him*, and then activated by a negatively evaluated discourse, i.e. *by their convulsive sectarian discourse.*

In certain cases, both actor-oriented and action-oriented de/legitimization strategies can be used in order to reinforce the effect of the de/legitimization process as shown in example 3 below.

Example 3: *Al-Maliki has bought votes by (giving out) plots of land or employment (positions in the public sector). If we truly have a state of law Al-Maliki would have been in jail by now.*

In example 3, the commentator delegitimized Al-Maliki's practices during the elections, which include the abuse of government recourses to guarantee votes, i.e. *(giving out) plots* of land or employment (positions in the public sector). *Al-Maliki's responsibility of these practices was established by agentializing the action of buying votes (van Leeuwen 2008, 66). The delegitimized action was evaluated negatively based on legal basis, i.e.* if we truly have a state of law Al-Maliki would have been in jail by now. *By so doing, the commentators implicitly de-authorized Al-Maliki and his political coalition as an illegitimate winner in the election as indicated by the original post when the author referred to the preliminary results. Using the actor-oriented delegitimization strategy of de-authorization, the commentator appealed to the concept representativeness (of the general public). In this example, it was the action-oriented delegitimization that reinforced the actor-oriented delegitimization, because the main topic of the comment-thread was related to discussion of the election results.*

Alternatively, in example 4 (below), the commentator combined an actor-oriented delegitimization with an action-oriented delegitimization in order to reinforce the effect of the latter.

Example 4: *Do you hold dialogue with the one who wishes to slaughter you?*

In example 4, taken from the second comment-thread, the commentator first attempted to delegitimize the Sunnis opposition, with whom the post-author urged the government to hold dialogue. Using the delegitimization strategy of negative representation of out-group actor, the commentator discursively represented the Sunni opposition by genericization (van Leeuwen 2008, 35) referring to them generically, i.e. *the one who wishes to slaughter you*. This type of representation criminalized the opposition presenting them as fit for prosecution not for a political dialogue. In doing so, the commentator attempted to irrationalize the political action, i.e. holding a dialogue with the opposition, by highlighting its consistency, because the Sunni opposition was perceived by the commentator as unfit to hold dialogue with. This political action was discursively represented in terms of objectivation (van Leeuwen 2008, 63–64), which refers to the substitution of a product of an action, i.e. dialogue, for an action, i.e. the process of holding a dialogue with the opposition or the process of negotiation.

A quantitative comparison between the three comment-threads is illuminating; it can elucidate the similarities and thematically related differences in the data. The numbers of de/legitimization instances identified were 67 (thread 1), 114 (thread 2), and 105 (thread 3). The comments that were identified as involving de/legitimization were coded using the eight different strategies of de/legitimization listed in Table 1. As mentioned in examples 3 and 4 above, some comments that had de/legitimizing function included multiple de/legitimizing strategies. In these cases, the occurrence of multiple strategies was accommodated in the analysis by quantifying each single occurrence of the different strategies; this means that the comments that included more than two de/legitimization strategies were coded twice. The results were then normalized in relation to the total numbers of de/legitimization instances identified in each comment-thread. Coding decisions regarding ambiguous cases of de/legitimization were made by using the interactional responses as evidence that the strategy was interpreted by the participants as serving either a legitimizing or delegitimizing function.

The quantitative analysis shows that actor-oriented delegitimization strategies are much more commonly used than the action-oriented de/legitimization strategies in the three comment-threads. This suggests that the political debates in the context of Facebook are characteristically personalized and infrequently agenda-oriented, because such debates tend to focus on the political actors and their images rather than their actions and agendas. Despite the thematically related individual differences among the three comment-threads, the frequencies of the actor-oriented and action-oriented delegitimization strategies stayed relatively the same across the three comment-threads, as shown in Figure 1.

However, the use of each de/legitimization strategy differed in terms frequency across the three comment-threads. In the first comment-thread, the most commonly used strategy was the negative representation of out-group members representing 39% of all strategies ($N = 26$) followed by authorization representing 16% of all strategies ($N = 11$) and then de-authorization ($N = 10$). Similarly, in the second comment-thread, the delegitimization strategy of negative representation of out-group members was by far the most commonly used representing 58% of all strategies ($N = 66$) followed by the legitimization strategy of positive representation of in-group members representing 18% of all strategies ($N = 20$). This was due to the commentators' persistent use of inter-communal criminalization to present other or out-group members negatively, and victimization to present in-group members positively, which seems to be related to the sensitive nature of the topic discussed, i.e. the government policies that were perceived as sectarianly biased by some Sunni opposition. In the third comment-thread, the strategy of authorization was the more commonly used representing 30% of all strategies ($N = 32$) followed by the strategy of negative representation of out-group members representing 29% ($N = 30$). Most importantly, the legitimization strategies of authorization and de-authorization were used very frequently ($N = 49$) representing 47% of all strategies. In light of the topic of

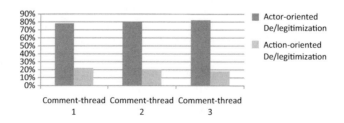

Figure 1.   Frequencies of actor-oriented and action-oriented de/legitimization strategies.

the comment-thread, which was about the results of the 2014 election, and with reference to the individual examples (as shown example 1), high frequency of de/authorization seems to be due to the commentators' interest in making claims about their favored political actors' ability to represent the general public. These differences suggest that the topic discussed in each comment-thread and the temporal context affect the commentators' choices of the de/legitimization strategies.

Positioning level 2: establishing alignments and forming political fronts

Analyzing the interlocutors' alignments vis-à-vis each other at positioning level 2 in the data analyzed in this paper has two advantages. First, it shows how the commentators flesh out their generalized relational identities, i.e. genre-specific roles, and turn them into particularized relational identities, i.e. politically defined alignments (cf. Sluss and Ashforth 2007). In the Facebook public commenting genre, the genre-specific roles, e.g. post-author vis-à-vis commentator, are known by virtue of generic structure of the interaction and made recurrently salient during the interaction according to the participants' emerging needs; these genre-specific roles can evolve into political roles of supporters or antagonists in regard to the topic in question. Second, positioning analysis at level 2 elucidates the dynamics of the interlocutors' relations to each other in the multi-participant and asynchronous Facebook public commenting genre, and as such these relations become polarized. This also entails identifying the 'interactional orders' (Langlotz and Locher 2012), which indicate to whom the comments are intended to be a response, especially because the collapsed context in Facebook comment-threads (cf. Marwick and Boyd 2011) makes it possible for a commenter to address the post-author, another commenter, or maybe both.

Examples 5 and 6 demonstrate how a commentator fleshed out his genre-specific role into a politically defined alignment that allowed him to join one of the political fronts constructed in the interaction.

Example 5:

DA: *This is a fact that we the non-politicians are aware of, how about (those) who call themselves politicians??????!!*

The commentator (DA) in the example above showed his agreement with the original argument made by the post-author about the ineffective strategies of the oppositions to depose the Prime Minister. This agreement was indicated by the statement, *This is a fact that we the non-politicians are aware of.* Such an agreement automatically established his genre-specific role as commentator in a comment-thread on Facebook, which bestowed on him certain rights and obligations associated with this role. Yet, his agreement with the post-author's argument did not establish the alignment that indicated his membership in one of the political fronts constructed in the interaction, e.g. pro-Prime Minster, con-Prime Minister, Pro-opposition, con-opposition, because he ambiguously voiced agreement with the main post without de/legitimizing any of the parties involved.

However, in later comment made by the same commentator, his genre-specific role evolved into a politically defined role that established his membership in a political front in the interaction, as shown in example 6 below taken from comment-thread 1.

Example 6:

HA: *Al-Malik is a successful politician … Even though I do not like him he managed to fund [make affective] his electoral campaign from his opponents via the demonstrations he even became the chosen one of this time.*

DA: *You mean a successful and arrogant dictator.*

In his response to HA who legitimized the former Prime Minister, DA attempted to nullify the HA's legitimization by using delegitimizing. HA used the actor-oriented strategy of positive representation of in-group actor to legitimize the former Prime Minister describing him as *a successful politician* and implying that he is a legitimate representative of his people, i.e. *he even became the chosen one of this time.* In response to this legitimization attempt, DA delegitimized the former Prime Minister using the actor-oriented strategy of negative representation, hinting at the former Prime Minister's success in abusing the power to which he is entitled as Prime Minister and becoming a dictator.

Example 6 above shows how DA's comment was intended as a response to a specific recipient, i.e. HA, by means of 'format tying' (Bolander 2012, 1616), which was made by reusing a lexical item and syntactic structure, i.e. *a successful politician*, in the first comment and *a successful dictator* in the other. By so doing, DA established his antithetical alignment to the other commentator and constructed his membership in the political front of opponent for the former Prime Minister's and as a likely support for the opposition parties. Polarizing the interaction between the two commentators, taking such an alignment oriented rapport toward challenge between the two commentators, which was likely to be interpreted as a face threatening (Spencer-Oatey 2008, 32).

Alternatively, commentators may manage rapport differently when interacting with multiple participants at different interactional orders. Example 7 illustrates how commentators can index responsiveness when interacting with multiple categories of addressees.

Example 7: *What a victory are the brothers talking about?! Can you enlighten me Father of XXX[2] [used honorifically] because my head is spinning?*

In example 7 above, the commentator responded to both the post-author and some of the commentators. He challenged the authorization attempt made by the post-author and some commentators in earlier comments about the former Prime Minister's victory in the provincial election implying that it is a uselessly indecisive victory. The commentator's use of the honorific expression *Father of XXX* indexed responsiveness to the post-author, while the responsiveness to the other commentators was indexed by the use of noun phrase *the brothers*, which was used honorifically. The commentator established an antithetical alignment to commentators who agreed with the post-author's argument about the former Prime Minister's victory. However, he avoided orienting rapport toward challenge when interacting with the post-author. Therefore, he directed the challenge to the commentators with whom he disagreed only, and involved the post-author as a verified witness in the discussion in order to mitigate the challenge and consequently any possible threat to post-author's face.

Analyzing the corpus qualitatively indicates that the polarized and conflictive interactions between the interlocutors involved out or in-group categorizations. These categorizations are made by the actor-oriented de/legitimization of representing out or in-group actors or the action-oriented de/legitimization of evaluating political actions associated with out or in-groups (see Strategies 1 and 4 in Table 1).

Positioning level 3: deindividuation and the formation of sociopolitical communities

The significance of positioning analysis at level 3 lies in its potential to connect the discursive construction of identity in the locality of interaction to the broader macro-level social processes (De Fina 2013, 40). Therefore, interlocutors enrich their genre-specific roles at positioning level 2 by the alignments they take and attributes they make salient during the course of the interaction to transform their situated identities into transportable identities (Zimmerman 1998, 106). In order to achieve their rhetorical goals, commentators may make generalizations about their own or others' sociopolitical identities, which may result in forming online communities.

The commentators' political identities derive 'from the establishment of rules and the fixing of meanings which condition and constrain political action by legitimizing certain agents and policies and delegitimizing certain others' (Mole 2007, 15). As one's sense of self is not unitary but rather versatile and multi-faceted given that it comprises different beliefs about one's own attributes and characteristics (Campbell et al. 2000, 67), a political identity may include different social attributes that comprise different sense of self. Consider the example below taken in comment-thread 1.

> Example 8: *Al-Maliki's [victory in the] election was originally sectarian-based. He has been and always will be a Prime Minister for one sect only.*

Example 8 above shows how the commentator indexed more transportable senses of self vis-à-vis the dominant discourses that frame the discussion. The commentator established a politically defined alignment as an opponent to the former Prime Minister by de-authorization depicting his previous victory in the election as unworthy, because it was made by appealing to sectarian emotions and bias, i.e. *Al-Maliki's [victory in the] election was originally sectarian-based*, which made him, the commentator argued, *a Prime Minister for one sect only*. Communicating his political stance against a political actor in such a way, the commentator did not only index his politically defined alignment, but also his sociopolitical identity as a non-sectarianist and nationalist. This is because identity is indexed, as argued by Bucholtz and Hall (2010, 21), by 'implicatures and presuppositions regarding one's own or others' identity position; [and] displayed evaluative and epistemic orientations to ongoing talk.'

In a fragile, consociational democracy like Iraq, it is typical for political identities to be intermingled with the ethno-sectarian identities of the parties and participants. In the three comment-threads analyzed in this paper, the political affiliations of the commentators are sometimes interwoven with the collective attributes that define their memberships in certain ethnic or sectarian groups to foreground particular sub-national identities. Example 10 below, which is taken from comment-thread 2, elucidates how a commentator constructed his sociopolitical identities that did not only indicate his political affiliation but also his collective membership in an ethnic community.

> Example 9: *This is not a just comparison, neither does Al-Maliki with all his corruption look like Saddam, nor 'the Shiites,' and I apologize for calling things by their names, exercised the same violence exercised by Sunnis.*

In example 9 above, the commentator attempted to delegitimize the post-author's call for the government to hold dialogue with the Sunni opposition. He also delegitimized the Sunnis as exercising excessive violence in comparison to the violence exercised by Shiites, hinting at the claim that the Shiites' exercise of violence can be proportionately tolerated. By so doing, the commentator took an antithetical alignment to the post-author, but more importantly he indexed his ethnic identity as a Shiite different from Sunnis by means of differentiation (van Leeuwen 2008, 40).

When commenters discussed a characteristically sensitive topic from an ethno-sectarian point of view as in example 9, they tended to index their ethno-sectarian identities almost always in order to highlight difference and divergence from other commenters and communities. Across the three comment-threads analyzed in this chapter, constructing ethno-sectarian identities was often perceived as an attempt to reinforce inter-communal tension or an impingement on the other communities' political rights. Despite the negative effect, commenters still indexed their ethno-sectarian identities either as an attempt to substantiate a fallacious and biased argument, or as a form of emotional discharge in response to the perceived grievances against their ethno-sectarian community (as shown example 9 above). An in-depth look at how commentators employed de/legitimization to position themselves in relation to each other revealed that there are two patterns of identifying commentators as members in certain communities. Calculating the frequency of legitimization strategies vis-à-vis delegitimization strategies in each comment-thread highlighted the different discursive patterns the commentators used to index their sociopolitical identities as shown in Figure 2.

Figure 2 shows that commentators in all comment-threads tended to delegitimization more commonly than legitimization. Nevertheless, in the third comment-thread, which was about 2014 election, the result was less polarized, because the commentators used the legitimization strategy of authorization more frequently to emphasize electoral representativeness. These results suggest that the commentators tend to construct their sociopolitical identities via negative identification, which is based on differentiation and exclusion. Negative identification refers to the process of defining self by negatively recontextualizing particular political actions and negatively characterizing particular political actors, i.e. through a delegitimization process that dissociates them from these disproved political actions and unfavorable political actors (cf. Bucholtz 1999 for similar tendencies in adolescent discourse). This supports the locus communis about the Iraqi public's lack of trust in the main political actors.

Upon constructing their sociopolitical identities, commentators emphasized difference from and deepened divisions with the commentators perceived as out-group members (cf. Garcés-Conejos Blitvich 2010, 541). As such, commentators may, consciously or unconsciously, pigeonholed each other into discursively formed communities. These

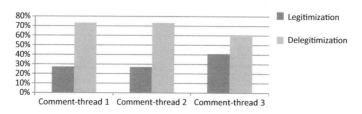

Figure 2. Frequencies of legitimization and delegitimization strategies.

communities were oppositional to each other due to the binary nature of the de/legitimization process that indexed the commentators' sociopolitical identities. Constructing online communities is motivated deindividuation, which is very common in highly polarized contexts (Garcés-Conejos Blitvich 2010, 542). Deindividuation refers to the tendency of conforming to the behavioral standards associated with a social group when confronting individuals perceived as out-group member(s) (Reicher et al 1995, 191).

The discursively constructed communities range from completely imagined communities to an online recreation of ethno-sectarian communities that existed in the offline world. Like any other functional sociocultural grouping, these formed communities presupposed the existence of a set of norms and ideologies that define how these communities function (van Dijk 1998, 142). The commentators often appealed to a set of symbolic norms assumed to be shared by the members of the imagined communities. Conversely, the online recreation of the actual communities seemed to be operationalized by the same norms and ideologies that underlie the original communities in the offline world. Example 10 (below) shows how commentators can construct an utterly imagined community.

Example 10:
38. *Post-author: XXX accuses me of being from Fakhri Kareem's group. hahahahahahahahahahahahahahahahahahahahahahahahahahaha*
39. *AT: obviously, XXX is not Magrood [dispossessed], therefore he has not read the book and he does not know the publishing house.*

In comment 38 (as shown in example 10 above), the post-author attempted to ridicule an accusation made against him by a commentator in an earlier comment. The post-author was accused of criticizing the former Prime Minister in order to flatter the owner of Al-Mada Publishing House, who was one of the former Prime Minister's opponents, as payback for publishing one of his books. The response to the commentator' accusation brought about an imagined community: that of the author's online fans and friends on Facebook. The commentator in line 39 positioned the accuser in the role of an outsider who did not belong to the community of the author's fans and friends, and by so doing he implied that he was a member in this community instead. He nicely evoked that imagined online community by using the title of the one of the author's books, i.e. *The Dispossessed*, excluding the accuser from this community stating that *obviously, XXX is not Magrood [dispossessed]*. The existence of this imagined community was also indexed similarly in several later comments.

Commenters could also form partially imagined communities, which were motivated by actual but fuzzy or indefinite political groupings in the offline world. Consider example 11 below.

Example 11: *Mr. XXX let go with this subject, 69!!— Mr. XXX Al-Maliki [garnered] at least 100 [seats] do not be part of the league of Al-Maliki's enemies. I want you to say the truth that Al-Maliki's rivals had lost the election, which is the truth. It is better for you to keep being independent.*

In example 11, the commentator voiced his disagreement with the post-author's speculations about the parliamentary seat the former Prime Minister's coalition. Rejecting the number of seats expected by the post-author (69), he authorized the Prime Minister coalition, which was discursively represented by individualization, i.e. *Al-Maliki*, by

DISCOURSE AND SOCIAL MEDIA

appealing to the expected number of the seats they would win. He also de-authorized all the other blocs describing them as the *league of Al-Maliki's enemies*, asking the post-author not to join this league. In doing so, the commentator formed an imagined league that included all the rivals of the Prime Minister, who are quite few but ineffectively disunited. Yet, this league was not totally imagined as it was motivated by the implicit agreement among most political parties not to support the Al-Maliki (the former Prime Minister) for another term in office. The commentator constructed his sociopolitical identity as a pro-Al-Maliki, as such as a member in the league of Al-Maliki's supporters.

Alternatively, commentators can discursively construct an online version of ethno-sectarian communities. Typically when the tension exacerbates, more commentators subscribe to these imagined communities and discursively behave in line with their ideological biases. Example 12 (below) shows how commentators discursively constructed an online version of ethno-sectarian communities.

> Example 12:
> 71. *AY: We rule and you blow up. May Allah help the sons of the ill-fated [victims]?*
> 72. *FO: Are you delighted that you rule? … and are you convinced that the other sect is blowing up?… when you lose a beloved one you will see who you blame the government.*
> 76. *AY: No I won't blame it and I am convinced that all the blowing up and explosions are from you. Do you think we are stupid?*

In comment 71 (in the example above), AY authorized his own sect, with the statement, *we rule*, and simultaneously delegitimized the opposing sect, *you blow up*. He implicitly indexed his sociopolitical identity as a Shiite by using the collectivized first person plural to refer to the majority sectarian community that rules the country, in which he was a member. By contrast, he indexed the identity of the opposing minority, i.e. Sunnis, whom he accused of the violent attacks against simple people referred to by the idiomatic expression *the sons of the ill-fated*. Understanding the implied ethnically biased accusation in 71, FO responded to AY in 72 in a bid to defend his ethno-sectarian group by rejecting the accusation, i.e. *are you convinced that the other sect is blowing up?,* and blaming the government for these actions. In comment 76, AY delegitimized the Sunnis again by reiterating the accusation of being responsible for the explosions and the violence I the country.

This extract demonstrates how two actual communities, i.e. Shiites and Sunnis, were discursively recreated as the homogenously Sunni-hating Shiite community, and homogenously Shiite-hating Sunni community by appealing to the stereotyped, i.e. enregistered (Agha 2009; De Fina 2015), identities. These mediated, ethno-sectarian communities attracted the attention of many commenters, and as such triggered inter-communal discursive conflict motivated by the ideological biases of offline communities. Therefore, this took the political discussion from mutual accusations by two commenters to a different level of inter-communal conflict in which many commenters participated.

Conclusion

At positioning level 1, the analysis indicates that, when discussing a political topic on Facebook, commentators de/legitimize preferred interpretations of political reality mostly by recontextualizing political actors rather than their political actions, which makes the political discussions in the context of Facebook characteristically personalized and infrequently agenda-oriented. By so doing, they flesh out their generalized relational identities, i.e. genre-specific roles, and turn them into particularized relational identities, i.e. politically defined alignments vis-à-vis the topic discussed at poisoning level 2. The analysis also shows that the de/legitimization strategies that trigger social and cultural categorization in terms of in-group and out-groups tend to polarize the discussion resulting in more conflictive interactions.

Positioning analysis at level 3 elucidates that the commentators' political alignment are interwoven with the collective attributes that define their memberships in certain ethnic, sectarian, or cultural groups in polarized contexts. However, the commentators tend to construct their ethno-sectarian identities via negative identification, which is based on differentiation and exclusion to dissociate themselves from the unfavorable/out-group political actors and their disproved political actions.

With respect to the research aim related to the sociopolitical communities constructed on Facebook, it is found that the commentators emphasize differences from and deepen divisions with the interlocutors perceived as out-group members in heatedly conflicted interactions. The analysis demonstrates that commentators, consciously or unconsciously, categorize each other into oppositional communities motivated by the binary nature of the de/legitimization process that indexes their sociopolitical identities. The constructed communities range from completely imagined communities to an online recreation of ethno-sectarian ones, which characteristically attract more attention from most commentators and trigger inter-communal discursive conflict.

Disclosure statement

No potential conflict of interest was reported by the author.

Notes

1. Arab Media Outlook Report 2011–2015, 224.
2. The name is anonymized by the author.

Notes on contributors

Thulfiqar H. Al-Tahmazi is based at the University of Leicester. Currently, he is working on his PhD thesis entitled 'The Struggle for Power in Iraqi Political Discourse across Mainstream and Social media: identities, interaction and impoliteness' as a scholarship holder of the HCED Iraq program. He is also an assistant lecturer at the Department of English Language and Literature, the University of Mustansiriyah, Baghdad-Iraq.

References

Agha, A. 2009. *Language and social relations*. Cambridge: Cambridge University Press.
Bamberg, M. 1997. Positioning between structure and performance. *Journal of Narrative and Life History* 7: 335–342.
Bolander, B. 2012. Disagreements and agreements in personal/diary blogs: A closer look at responsiveness. *Journal of Pragmatics* 44, no.12: 1607–1622.
Bou-Franch, P., and P. Garcés-Conejos Blitvich. 2014. Conflict management in massive polylogues: A case study from YouTube. *Journal of Pragmatics* 73: 19–36.
Bourdieu, P. 2005. The political field, the social science field, and the journalistic field. In *Bourdieu and the journalistic field*, ed. R. Benson and E. Neveu, 29–47. Cambridge: Polity Press.
Bucholtz, M. 1999. "Why be normal?": Language and identity practices in a community of nerd girls. *Language in Society* 28: 203–223.

Bucholtz, M., and K.H. Hall. 2010. Locating identity in language. In *Language and identities*, ed. C. Llamas and D. Watt, 18–28. Edinburgh: Edinburgh University Press.

Campbell, J., S. Assenand, and Di Paula. 2000. Structural features of the self-concept and adjustment. In *Psychological Perspectives on Self and Identity*, eds. A. Tesser, R.B. Felson, and J.M. Suls, 67–87. Washington, D.C. American Psychological Association.

Cap, P. 2008. Towards the proximization model of the analysis of legitimization in political discourse. *Journal of Pragmatics* 40: 17–41.

Cap, P. 2010. Proximizing objects, proximizing values: Towards an axiological contribution to the discourse of legitimization. In *Perspective in politics and discourse*, ed. U. Okulska and P. Cap, 119–142. Amsterdam: John Benjamins Publishing Company.

Chilton, P. 2004. *Analysing political discourse: Theory and practice*. London: Routledge.

Chilton, P.A., and C. Schaffner. 2002. Introduction: Themes and principles in the analysis of political discourse. In *Politics as text and talk: Analytic approaches to political discourse*, ed. P. A. Chilton and C. Schaffner, 1–41. Amsterdam: John Benjamins.

Chovanec, J. 2010. Legitimation through differentiation: Discursive construction of Jacques Le Worm Chirac as an opponent to military action. In *Perspective in politics and discourse.*, ed. U. Okulska and P. Cap, 60–82. Amsterdam: John Benjamins Publishing Company.

Dahlberg, L. 2007. Rethinking the fragmentation of the cyberpublic: From consensus to contestation. *Journal of New Media and Society* 9, no.5: 827–847.

Davies, B., and R. Harré. 1990. Positioning: The discursive production of selves. *Journal for the Theory of Social Behaviour* 20, no.1: 43–63.

De Fina, A. 2013. Positioning level 3: Connecting local identity displays to macro social processes. *Narrative Inquiry* 23, no.1: 40–61.

De Fina, A. 2015. Enregistered and emergent identities in narrative. In *Researching identity and interculturality*, ed. F. Dervin and K. Risager, 46–66. London: Routledge.

De Fina, A., and A. Georgakopoulou. 2012. *Analyzing narrative: Discourse and sociolinguistic perspectives*. Cambridge: Cambridge University Press.

Diamond, J. 1996. *Status and power in verbal interaction*. Amsterdam: John Benjamins Publishing Company.

Douai, A., and H.K. Nofal. 2012. Commenting in the online Arab public sphere: Debating the Swiss Minaret Ban and the "Ground Zero Mosque" online. *Journal of Computer-mediated Communication* 17, no.3: 266–282.

Dubai Press Club. 2012. *Arab media outlook report 2011–2015: Exposure and transition*. 4th edition.

Fetzer, A. 2013. The multilayered and multifaceted nature of political discourse. In *The pragmatics of political discourse. Explorations across cultures*, ed. A. Fetzer, 1–20. Amsterdam: John Benjamins.

Gee, J.P. 2005. *An introduction to discourse analysis: Theory and method*. New York: Routledge.

Gracés-Conejos Blitvich, P. 2010. The YouTubification of politics, impoliteness and polarization. In *Handbook of research on discourse behavior and digital communication: Language structures and social interaction*, ed. R. Taiwo, 540–563. New York: Information Science Reference.

Halliday, M., and C. Matthiessen. 2004. *An introduction to functional grammar*. 3rd Edition. London: Arnold.

Khosravinik, M. 2010. Actor descriptions, action attributions, and argumentation: Towards a systematization of CDA analytical categories in the representation of social groups. *Critical Discourse Studies* 7, no.1: 55–72.

Langlotz, A., and M.A. Locher. 2012. Ways of communicating emotional stance in online disagreements. *Journal of Pragmatics* 44: 1591–1606.

Linell, P. 1998. Discourse across boundaries: On recontextualizations and the blending of voices in professional discourse. *Text* 18, no.2: 143–157.

Markham, A., and the AoIR ethics working committee. 2012. Ethical decision-making and Internet research: Recommendations from the AoIR ethics working committee (Version 2.0). Approved by AoIR, 12/2012. http://aoir.org/reports/ethics2.pdf, accessed on 13 September 2013.

Marwick, A.E., and D. Boyd. 2011. I tweet honestly, I tweet passionately: Twitter users, context collapse, and the imagined audience. *New Media and Society* 13, no.1, 114–133.

Moissinac, L. 2007. "Mr. Lanoe hit on my mom": Reestablishment of believability in sequential 'small stories' by adolescent boys. In *Selves and identities in narrative discourse*, ed. M. Bamberg, A. De Fina, and D. Schiffrin, 229–252. Amsterdam: John Benjamins.

DISCOURSE AND SOCIAL MEDIA

Mole, R. 2007. Discursive identities/identity discourses and political power. In *Discursive construction of identity in European politics*, ed. R. Mole, 1–24. London: Palgrave Macmillan.

Reicher, S.D., R. Spears, and T. Postmes. 1995. A social identity model of deindividuation phenomena. *European Review of Social Psychology* 6, no.1: 161–198.

Reisigl, M., and R. Wodak. 2001. *Discourse and discrimination*. London: Routledge.

Reyes, A. 2011. Strategies of legitimization in political discourse: From words to actions. *Discourse and Society* 22, no.6: 781–807.

Rojo, L.M., and T.A. Van Dijk. 1997. "There was a problem and it was solved!" Legitimation the expulsion of 'illegal immigrants in Spanish parliamentary discourse'. *Discourse and Society* 8, no.4: 523–566.

Shi-xu. 2015. Cultural discourse studies. In *International encyclopedia of language and social interaction*, ed. K. Tracy, C. Ilie, and T. Sandel, 212–223. Boston, MA: Wiley-Blackwell.

Sluss, D.M., and B.E. Ashforth. 2007. Relational identity and identification: Defining ourselves through work relationships. *Academy of Management Review* 32, no.1: 9–32.

Sowińska, A., and T. Dubrovskaya. 2012. Discursive construction and transformation of 'us' and 'them' categories in the newspaper coverage on the US anti-ballistic missile system: Polish versus Russian view. *Discourse and Society* 6, no.4: 449–468.

Spencer-Oatey, H. 2008. Face, (Im)Politeness and rapport. In *Culturally Speaking: Culture, Communication and Politeness Theory*, ed. H. Spencer-Oatey, 11–47. 2nd Edition. London: Continuum.

Thomas, R., and A. Davies. 2005. Theorizing the micro-politics of resistance: New public management and managerial identities in the UK public services. *Organization Studies* 26, no.5: 683–706.

Van Dijk, T.A. 1998. *Ideology: A multidisciplinary approach*. London: Sage.

Van Dijk, T.A. 2008. *Power and discourse*. London: Palgrave Macmillan.

Van Leeuwen, T. 2007. Legitimation in discourse and communication. *Discourse and Communication* 1, no.1: 91–112.

Van Leeuwen, T. 2008. *Discourse and practice: New tools for critical discourse analysis*. New York: Oxford University Press.

Wodak, R. 2011. *The discourse of politics in action: Politics as usual*. London: Palgrave.

Zimmerman, D. 1998. Identities, context and interaction. In *Identities in talk*, ed. Charles Antaki and Sue Widdicombe, 87–106. London: Sage.

YouTube as a site of debate through populist politics: the case of a Turkish protest pop video

Lyndon C.S. Way

Department of Media and Communications, İzmir University of Economics

> During and immediately after the 2013 anti-government protests in Turkey, while there was almost complete state control over mainstream media, anti-government pop videos posted on YouTube became a symbolic rallying point for protest movements and attracted vast amounts of posted comments. These were widely shared and became sung in public places and during clashes with the police. These videos and the comments posted below them can be examined in the light of scholarly debates about the role of social media in public debate and protest movements. For critical discourse analysis, this provides the challenge to analyse the discourses realised in both the video and in the comments themselves. In popular music studies, it has been suggested that pop songs have been unsuccessful at communicating more than populist political sentiments. From a discursive point of view, the paper shows that this is indeed the case for one Turkish iconic protest video. It also finds that comments do not deal with the actual events represented in the video but seek to frame these in terms of wider forms of allegiances to, and betrayal of, a true Turkish people and in the light of homogenised and reduced forms of history.

Introduction

During and immediately after the 2013 anti-government protests in Turkey, while there was almost complete state control over mainstream media, pop videos posted on Youtube became a symbolic rallying point for the protests, attracting vast amounts of posted comments. These were widely shared and became sung by those against the government in public places and during clashes with the police. Despite government efforts to control the Internet, these videos appeared as oppositional whilst the mainstream media, for the most part controlled by the government, either ignored or glossed over the protests. On the Youtube pages where they were posted they became hubs for discussion and airing of opinions about both the music itself and the political situation. While scholars have begun to investigate the potential of social media to facilitate civic debate and also to play a role in protest movements, there is little discursive work in multimedia on social media sites, on how posted images and film clips, themselves carrying discourses become focal points for discussions, comments and online interactions (Georgakopoulou 2014). There has also been much less work around the way that discourses are realised multimodally through entertainments media, where critical discourse analysis (CDA) has tended to deal more with ideologies in official speeches and news media (Machin and van Leeuwen 2005). In this particular case, I am interested in the discourses communicated by an iconic popular protest song, through its lyrics, the images it carries and its sounds, and how these then related to posted comments.

In CDA, it has been argued that political discourses should be investigated not only in political speeches and news media but in entertainment media (Machin and Richardson 2012) where they are also disseminated and legitimised. And in the field of popular music studies, there has been much debate as to the way that popular music has been able to play a useful role in the communication of coherent political ideas (Lynskey 2010).

In this paper, I first carry out a multimodal analysis of the music video, asking what kinds of political discourses are communicated. In the field of popular music studies, there has been much debate as to the way that popular music has been able to play a useful role in the communication of coherent political ideas (Lynskey 2010), but there has been a call for CDA to pay more attention to such processes where it has been shown that music has been deployed for its specific ideological purposes (Machin and Richardson 2012). I then go on to analyse the political discourses found in the posted comments, which in this case clearly come from both protesters, those in favour of the song, and government supporters, those against the song. I begin by giving a brief account of the situation which the video represents and about which the comments are posted.

Among its paradigmatic and practical issues, cultural discourse studies investigate divergent and competing human discourses especially from the perspectives of less known, marginalised and disadvantaged communities in order to reverse ethnocentrism favouring the West in the academic study of discourse and communications (Shi-xu 2015, 2). This paper presents a case where a divergence of discourses (both marginal and dominant within Turkey) interacts and competes in a non-Western context. Though the case study is restricted to Turkey, it is hoped it sheds light on the role of music videos and related Internet comments more universally.

The Turkish situation

On the 28th of May 2013, a protest began in Istanbul's Gezi park to save a public green space marked for development into a shopping mall. What started with a few city planners and environmentalists quickly grew to involve millions of people demonstrating against the government in cities across Turkey. Gezi park had become symbolic for many people who were critical of the Justice and Development Party (AKP – the government at the time), and particularly Recep Tayyip Erdoğan (the prime minister at the time), regarding perceived infringements on democracy, freedom, repressive police tactics and a range of intolerant government policies. The authorities responded to the protests by deploying the police who used live ammunition, tear gas, water cannons, plastic bullets and beatings which resulted in over 3000 arrests, 8000 injuries and 6 deaths (Amnesty International 2013).

These large-scale protests can be seen in one sense as a manifestation of divisions in Turkish politics and society between secularists, whose ideas are rooted in those of the founder of the modern Turkish Republic, Mustafa Kemal Atatürk, and Turkey's ruling AKP (de Bellaigue 2013) who came into power in 2002. AKP is an economically neo-liberal and socially conservative political party with a strong emphasis on a particular sense of Islam (Yeşiltaş 2009). While there have been claims to success in some sectors of Turkey's economy, there has also been record unemployment and poverty (Sümer and Yaşlı 2010, 17). AKP has sought to systematically privatise public/state institutions

DISCOURSE AND SOCIAL MEDIA

across communication, transportation, industry and energy (Uzgel and Duru 2010, 24). Gezi park, with the plan to allow private commercial appropriation of a public space, should be seen in this context.

During the protests and in the following period, those involved have continued to be harassed by the government (Amnesty International 2013) whilst the mainstream media initially ignored the protests and then undercovered events. There is a history of close relations between media and politics in Turkey (Özguneş and Georgios 2000, 414) and it has been argued that AKP has taken even more tight control than their predecessors (Jenkins 2012). The AKP government has put pressure on existing media to become less critical whilst acquiring more of its own (Sümer and Yaşlı 2010, 17).

The popular music industry operates within this tightly controlled mediascape. AKP has had clear policies oriented to eliminate nationally based commercial popular music, in terms of its production, dissemination and live performance, where members of bands have been arrested for spreading 'propaganda' (Solomon 2005, 6). AKP has supported what are presented as more traditional forms of music, especially where the artists openly support the government (Way and Gedik 2013).

It is into this context that we must place the Youtube clip and the posted comments that will be analysed in this paper. Such songs, since they appear against specific government policy, are appealing as symbols of the wider protest. And such comments forums, while they can be deleted cannot all be monitored and can be unregulated spaces where citizens are able freely debate the situation.

Social media

On the one hand, the Internet is seen by some commentators as a place which has opened the public sphere, making it more democratic. Von Hippel (2005) believes networked media challenge centralised control of media production and distribution by traditional organisations, whilst Jenkins (2006) claims these have reconfigured communicative power relations. Vatikiotis (2014) points to cases where networked media can be seen as democratic. He cites Internet users as citizen-reporters, who contribute 'to the setting of the agenda and performing a watchdog role ... enhancing political participation' (Vatikiotis 2014, 297). And some scholars have presented highly optimistic views of social media being instrumental in successful protest movements.

On the other hand, numerous approaches have acknowledged the dubious democratic affordances of social media practice. Vatikiotis (2014, 298) outlines the various reasons for scepticism regarding democracy and social media. At a fundamental level, these include the lack of access to technology and inequalities of technological literacy (Hargittai 2008); the degradation of economy, culture and values due to the demarcation between professionals and amateurs (Keen 2007); the limited analytical and critical value of alternative forms of journalism (Scott 2007); lazy online forms of activism ('slacktivism') that have no political impact (Morozov 2009); and weak social ties of movements initiated by social media (Andrejevic 2013). Other scholars have pointed to the way that many online forums tend to be characterised by hard language and insults (Coffey and Woolworth 2004). Dean (2010) points to the way that forums tend to find people more oriented not to attending to new and fresh points of view but to falling back on what is known and comfortable. Lindgren (2010) suggests that Youtube comments tend to not focus on analysis of situations represented in video clips but rather to frame them in terms of pre-existing personal and social interests or prejudices. Following the work of Lindgren (2010) and Georgakopoulou (2014), I want to first analyse how a particular video represents a set of events and then consider the nature of the comments. First I consider some important comments made by scholars about the political potential of popular music.

Pop music, resistance and popular politics

There is considerable debate about the relationship between popular music and politics (Hesmondhalgh and Negus 2002, 7). Some scholars have been highly optimistic as regard the ability of music to represent and promote socio-political interests or particular cultural values (Korczynski 2014; Lorraine 2006; Shoup 1997). However, other scholars have rather pointed to its limitations. Frith (1988, 1981) and Street (1988) highlight how production and promotion, by large corporations, along with social and consumption contexts constrain potential meanings in pop. Of course, we might expect the new media environment to have greatly shifted these possibilities. However, scholars such as Street (1988) and Frith (1988, 472) point to an incompatibility between pop and conventional politics. Political pop songs tend to be highly populist rather than about specific issues (Street 1988), where pop musicians allow a sense of being anti-mainstream and anti-authority, where this is connoted rather than specified and where fans will also hold down mainstream jobs and have broader investments in this so-called 'mainstream' society. Even with artists known for their 'politics', Street (1988) points out lyrics are in fact highly ambiguous and the way they are performed, and marketed, plays a big role in how they are received. Also, Grossberg (1987) argues much of meanings are put there by listeners themselves.

The idea that popular music is more about popular politics is important for the analysis in this paper and a number of scholars have looked to unpacked the nature of such discourse. Populist politics involves 'representing popular interests and values' (Williams 1976, 238) including a universal 'appeal to the people and anti-elitism' (Laclau 2005, 7). In fact, 'the people' pitted against 'an elite' other are essential to the concept of popularism (De Cleen and Carpentier 2010; Laclau 2005; Storey 2003). According to Laclau (2005, 74) and De Cleen and Carpentier (2010), 'the people' is an important notion where meaning is shifting and fought for by different groups (Laclau 2005, 74). For example, De Cleen and Carpentier (2010) identify how the people are constructed differently by Belgian extreme right-wing political groups and those opposed to them. This discursive construction is in conjunction with 'the formation of an internal antagonistic frontier separating the "people" from power' (Laclau 2005, 224). Populism 'pretends to speak for the underdog whose political identity is constructed by opposing it to an elite' (De Cleen and Carpentier 2010, 180). One problem with such popular discourses is that they inhibit actual civic debate of issues (McGuigan 1992). I draw on these ideas in the subsequent analysis of the Youtube music video and the comments that are posted.

It is how these discursive constructs of the people and the elite and their actions are represented during the time of Turkey's protests that are of interest in this paper. Discourse analysis can supply the necessary methodology to uncover the fine details in texts, the micro details which articulate broader discourses. In this case, discourses which articulate politics conducive to political debate around issues Gezi Park protests raised.

Methodology

This paper follows the broader aims of CDA (Wodak 2001). It looks to reveal the discourses in the Youtube pop video and those found in the comments. Here, discourses are thought of models of the world and project certain social values and ideas which contribute to the (re)production of social life. The aim of the analysis is to reveal what kinds of social relations of power, inequalities and interests are perpetuated, generated or legitimated in texts both explicitly and implicitly (van Dijk 1993). Discourses can be thought of as a kind of 'script' (van Leeuwen and Wodak 1999) that involves identities, ideas, values, attitudes, settings and the likes. These scripts have a dialectical relationship with actual social practices, both helping define them and being defined by them. In a given setting texts will be shaped by the interests of their authors to try to shift and re-contextualise social practices in their own interests (van Leeuwen and Wodak 1999). The task of CDA is to identify and reveal the details in texts through which this is accomplished. Van Leeuwen and Wodak (1999) suggest that we can look for the way that social practices are re-contextualised through parts of them being absent from an account, for example, such as certain participants or actions. Other participants or actions may be substituted for these. The causal sequence of a particular event can be changed. These are highly useful in this analysis where the aim is to reveal how the Youtube video and then the comments made by voices representing different ideologies re-contextualise specific events in Gezi park.

Since the Youtube video realises discourses not only through language, but also through video and sound the analysis draws on a number of tools from multimodal CDA (Machin 2007). Here too, it has been argued that the task is to draw out the details of how broader discourses or the 'scripts', the 'doings' of discourse are communicated and how the different modes play slightly different roles (Machin and Mayr 2012). Here I look at the lyrics, video and music as a multimodal ensemble (Norris 2004). I look at the way that social actors and transitivity are represented in the video (Machin and Van Leeuwen 2005: Machin and Mayr 2012) and how music too can be shown to communicate ideas, attitudes and identities, through cultural references and through specific meaning potentials (Machin 2010; Machin and Richardson 2012; van Leeuwen 1999).

Analysis of the Youtube video

The video analysed below is one example of a raft of similar anti-government songs that appeared on Youtube at the time of and after the protests. The track is called *The Spring of War* by a band called The Ringo Jets, who have formerly released one CD. This video received 143,300 views. The song is a blues type tune, with lyrics that comprise three repeated lines. The video, like others released at the time, uses the limited amount of footage of the protests also made available online.

In the first place we can ask how participants are represented. In the lyrics we find no individual social actor's names only the use of the collective pronouns 'they' and 'us'. This lack of specific social actors has been noted as one characteristic of popular music lyrics. In CDA, it has been shown that pronouns are one of the best grammatical categories for the expression and manipulation of social relations, status and power (Van Dijk 1993, 203). And importantly such pronouns can rapidly shift to include and exclude (Fairclough 2003). This video is not about a simple people against the government and its forces. The video in contrast does show participants who are collectivised. We see protesters and the police, though the police are foregrounded and given salience (van Leeuwen 2005) as seen in Figure 1. But they are never individualised. We see a single generic (van Leeuwen 1996) protester being beaten behind the police, but it is the brutality of the police that is prioritised here rather than the suffering of their victim. We also find the police named in captions as seen in Figure 3. Protesters are not

Figure 1. Collectivised representations of police and brutality.

individualised but seen in large groups moving in the same direction, but within the group we see a range of ages, genders and even children. It has been observed (Bouvier 2014) that in news footage of people's uprisings in Arab countries children were represented as a strategy to suggest this is really the people, including families, where children represent an innocent truth.

We do get individualisation where the Prime Minister is shown in a still to the right of the screen, as seen in Figure 2. We also find members of the government represented through honorifics, but not named, in captions, 'minister of state' and 'prime minster'; as is seen in Figures 1 and 2. This signals that these are officials who are at fault, part of a discourse about a wider criticism of the elite.

Machin and Mayr (2012) point to the way that poses are one important way that participants can be represented. In Figure 2, we see the prime minister looking upwards with arms uplifted in a pose of prayer. These both remind viewers of the government's anti-secular stance and also connote self-grandeur. We also find the caption 'I gave the

Figure 2. Band member closeness and arrogant politicians.

Figure 3. Poretesters' unity and strength.

order' and 'Our police wrote an epic legend', pointing to his arrogance in the face of the violence seen in the video, while lyrics keep reminding that this is about 'them' and 'us'.

The most individualised participants are the band members, who comment on the events as they sing in the fashion of a news reader, reporter and weather man. They are shown in close shot and allowed to engage directly in a 'demand relationship' with the viewer creating a sense of social intimacy (Kress and Van Leeuwen 2001). All are in relative close-up and directly address the viewer creating a point of identification with the viewer.

The authorities, or 'they' are represented with material verb processes in the lyrics, pointing to their force:

Well they are isolating, manipulating, toxicating and its suffocating us.

These four material process activations with material effect connote negative power (van Leeuwen 1995, 90). However, there are abstractions as in 'isolating' and the metaphors 'toxicating' and 'suffocating'. These are common devices in generalisations (van Leeuwen 1995, 99) and here play their role in a populist discourse where leaders are represented as extreme despots.

Setting, context and causalities also become abstracted. For example,
And it is complicated, tolerated, formulated and it humiliated us.

The pronoun 'it' obscures agency. Here, 'it' represents 'the present situation in Turkey caused by the government'. But what is 'complicated, tolerated, formulated' and what 'humiliates' is not articulated. This list is a criticism of the government. But it is not specified what exactly the government has done or if it is responsible for all of these things. It is formulated not simply as a government with an ideology or set of policies which it opposes but as a despotic govern which acts against the people, who tolerate the situation. And these populist discourses, such as unemployment which is common across much of Europe at the time of writing, are rooted in broader shifts in the global economy, and here become fused together.

> In the chorus of the lyrics we find personalised communication as 'you' is addressed.
> You can smell in the air, the spring of war is here.

And we find a passive clause where 'the spring of war is here'. No agent is indicated as to starting the war. But there is a sense that this is just a beginning.

As regard transitivity in the video we find much police brutality and scenes where large numbers of protesters are seen moving purposefully in the streets as seen in Figure 3. They are activated as they are shown energetically walking, shouting and waving their arms. We also see scenes where protesters throw objects and push back at the police. There is a sense, visually, that while the police and authorities are ruthless and cruel, the people are fighting back.

The music itself also plays a role in communicating discourses about the events. The actual genre of music is blues which is associated with melancholic sentiments and also with authenticity (Frith 1993). The piece itself emphasises low pitched notes which suggest sadness and gravity (van Leeuwen 1999). Higher notes tend to be associated with optimism and higher levels of energy (Machin 2010). The sounds are also rough with distorted guitar sounds which suggest dirt and grittiness, rather than smooth and rounded. Such sounds are associated with certain kinds of truthfulness through a lack of polish or restraint. Sadness and inward contemplation are communicated by the vocal melody which has repeated descending lines. Each time the ending note is lower than the starting note. The rhythm of the song drags and feels somewhat laboured. There is no bounce nor lightness nor sense of joyful energy.

To summarise the multimodal ensemble works in the following way. The lyrics describe an 'us' who have tolerated and are put up on by a unnamed 'they' who are ruthless although what 'they' have done is not specified and is represented only through abstractions while we are told this is the spring of a war. Titles on the screen using the genre of news use the honorifics 'minister', 'prime minister' to attribute acknowledged guilt by these people. Visually, we see police brutality and protesters crowding the street often moving together and fighting back. There is no sense of difference at any level in this representation of protesters, in this 'us', as regard issues of poverty and unequal access to resources and opportunity that cut across Turkish society irrespective of religious/secular affiliations. We see the prime minister gesticulating and the members of the band communicating with us personally and sincerely. The music adds ideas of sadness and graveness. Overall, there is a sense of a brutal regime and people who will tolerate it no longer. It is a situation that must be changed. But no specifics are given in any of the modes. As scholars in popular music studies might suggest (Grossberg 1987; Street 1988), this is highly ambiguous as a political message and draws heavily on a range of connotations and relies on the audience to piece it together. What I want to do now is look at the way that the comments posted on Youtube below the video draw, explain or frame it.

Analysis of the Youtube comments

The video had received over 200 comments at the time of writing. These are originally in Turkish. Though best avoided, translations are commonly used in CDA (van Leeuwen and Wodak 1999; Wodak 1991). To overcome any bias, I had comments translated by three individual translators, including myself. Any discrepancies between translations were discussed and if we could not agree on a phrase or sentence, it was not used in the analysis. Comments comprise four loose categories. Some support the band saying simply 'well done', or repeat words or lines from the song. Another category repeats slogans and key phrases associated with the protest movement such as 'freedom' and 'the spirit of Gezi'. The third category is where people simply abuse and insult each other. In fact it is this category that is most in the form of a dialogue with interactions between posters. Other comments link to themes but not in a sense of an obvious interchange. Of course, these form an important part of the stream of comments and I will address these later in the analysis. But the last category, which is of main interest for the analysis here, is more fully developed comments about the protest and the situation itself as this allows us to access the kinds of discourses that they use. Posters who write these fall into two groups: those who are against the government and those who support it. In the analysis that follows I first analyse the two sets of comments in turn, to establish the kinds of discourses that are found over the 200 comments. Then I analyse a sequence which takes the form of a more developed interchange, to look at the way that these discourses interact.

Anti-government comments

What we find in these anti-government comments is not unlike the discourses found in the video itself. In the first place, we have a sense of the knowing people. For example:

> I open my eyes, I don't jump into the games which are played on us, I read, I don't follow something blindly. I wish our people would lose the blinders and see what is going on.

Although in this case not enough of the people 'know' only the protesters. What is to be known is not stated but expressed metaphorically through the removal of 'blinders'. And what is already known once eyes are opened is not expressed in concrete terms but as a game being played on the people. Like the video we also find the sense of an 'us' a single 'people' who are the victims of the game. Pronouns act as an important way of framing the wider events. But in this case, there is no agent acting against the people. But that it is a game being played on the people points to something deliberate and malicious.

In a comment further down the same stream of comments we find the 'blinders' metaphor taken up:

> All of this happens because the blinders started to fall. Be careful they only started to fall now. Think about what would happen when they fall completely.

Such a way of talking about gaining vision, clarity, the people no longer being blinded, that the government seeks to blind the people is typical of the way 'what is wrong' is formulated without specific details. A truth is being revealed but its actual nature is not stated.

Many anti-government comments also represent government supporters as being non-thinking. But this can also sometimes suggest that they may indeed be part of 'the people' and are victims. For example:

> What happens if you win elections, you keep sinking. Win the election, it is nothing. What does it mean if crowded, useless herds win? It is good to see you struggle. Now fuck off.

Throughout these comments, there is a lack of specificity as regard to who may characterise the different sides of the matter. There is a shifting sense of people and of us and them in the fashion described by Farclough (2003), where sometimes government supporters are blinded at other times part of 'crowded, useless herds' and other parts of the self-interested elite. We see this in the following comment:

> You are the one negotiating with PKK, it is your prime minister who is dancing because he made Kurdistan, you have the shoeboxes, you are the thieves, you are the ones who slander people ... you are the one who is continuing to cut trees which was illegal from the beginning although the court gave a stop order ... So are we – the ones that are objecting to these – the traitors? Fuck off you are the traitors.

This comment is in response to a pro AKP comment. 'You' here refers to the AKP government and its supporters. Here 'you' are the elite represented as powerful, activated in a range of verb processes. These all vaguely point to events reported in the press. For example, 'you have the shoeboxes' references a corruption case involving millions of dollars found at the manager of the Halk Bank, run by the government. But in no place are issues such as Kurdistan discussed, nor the processes of privatisation of which Gezi was a part, nor the huge numbers of unemployed youth, as is characteristic of many contemporary societies across Europe. Important in this comment also is the sense of the 'we' who stand apart from 'you' and the set of injustices. In populist politics, 'the people' can easily stand removed from responsibility from any kind of issues, even if at one time such actions were themselves popular and called for by 'the people'.

What is clear across these comments is that in the first place, rather than analysing or commenting on the actual events or even on how they are represented in the pop video, they frame the events around a set of personal interests flexibly including diverse events through a shifting use of pronouns. This involves, in the fashion described by Georgakopoulou (2014, 532) as to how the Greek crisis was discussed on social media, an exchange of popularised and slightly xenophobic versions of history, what he describes as a process of 'homogenisation and reduction'.

An important part of these anti-government comments is that nationalistic discourses are used to frame the events. For example, in the comment above the government's negotiations with Kurdish leaders are represented as 'dancing as he made Kurdistan'. In fact, this is part of a discourse which points to the Prime Minister being a traitor. This in itself is a complex issue, sometimes interwoven with more far right and xenophobic views. But here it becomes thrown together as part of a list serving to de-legitimise. The idea of the 'traitor' is also recurrent as a naming strategy. Clearly, politicians serve their own ideologies even if we dislike them. Yet the idea of using the concept of traitor, part of the nationalist discourse, is an act of claiming what are the deeper interests of a coherent and monolithic citizenship and people, rather than constructing these as ideological differences that cut across society at this present time, ones that we need to discuss and understand.

Nationalist discourses can also be found in comments which show their support for Mustafa Kemal Atatürk. For example:

> But your prime minister himself can't say I am Turk. He can't even call Atatürk 'Atatürk'.

In this case, patriotism and national identity is called into question. This is partly in reference to Erdoğan and AKP prioritising Islam as an identity marker over being

Turkish. In this sense, the argument shifts away from the neo-liberal drive to privatisation that Gezi first symbolised to issues related to Atatürk, the founder of the modern secular Turkish Republic. Until very recently, it was unthinkable for any public figure to do anything but praise Atatürk. Comments do not make it clear whether or how such identity formulations align with those who are blinded or not.

> Clear links are made between those who the protesters are against and religion. For example:
> Youtube shows what the religious gang in the government does to its people, the shoeboxes, the way it benefits some individuals and itself.

It was, of course, not clear that such a religious/secular divide characterised those who protested and those who did not. Conservative Islamic groups such as The Radical Muslims and individual women who wore clothes associated with Islam were amongst protesters in Gezi. In this manoeuvre, religion is connected to the elite, a 'gang' who are self-interested and pitted against the knowing people. Choosing to name the government as a gang points not to a democratic body but to a group who use violence and bullying to achieve their aims. This discourse about the prime minister's rule is common in popular expressions. This is important in the current Turkish political landscape where opposition political parties are based firmly in Kemalism and secularism and where the years of AKP have seen a shift to increasing state control of things like alcohol consumption and women's dress. But these things are not discussed or raised specifically.

In sum, these comments represent the government as bullying, a religious gang, self-serving, an elite who acts against the interests of and who bullies a people with common interests. This elite is also challenged on the grounds of national identity. There is a sense of people being blinded which prevents a more dramatic kind of event. But overall a range of complex issues are hinted at but never fully articulated. Given what Gezi was about in the first place as regard privatisation of public property, what this meant for Turkey, the anti-government comments are about something slightly different.

Pro-government comments

What we find in the pro-government comments are a similar lack of specific details about policies – the same homogenisation and reduction. There is a similar kind of attempt to frame the events in terms of wider interests using pronouns. Here, posters try to define just who are 'the people' and who are the distant, self-serving elite. As with the anti-government comments, these are not actually about Gezi at all, nor privatisation, nor specific policies and which sections of the population benefit or not and in which ways. It is more about legitimacy of identity.

In the following comment, see how 'the people' are to be thought of as government supporters and the government:

> You are 'çapulcu' (translation: street person) and …. God know you didn't even leave your village you wannabe. Wannabe wannabe again wannabe. Ahh ahh you empty-headed çapulcu.

Çapulcu is the name protesters were given by Prime Minister Erdoğan. It is an insult, but it was a strategic way to represent the millions of students, professionals, multi-religious and secular groups who were protesting for various reasons. They are collectivised as a 'you'. These people are 'empty-headed' and do not understand things represented by reference to them being from a village. In other comments, çapulcu's lack of education is connoted in they 'haven't read a decent book in all their life and didn't improve themselves'. The value of the protests and protester's actions are questioned by being called a wannabe, repeatedly with a sense that there were people looking for their moment of fame.

As with the anti-government discourse, the idea of a self-serving elite is also important though here it is represented by governments that preceded AKP. Pro-government comments often use a sense of past versus future. In some instances, the corruption is connected to a wider elite that exists internationally although the links are never clearly specified. For example:

> Did you start to pay taxes after Erdoğan became prime minister? You paid taxes before Erdoğan so where did this tax money go? Why are you always biased? But of course US and Israel was ruling the country before so you didn't raise your voice. We, including our prime minister's voice, were heard like ships ... Most importantly he paid the debt to IMF. Why the previous governments couldn't do that? Because they were busy eating and none of them cared about the country.

The elite here include former governments who are represented as corrupt and uncaring, activated in 'busy eating' and not caring connoting a despotic rule. But this elite also includes the USA and Israel 'ruling the country'. This is a popular largely anti-American discourse criticising both former governments and AKP. Presented in this way it serves to gloss over the complexities of what in some ways have been a mutually beneficial web of relationships although not without problems. But here it is used to connote that those against the government are somehow in favour of relations with the USA and Israel, here represented as them 'ruling' Turkey.

Importantly, many of the pro-government comments name the prime minister in ways which connote inclusiveness and respect. While in anti-government comments, he is named through abusive terms or as 'your prime minister' here he is named not only formally as Erdoğan and Prime Minister, but 'our prime minister'. The sentence 'We, including our prime minister's voice, were heard ...' makes clear the Prime Minister is a part of the people, activated positively in unison, opposing corruption and collusion with the USA and Israel. What exactly the people are doing is unclear, but a discourse of populism where the people are pitted against the elite is communicated.

Unsurprisingly, the pro-government comments represent AKP positively working for the people, but again never in specific terms. These comments usually are contrasted with negative ones of previous governments. For example:

> This country will grow, develop and other countries will shrink. Look at today's Gezi park, not yesterday's. It is better and good people will always win. As long as AK Party exists my country will be better.

Here, 'this country' is conditionally attributed with future growth and development. Gezi park is 'better'. Though not directly attributed with these positive attributes, the last line of the comment does just that, by claiming AKP's existence ensures 'my country will be better'. Overall, it is in the co-text of 'my country', 'grow', 'develop', 'better', 'good people' and 'win', connoting more positivity.

The AKP government is also represented as leaders of the people, performing positive actions for the people and the country. Again, no details are given, just abstract positive attributes. These positive attributes are contrasted with other countries which 'will shrink' and yesterday's Gezi park, yet another vague reference to the times before AKP's governance.

So in sum what we find is government actions and policies related to Gezi are absent. Police actions are also absent. Instead, posters concern themselves with constructing the people as AKP and its supporters. AKP works for the good of the country whilst its supporters are clever. The elite pitted against them are former governments, protesters and even the USA and Israel.

What characterises the discourses of both sides are that the events and the video are not commented upon in detail but rather there is an attempt to frame them by setting them into the interests of a shifting notion of a legitimate Turkish people at the mercy of self-interested elites. To accomplish this, popular history and reduced versions of events without connection are thrown together. The pressing socio-political issues in Turkish society, even issues like police brutality, or unemployment, are not discussed. What becomes clear is that like the pop video this is populist politics where there is an easy and trustworthy mass public consensus and there are ignorant, self-interested elites.

Exchange of views

In this final section, having looked at the political discourses used by the pro and anti-government Youtube posters, I want to look at the way that these interact on the forum. As stated earlier, many of the comments appear to have little relationship to previous posts, but air an opinion. Arguably, it is this tone of a lack of specific details and challenges to the collective other 'you', that leads to more comments of this type. As Coffey and Woolworth (2004) point out such forums tend not to be characterised by attempts at deeper understanding of social relations. But in several occasions, there were some clear interactions. Here, I examine one of these involving three posters. These provide an excellent opportunity to understand how these discourses interact.

The example starts after poster two claimed that the prime minister is great. Here is how the populist discourses held by each unfold when they meet:

> Poster one: Alright, you are used to being hoodwinked. They are stealing but show you that they are not. When you see reality, you will be shocked.
>
> Poster two: Actually the ones that came before are the ones that robbed the country. You can't see the service that the government gives, I guess. Investments that are worth billions are made for the country. Go and look at how much money the third bridge which is being built now costs. Talking is not service. They didn't even drive a nail.
>
> Poster three: Oh leave them alone, they love waiting in the sugar queues.
>
> Poster one: Is there only Istanbul? The whole of Turkey. I don't live in Istanbul and I don't care about a third bridge. What has the government done as a service to this country? They used the earthquake money to make benefits available to their friends. They made 3 metres of road. It was ten times more than what it was worth. That money was my taxes. They didn't even deny all these accusations. There isn't a parallel state, is there any proof? What shall I do with this service if the people are not happy?

Poster one is anti-government while posters two and three are pro-government. Poster one begins by constructing an elite who are distinct from 'the people', some of whom are 'hoodwinked' and some who know. The government is represented through the pronoun 'they' who are activated by 'stealing'. Poster two is accused of being ignorant.

Poster two replies by explaining that it was the former regime who are responsible for present problems. Rather general evidence is given for what the present government is

DISCOURSE AND SOCIAL MEDIA

offering in 'investments worth billions' and the building of a bridge, which in itself has come under much criticism from environmentalists and for being a poor use of money. Notably, this comment begins cordially with 'you cant see that …'

Poster three throws in a snark comment drawing on the discourse of the protesters being uneducated peasants.

Poster one replies 'I don't live in Istanbul and I don't care about a third bridge' and asks 'What shall I do with this service?' Though this lays out an argument for why he dislikes AKP, this poster personalises his complaints and gives very few details of the actual problems with AKP. Poster one's comments also include vague references to AKP's clamp down on opposition after the banking scandal in 'there isn't a parallel state'. AKP's response to the banking scandal was to claim there was a parallel state within Turkey's judiciary, police and politics headed by Fethullah Gülen which is out to usurp AKP's power. This poster's flat denial of the parallel state is backed up with no counter claims or proof. This same lack of detail and context is seen in 'You didn't even deny all these accusations'. These serve the purpose of connoting a self-serving arrogant elite.

What is of note in this interaction is that we do find hints and fragments of actual issues which become fuzzy, fused with personalised perspectives and framed in terms of established alignments and prejudices. What we might argue is that here we get a clearer sense of how many people do in fact manage the knowledge they come across about events and persons in civic society and in politics. Stuart Hall (1983) writing on the way that the 1980s British working classes voted for a government that appeared completely against their interest, pointed to the way that this government, headed by Margaret Thatcher, understood the processes and the ways that understandings of events were largely reduced and fused with the personal. Fiske (1989) suggested that tabloid newspapers also operate at this level. And perhaps much public debate, that we see here, is more like a poorly informed shouting match than a debate, unlike a Habermasian coffee shop.

Conclusion

This paper's aim was to look at the kinds of political discourses found on Youtube in a video and its comments which represented a specific event in Turkey, a place with tight government control over mainstream media. This analysis supports other studies which characterise such forums not as sites of engagement and debate but where comments seek to frame events into pre-existing alignments using a populist form of politics. Overall, the exchange of ideas is closer to the accounts scholars give of political populism, where the complicities of policy, economics, social and civic matters are homogenised, reduced and used to position who is a good national citizen and who is not.

The pop video analysis supports the views of those who point to the limitations of popular music to communicate more specific political ideas. This is not to say that this can play no positive role. It allows the public sharing of a discourse which connotes protest and challenge to the government. Such Youtube videos do indeed allow a greater variety of viewpoints to be accessed when the mainstream media is so restricted, exposing nearly 150,000 people to this view on the Gezi park protests. But we can be mindful of the way that while there may be pleasure and some sense of unity in deriding those in power, this can distract from on-going concrete issues that may sit behind the individuals being attacked on this occasion. Turkey is influenced by the trajectory of global capitalism, the shift to neo-liberalism and power of international banks. In Europe even more left-wing governments have found these forces impossible to stop. The populist criticism does little more than make simplistic social divisions around issues of religion and political alignment across which great divides in poverty, access to education, health care and broader opportunities run. In CDA, it is said that discourse has a dialectical relationship with social practice. In this sense rather than challenging a power elite such protest discourses are in danger of perpetuating and reproducing different kinds of inequalities. Both sides of the argument, rather than picking apart the issues that face them, seek precisely to gloss over these to create a sense of a homogenous 'people'; either for or against the government.

Of course, Youtube is not all social media. And I would suggest that critical discourse studies need to do more work around different kinds of sites, how discourses run across them, and how they are engaged with or framed by users and how this is done multimodally. A larger study would be able to follow representations of the Gezi protests across different kinds of social media. Presently, we simply do not know enough about what people do on different sites. Do some of the more or less xenophobic posters studied in this case behave differently on other forums? Do these dissolve into ghettos? And it would of course be useful to situate such a cyberethnography in the everyday lives of these individuals. Concurring with the introduction to this collection, it is suggested that what we find online is a complex thing which we are yet to fully understand.

Disclosure statement

No potential conflict of interest was reported by the author.

Notes on contributors

Lyndon C. S. Way received his Ph.D. in Journalism from Cardiff University and teaches media and communications at Izmir University of Economics (Turkey). He has published concerning news representations in *Social Semiotics* (2011), *CADAAD* (2011), *Global Media Journal* (2010 and 2012), *Journal of African Media Studies* (2013), *Journalism Practice* (2013) and *Journalism and Discourse Studies* (2015). He has published on popular music in *Multi-modal Communication* (2012), *Social Semiotics* (2013) and *Kültür ve İletişim* (2014). Presently, he is editing a book on music as multimodal discourse.

References

Amnesty International. 2013. Gezi Park protests: Brutal denial of the right to peaceful assembly in Turkey. http://www.amnesty.org.uk/news_details.asp?NewsID=20991.
Andrejevic, M. 2013. Estranged free labour. In *Digital labour: The internet as playground and factory*, ed. T. Sholtz, 149–164. New York: Routledge.
Bouvier, G. 2014. British press photographs and the misrepresentation of the 2011 'Uprising' in Libya: A content analysis, In *Visual communication,* ed. Machin, 281–299. Berlin: De Gruyter Mouton.
Coffey, B., and S. Woolworth. 2004. Destroy the scum, and then neuter their families: The web forum as a vehicle for community discourse? *Social Science Journal* 41, no. 1: 1–14.
de Bellaigue, C. 2013. Turkey: Surreal, menacing…pompous. *New York Review of Books.* www.nybooks.com/articles/archives/2013/dec/19/turkey-surreal-menacing-pompous/.
De Cleen, B., and N. Carpentier. 2010. Contesting the populist claim on "the people" through popular culture: The 0110 concerts versus the Vlaams Belang. *Social Semiotics* 20, no. 2: 175–196.
Dean, J. 2010. *Blog theory.* Cambridge: Polity Press.
Fairclough, N. 2003. *Analysing discourse: Textual analysis for social research.* London: Routledge.
Fiske, J. 1989. *Understanding popular culture.* London: Routledge.
Frith, S. 1981. *Sound effects.* New York: Pantheon books.

DISCOURSE AND SOCIAL MEDIA

Frith, S. 1988. Art ideology and pop practice. In *Marxism and the interpretation of culture*, ed. Grossberg, L., and C. Nelson. Chicago, IL: University of Illinois Press.

Frith, S. 1993. Youth/ music/television. In *Sound and vision*, ed. Frith, Goodwin and Grossberg, 67–84. New York: Routledge.

Georgakopoulou, A. 2014. Small stories transposition and social media: A micro-perspective on the 'Greek crisis'. *Discourse and Society* 25, no. 4: 519–539.

Grossberg, L. 1987. Rock and roll in search of an audience. In *Popular music and communication*, ed. Lull, J. Beverly Hills: Sage.

Hall, S. 1988. *The hard road to renewal: Thatcherism and the crisis of the Left*. London: Verso.

Hargittai, E. 2008. The digital reproduction in inequality. In *Social stratification*, ed. D. Grusky, 936–944. Boulder: Westview Press.

Hesmondhalgh, D., and K. Negus. 2002. Popular music studies: Meanings, power and value. In *Popular music studies*, ed. Hesmondhalgh, D., and K. Negus, 1–10. London: Arnold.

Jenkins, G. 2012. A house divided against itself: The deteriorating state of media freedom in Turkey. *Central Asia-Caucasus Institute*. http://www.silkroadstudies.org/new/inside/turkey/2012/120206A.html.

Jenkins, H. 2006. *Fans, bloggers and gamers: Media consumers in a digital age*. New York: New York University Press.

Keen, A. 2007. *The cult of the amateur*. New York: Doubleday.

Korczynski, M. 2014. *Songs of the factory: Pop music, culture, and resistance*. Ithaca, NY: Cornell University Press.

Kress, G., and T.van Leeuwen. 2001. *Multimodal discourse: The modes and media of contemporary communication*. London: Hodder Education.

Laclau, E. 2005. *On populist reason*. London: Verso.

Lorraine, L. 2006. Music and national culture: Pop music and resistance in Brazil. *Portuguese Cultural Studies* 1, no. 1: 36–44. http://scholarworks.umass.edu/p/vol0/iss1/4.

Lindgren, S. 2010. At the nexus of destruction and creation: Pirate and anti-pirate discourse in Swedish online media. In *New media and interactivity [NMIC2010 proceedings]*, eds. Uğur Dai et al., 229–236. Istanbul: Marmara University.

Lynskey, D. 2010. *33 Revolutions per minute: A history of protest songs*. London: Faber.

Machin, D. 2007. *Introduction to multimodal analysis*. London: Hodder Education.

Machin, D. 2010. *Analysing popular music: Image, sound, text*. London: Sage.

Machin, D., and A. Mayr 2012. *How to do critical discourse analysis: A multimodal approach*. London: Sage.

Machin, D., and J.E. Richardson. 2012. Discourses of unity and purpose in the sounds of fascist music: A multimodal approach. *Critical Discourse Studies* 9, no. 4: 329–345.

Machin, D., and T. van Leeuwen. 2005. Computer games as political discourse: The case of Black Hawk Down. *Journal of Language and Politics* 4, no. 1: 119–141.

McGuigan, J. 1992. *Cultural populism*. London: Routledge.

Morozov, E. 2009. The brave new world of slacktivism. *Foreign policy*. http://neteffect.foreign policy.com/posts/2009/05/19/the_brave_new_world_of_slacktivism.

Norris, S. 2004. *Analyzing multimodal interaction: A methodological framework*. London: Routledge.

Özguneş, N., and T. Georgios. 2000. Constraints and remedies for journalists reporting national conflict: The case of Greece and Turkey. *Journalism Studies* 1, no. 3: 405–426.

Scott, T. 2007. Analyzing political conversation on the Howard Dean candidate blog. In *Blogging, citizenship and the future of media*, ed. M. Tremayne, 39–59. New York: Routledge.

Shi-xu. Forthcoming. Cultural discourse studies. In *International encyclopedia of language and social interaction*, ed. Tracy, K., C. Ilie, and T. Sandel. Boston, MA: Wiley-Blackwell.

Shoup, J. 1997. Pop music and resistance in apartheid South Africa. *Journal of Comparative Poetics* 17, no. 17: 73–92.

Solomon, T. 2005. 'Living underground is tough': Authenticity and locality in the hip-hop community in Istanbul, Turkey. *Popular Music* 24, no. 1: 1–20.

Storey, J. 2003. *Cultural theory and popular culture. An introduction*. Harlow: Pearson Education.

Street, J. 1988. *Rebel rock: The politics of popular music*. Oxford: Basil Blackwood.

Sümer, Ç., and F. Yaşlı. 2010. *Hegemonyadan Diktoryaya AKP ve Liberal-Muhafazakar İttifak* [From hegemony to dictatorship AKP and Liberal conservatism]. Ankara: Tan Kitapevi Yayınları.

Uzgel, İ., and B. Duru. 2010. *AKP Kitabı Bir Dönüşümün Bilançosu* [A balance sheet of AKP transformations]. Ankara: Pheoenix Yayınevi.

van Dijk, T.A. 1993. Principles of critical discourse analysis. *Discourse and Society* 4, no. 2: 249–283.

van Leeuwen, T. 1995. Representing social action. *Discourse and Society* 6, no. 1: 81–106.

van Leeuwen, T. 1996. *The representation of social actors*. In *Texts and practices – readings in critical discourse analysis*, ed. Caldas-Coulthard and Coulthard, 32–70. London: Routledge.

van Leeuwen, T. 1999. *Speech, music, sound*. London: Macmillan Press.

van Leeuwen, T. 2005. *Introducing social semiotics*. London: Routledge.

van Leeuwen, T., and R. Wodak. 1999. Legitimising immigration: A discourse historical approach. *Discourse Studies* 1, no. 1: 83–118.

Vatikiotis, P. 2014. New media, democracy, participation and the political. *Interactions: Studies in Communication and Culture* 5, no. 3: 293–307.

Von Hippel, E. 2005. *Democratising innovation*. Cambridge, MA: MIT press.

Way, L., and A. Gedik. 2013. Music and image: Popular music's resistance to conservative politics. Paper presented at Ege University 14th cultural studies symposium – Confinement, Resistance, Freedom. İzmir, Turkey May 8–10.

Wodak, R. 2001. *The discourse-historical approach*. In *Methods of critical discourse analysis*, eds. Ruth Wodak and Michael Meyer, 63–94. London: Sage.

Williams, R. 1976. *Key words*. London: Fontana Press.

Yeşiltaş, M. 2009. Soft balancing in Turkish foreign policy: The case of the 2003 Iraq War. *Perceptions* 14, no. 1: 25–51.

'Should each of us take over the role as watcher?' Attitudes on Twitter towards the 2014 Norwegian terror alert

Joel Rasmussen

Department of Media and Communication, University of Oslo, Oslo, Norway

Research on securitization – the process of politicization aiming to increase security – stresses how important it is for security authorities to gain public support for their representation of threats and security measures. However, there is little research on how people understand and respond to securitization and even less so via social media. Research on security and antiterrorism discourse has rather focused on policy documents and journalism. This article analyses attitudes on Twitter in the wake of the Norwegian terror alert in July 2014. Using discursive psychology it provides novel insights into securitization as an argumentative process that has entered social media. The study analyses all tweets with the hashtag #terrortrussel (Eng. #terrorthreat) from individual users and, in addition, the initial statements by the Norwegian authorities. The results demonstrate that Twitter users are creatively using social media in response to securitization, endorsing attitudes regarding a number of themes: (1) the authorities' announcement and ways of representing the terror alert; (2) the diffusion of responsibility to lay people for monitoring suspicious events and actors; and (3) the issue of ethnicity and blame. The study contributes to two research streams: studies of securitization and studies of antiterrorism discourse in discourse analytical research.

Introduction

On 24 July 2014, the Norwegian minister of justice, the Norwegian police and security police (PST) issued a terror alert. They stated to have information that people associated with an 'extreme Islamist group' in Syria may intend to carry out a terrorist act in Norway (Bjørnland 2014; Norwegian Government 2014). The otherwise unarmed police force was hastily armed, and border controls were intensified at airports, ports and border crossings. Just three years after Anders Behring Breivik's far-right terrorism struck the country, killing 77 innocent victims, terrorism was again brought to the fore in both traditional and social media.The Norwegian case presents opportunities for insight into securitization – a dynamic process of political moves towards a supposedly more secure society, which for its success needs public understanding and support (Buzan et al. 1998). Today's networking sites and microblogs comprise platforms that add to the diversity of viewpoints in public debates (Baden and Springer 2014). In comparison with traditional media, social media facilitate unfiltered opinion sharing (Gillmor 2006) that may both support and critique securitization. Little is known, however, about the potentially divergent attitudes articulated on social media regarding securitization.

This study will begin to fill a gap in research on securitization and explore in detail argumentative processes on social media. No studies in international relations, where securitization theory is most commonly used, have focused on social media responses to the communication of securitizing actors, the latter being the governments and authorities 'who securitize issues by declaring something – a referent object – existentially threatened' (Buzan et al. 1998, 36). Neither have they applied discourse analysis at the micro level to examine public responses to securitization. Moreover, in discourse analysis, securitization theory is an untapped source of insight since it has only been used in a few studies (e.g. Lorenzo-Dus and Marsh 2012).

In combining securitization theory and close discourse analysis of Twitter communication, the study will bring novel insights into securitization as an argumentative process that has entered social media. As a case in point, it aims to analyse the articulation and variability of attitudes on Twitter in the wake of the Norwegian terror alert in July 2014. The study answers three research questions that comprehensively meet this overall aim:

(1) What are the prominent themes that Twitter users emphasize after the Norwegian terror alert in July 2014?
(2) How do the tweets articulate, and call on readers to align with, attitudes regarding the terror alert?
(3) How can we understand attitude expressions on social media as part of an argumentative securitization process?

The article analyses all tweets with the hashtag #terrorthreat (No. #terrortrussel) from individual users between 24 July and 31 July, totalling 211 messages. To give context to this twitter communication, it also examines the Norwegian authorities' initial terror alert announcement on July 24.

The study uses discursive psychology (DP; Potter and Wetherell 1987) in order to analyse attitudes as performative stances produced through discursive means. DP is a strand of discourse analysis particularly suitable for studies of attitudes – approached here as performed evaluations rather than preformed mental states. It furthermore emphasizes that discourse encompasses both localized, here-and-now interaction and more 'global' webs of practices and meaning (Potter 1998). This view of discourse as involving, interactional and ideological dynamics is similar to that of cultural discourse studies (Shi-xu 2015 forthcoming). The present study deals with both these analytical levels as it analyses in detail tweets concerning a local event, and simultaneously draws on the theory of securitization, which focuses on a more global political trend. The study thus attempts to offer new insights on how to understand securitizing efforts and the particulars of local responses via social media. By contrast to cultural discourse studies (Shi-xu 2015), however, there is no deliberate focus on non-Western discourses, and perhaps more emphasis on the minutiae of interaction.

The article will be organized as follows. First, conceptualizations and previous research regarding securitization, antiterrorism discourse and social media will be presented. Second, the article will describe the empirical material and methodology. Third, the results section will begin with a description of the securitizing actors' communication, and then move over to analysing tweets about the terror alert. Finally, the article draws conclusions and specifies its contribution to existing knowledge.

Conceptualizations and previous research

Securitization

This section will give a brief introduction to the concepts of security and securitization, and then clarify two important aspects of security discourse, namely the dispersion of responsibility to laypeople and masculinity as a dominant norm.

Although the concept of securitization has been developed mostly in international relations research (Buzan et al. 1998; Waever 1995, 1997), it has roots in Foucault's later development of an understanding of power and governance, where he examines how the population's welfare and health become objects of national control and patronage. According to Foucault (2009), the first large-scale, health promotion project in the nineteenth century in the West, the treatment of smallpox, paves the way for more refined governing techniques aimed at the population. Through a combination of new research findings and a realization of the need to manage everyday issues that affect the people, an administration begins to develop that includes economy, opinion building, risk assessment, surveillance and prevention, i.e. ways of foreseeing threats and ensuring the security and safety of a nation's human resources. For the first time, statistics were used for better understanding of the community, and likewise 'cases' to draw lessons from. *Sécurité* appears as a form of power that is different from both the sovereign power of the law and the disciplinary power applied in the institutions. Its intentions are forward-looking; it predicts and prevents risks, threats and damage (McInnes and Rushton 2013). Its function is to 'respond to a reality in such a way that this response cancels out the reality to which it responds – nullifies it, or limits, checks, or regulates it' (Foucault 2009, 47). Moreover, security becomes an assemblage of technologies of power that, later on, is applied to more and more domains – migration (Bigo 2002), poverty (Lorenzo-Dus and Marsh 2012), HIV/Aids (McInnes and Rushton 2013), the environment (Buzan et al. 1998) and so on.

Securitization, then, is the process in which security measures are established in place of previous policies and routines. It requires the establishment of an existential threat that potentially is devastating enough to have political effects. For the threat to be established as 'real', some intersubjective agreement has to be created between the securitizing actors and citizens (Buzan et al. 1998, 25). Consequently, 'persuading the audience to accept that the issue is an existential threat is the key to the success of securitization' (McInnes and Rushton 2013, 119). Securitization has come to be seen, more and more, as a dynamic, intersubjective and argumentative process, rather than as a process that either succeeds or fails completely (McInnes and Rushton 2013).

Often in tandem with securitization, another process, responsibilization, ensures that cautious, safe behaviour becomes a 'duty to the self' among citizens. It represents the development that Western governance tends to abandon welfarism – meaning collective risk solutions, collective insurance, hierarchical expert dependency and a nonmoralizing vocabulary – and adopts prudentialism, which implies increasing individual effort and responsibility, less hierarchical expert dependency, at least a rhetorical de-emphasis of hierarchy, and a moralizing vocabulary (O'Malley 1996; Rose 1999). Hence, an increasing burden of responsibility is placed on the general public to monitor and communicate risks.

Moreover, security is traditionally – and continuously – conceived of as a masculine affair. Processes of securitization are thus informed by virtues associated with masculinity. In addition to other unfortunate effects, this presents obstacles for women. Obdradovic (2014) explains that when women have managed to achieve leadership positions in security and military contexts, historiography has belittled their accomplishments to consist of assisting or inspiring the men who purportedly do the significant work. Although women's participation in the security sector and military has increased, 'military masculinity continues to inform the way we conceive of and study security' (Obdradovic 2014, 17). Feminist scholars also critique the euphemistic language of securitization. Although the term 'security' has a variety of meanings, and at the individual-psychological level means freedom from danger and anxiety, its concrete meaning in processes of securitization is narrow. Cohn (2009) contends its main referents are weapons and war.

Antiterrorism discourse

A related area of securitization research, studies of antiterrorism discourse, has mostly analysed traditional press and policy documents. Some of the conclusions are that the language of antiterrorism has the effect of dehumanizing the enemy and spreading stereotypical images and labels of Islam and Muslims (Appleby 2010; Baker-Beall 2014; Bartolucci 2012; Holland 2013). It also spreads fear and uncertainty, which serves the purpose of terrorists. But the fear also facilitates supportive public opinion of powerful government counteraction (Altheide 2007; Bhatia 2008; Hodges and Nilep 2007; Mythen and Walklate 2006). It has been common for politicians, police and military, to describe 'a new era' when terrorist attacks have occurred. Seemingly natural, the new era brings a change of security regimes. These labels of a new age and a new international situation anticipate criticism of changing policies, since the change has already been defined as something that has suddenly come upon the nation. Military action against suspected terrorists and additional monitoring and control of citizens are therefore constructed as a matter of course (Kettell 2013).

While these results are important, I will describe two studies in more depth because they treat the language of evaluation and attitudes in antiterrorism discourse in some detail (see, MacDonald et al. 2013; Stenvall 2003). First, however, I will briefly define terrorism. The views on how terrorism should be defined differ because of varying political interests, and its meaning seems to change. The Oxford English Dictionary defines terrorism as the 'unofficial or unauthorized use of violence and intimidation in the pursuit of political aims' ('Terrorism' n.d.). Stenvall (2003) argues, however, that terrorism has increasingly become associated with a constant and undefined threat rather than the actual use of violence. Her discourse analytical study, which compares the news agencies' Reuters and AP's antiterrorism discourse before and after 9/11, shows that antiterrorism discourse is characterized by vagueness. This is manifested through several features.

First, the discourse is future-oriented and most events that are described are unproven. Modal nouns, such as possibility, risk and threat, are frequent. The journalists are thus mainly writing about negative events that might occur in the future (Stenvall 2003). The same observation applies to UK policy documents, where prevent – which is also future-oriented – becomes the most common keyword in documents after the 7/7 attack in London (MacDonald et al. 2013). Moreover, common modality markers like allegedly and alleged or claim all signal that the writer does not regard the reported statements proven (Stenvall 2003).

Second, quite abstract metaphors and concepts become important in the antiterrorism discourse, such as network, violent extremism and of course terrorism. By constructing the terrorist using the metaphor of a 'terrorist network', it is suggested that the terrorists have a lot of links and relationships and can expand, as networks do. Unfortunately, the metaphor has been used to legitimize that the target in the war on terror becomes wider. If affiliated somehow with the 'network', civilians and even children have become military targets (Stenvall 2003, 390). Similarly, common concepts like violent extremism, terrorism and terror threat are all nominalizations that turn concretes into abstracts. Although these concepts are used in policy documents, there is 'no explicit identification of any social group or subculture to which these tendencies are attributed' (MacDonald et al. 2013, 462). The subject matter thus remains abstract.

The vagueness of the discourse means, for instance, that agency is ambiguous. It is not clear exactly who is concerned or worried about a terrorist threat, or who among 'the Americans' is perceiving a security measure to be in their best interest (Stenvall 2003). This imprecision helps counteract political disagreement and fragmentation, and strengthens 'community cohesion', which MacDonald et al. (2013) found to be salient terms in policy discourse.

Social media and Twitter

Social media are digital platforms with applications that allow for many-to-many interaction (Hogan and Quan-Haase 2010, 313). Uses of social media feature rituals such as following, befriending and liking actors and content, but also exchanging, commenting and even manipulating (wikis) texts and audio-visual material. In Norway 932,000 people have Twitter accounts (Metronet 2014), an 18% of the population. Despite a large amount of users, Twitter 'remains an elite medium, primarily understood as used by an urban, well-educated "twitterati"' (Larsson and Moe 2014, 11).

Although all media are somewhat 'social' and interactive in nature (Hogan and Quan-Haase 2010; Thompson 1996), these platforms offer something new. Social media such as Facebook, Twitter and YouTube offer anyone with the necessary knowledge and Internet access the opportunity to gather a large number of geographically distant users around a message. One of the optimists regarding the potential of social media, Gillmor (2006) says that social media make sure that a greater variety of ideas and unfiltered opinions are available in the public sphere. Others, such as Cammaerts (2008) claim that the socio-economic elites who have previously been powerful in the media landscape continue to be so. It is even said that commercial forces 'colonize' social media. However, research shows that individual citizens indeed can get their one-liner shared or retweeted the most despite the competition from elites (Larsson and Moe 2014).Some of the imagery from the Boston marathon-attack in April 2013 that became most widespread was citizen-produced and entirely different from mainstream news photography (Allan 2014).

Compared with other social media, Twitter, with its 140 sign limit, is best used for sharing condensed news updates, opinions and links to drive traffic to news articles, blogs and webpages that provide a richer story. It features some unique discursive devices, three of which are the hashtag, retweet (RT) and the @-character. Hashtags render tweets searchable. They serve the function of flagging a subject, and people with a particular interest can thus search for the hashtag and get a unified result. In other cases, hashtags intensify evaluation and functions as a tool that connects twitterers who share a similar sentiment (Zappavigna 2011, 2012). Hashtags often consist of words that are abbreviated or written together. The following tweet is an example from the current study's sample that communicates both a theme and an evaluation:

Despite the #terrorthreat I will soon walk from Birkelunden to Sandaker. I know it is a little daring, but you have to take some chances. #yolo

Here, a theme is defined using the hashtag #terrorthreat (No. #terrortrussel). The action that is then described, a walk from Birkelunden to Sandaker, is completed with the hashtag #yolo. The latter is an abbreviation of 'you only live once', and thus endorses an attitude towards the terror threat and a coping strategy.

In contrast to hashtags, the @-character, which is placed before a username, functions as a form of address directed to a user and to users who follow him or her. You can subscribe to and track @-references, and for instance collect others' tweets about an organization. Another way of addressing a larger crowd is by 'retweeting' another user's post or parts of it, using the abbreviation RT followed most commonly by the @-character and the source's username. Moreover, retweeting is a form of display of engagement (Zappavigna 2011, 2012).

Although research on social media in risk and crisis contexts has grown immensely in the last few years, studies dealing with securitization or terrorism-related topics are largely absent. The exceptions that exist focus on how ordinary citizens' photos from terrorist attacks – spread via social media – challenge traditional news photography (Allan 2014) and how journalists may handle and make use of the evolving 'war and terror' blogosphere (Bennett 2013). Consequently, by focusing on securitization as a process that involves various publics through social media, the present study will add value to existing research.

Methodology

In line with case study methodology (Yin 1984), the project that this study is a part of uses a number of methods and data – semistructured interviews and document analysis – in addition to social media content. However, this article takes data drawn from Twitter as its main foci.

The particular case was chosen because terrorism is topical in Norway after what the Norwegians label 'July 22'. On 22 July 2011, Anders Behring Breivik killed 77 victims in two terrorist acts, the first against the government quarter in the Oslo city centre and the second against the Labour Party's youth federation, which held a summer camp on the island of Utøya. The 22 July-Commission that investigated the Norwegian preparedness and crisis response capability proposed a set of measures, such as a legal ban on semiautomatic weapons and participation in terrorist training, and several improvements in PST's work routines (NOU 2012). Hence, when the Norwegian government, police and PST issued a terror alert on 24 July 2014, they did it with this tragedy as a back story that had triggered a national securitization process.

Concretely, the paper analyses all tweets between 24 July and 31 July with the Norwegian hashtag 'terrortrussel' (Eng. 'terrorthreat'). This selection rendered 211 tweets, which is comparable with the volume of data analysed manually in other studies of Twitter (e.g. Zappavigna 2011). To give context to this twitter communication, it also examines the Norwegian authorities' initial terror alert announcement via a press conference, a press release and Twitter. Using the hashtag for the selection process was suitable because hashtags have the function of both representing a theme and expressing evaluations (Zappavigna 2012), which is exactly what the study focuses on. Other hashtags existed, such as #terrorberedskap (Eng. #terrorpreparedness) and #terrorisme. However, #terrortrussel was more popular and in addition unique to the Norwegian

DISCOURSE AND SOCIAL MEDIA

language that facilitated relevant search results. On 24 July, there were 101 tweets posted with the hashtag #terrortrussel, and a further 113 until 31 July, the day when the threat level was lowered. The hashtag then became sporadic, with only 20 tweets between 1 August and 7 November, and therefore the study focuses on the first intense week. The tweets and quotes that are used as examples in this article were translated from Norwegian into English.

A quantitative review of all tweets with the hashtag #terrortrussel, aside from those from the authorities, revealed 160 unique Twitter users. Some twitterers produced several messages and 10 at the most. The accounts had a median follower crowd of 528 users. The five users who topped the list had 14,000, 13,000, 10,900, 6998 and 6287 followers, while the five users at the bottom of the list had 18, 18, 19, 21 and 21. A software developer had the most followers. Among these 211 tweets, an average of 0.64 was retweeted and 24 times at the most. The Police Directorate and PST's 19 tweets during the same period were retweeted on an average of 31 times.

Researchers should be alert to the fact that tweets are deleted after a period of time and show how they manage it, since it could potentially be a serious validity problem (Kelley et al. 2013). Accordingly, at monthly intervals from August to October, I did searches on the hashtag ('#terrortrussel') and came up with the same results for the selected period, which showed that, over time, no tweets had yet been lost.

As for the detailed empirical analysis, the study uses DP, which is a form of discourse analysis that focuses on how social psychological themes are expressed through interaction. It was first introduced by Potter and Wetherell (1987) and further defined by Potter and Edwards (1992), where some of the linchpins of the approach were declared. The paper draws from DP a few analytical procedures and categories. The analysis begins by coding the themes that were evaluated by twitterers. Second, a great deal of attention is given to the question of how discursive devices are used to articulate particular attitudes. DP does not assume that attitudes are something static cognitively within us, but attitudes are performed and shaped in communication in actual settings. Attitudes are thus performed rather than preformed (Potter 1998, 246). Furthermore, DP neither presupposes a static object that we have attitudes about. Instead, attitudes can be seen as being involved in shaping the reality we perceive (Billig 1996/1987; Potter and Wetherell 1987). So, the focus is on the action-orientation of human interaction, that is, on what is being done through the discursive choices made. The analysis draws attention to discursive devices that have been found to be important for the expression of attitudes, such as reported speech, rhetorical questions, concede and counter pairs, graduation, intensification and modality (Halliday 2014; Martin and White 2005), but also how these discursive moves may be combined with features that are unique to Twitter.

Results

Securitizing actors' communication

To give context to the twitter messages from individual users that are analysed in the next sections, I will outline the Norwegian securitizing actors' initial communication in connection with the terror threat.

On July 24, the minister of justice, Anders Anundsen, along with the chiefs of the Norwegian security police (PST) and Police Directorate, Marie Benedicte Bjørnland and Odd Reidar Humlegård, held a press conference. At this meeting, Anundsen said:

DISCOURSE AND SOCIAL MEDIA

Excerpt 1. We are now in a situation where there is a concrete threat against Norway, and measures are implemented to meet this threat (Norwegian Government 2014).

A first thing to note is how modality can be used to express different levels of certainty and control (Halliday 2014). While Anundsen used a high degree of certainty (e.g. 'there *is* a *concrete* threat to Norway'), other statements were much vaguer. At the same press conference, Marie Benedicte Bjørnland read verbatim a press release that was published on the same day on PST's website and further shared via their Twitter account. Formulations are used, which provide low modal force:

Excerpt 2. PST recently received information that people associated with an extreme Islamist group in Syria *may* intend to carry out a terrorist act in Norway (Bjørnland 2014, my italization).

The use of negatives (Halliday 2014) regarding information contributes to the expression of a low level of certainty:

Excerpt 3. We have *no* information about who, how, what goal or the manner in which such a possible attack is planned [...] Because the information is *nonspecific* and *little* concrete, yet credible, it will be *difficult* to advise citizens in the country about how they should deal with this (Bjørnland 2014, my italization).

The professional jargon of PST and its director was quoted widely. In August when the alert level had been lowered, a search on Google on 'terror threat' (No. 'terrortrussel') and 'nonspecific but credible' (No. 'uspesifikk men troverdig') gave 2550 hits.

A second characteristic to note about the securitizing actors' communication is the responsibility allocated to the public. At the initial press brief, Anundsen gave the following request to the public, and on the police website, and in a press brief with the Oslo Police Commissioner, Humlegård, similar expressions were used:

Excerpt 4. It is important in this situation to follow the advice that the police provides and perhaps also, as citizen, be a little extra watchful in the situation that we now will outline (Norwegian Government 2014).

Excerpt 5. The police still ask people to be vigilant. If you see anything suspicious, call the police [...] (Norwegian Police 2014).

Excerpt 6. But we ask the individual to be vigilant and notify [the police] if something is suspicious (TV2 2014).

Seen through a Foucauldian lens, the securitizing actors encourage citizens to assume care for the self and others through individual acts of lay surveillance (Rose 1999). However, in anticipation of the risk that certain ethnic groups would be kept under surveillance, blamed and discriminated against, Anundsen declared that 'it is important that we, as citizens, do not condemn or react against particular groups in society' (Norwegian Government 2014).

The Police Directorate, PST and the Oslo Police informed the media and the public continuously until the threat was considered reduced and the police went back to normal preparedness on 31 July. Twitter was an information tool used frequently, with the Police Directorate publishing 17 tweets, and PST publishing two, during the eight days the threat was imminent. However, they never responded to others' tweets when they were addressed through the @-character or when they were given feedback on their own tweets. Their tweets were mostly unmodalized, nonevaluative messages with a focus on concrete actions and advice. An exception is the first tweet from PST on 24 July:

> Excerpt 7. Possible terror threat against Norway | PST pst.no/media/pressme... via@PST-Norway. (24 July)

As with PST's statements at the press conference and in the press release, evaluation appears in the form of low modal force regarding the existence of a threat ('*Possible* terror threat'). This confirms the previous research findings (Stenvall 2003) that antiterrorism discourse is characterized by ambiguity and future-orientation. Notably, however, different actors chose to express themselves with different amounts of certainty, and most tweets from the Police Directorate contained straightforward, nonevaluative information.

Attitudes towards securitizing actors' communication

Among the 211 tweets with the hashtag #terrorthreat (No. #terrortrussel), there are those that criticize and those that commend the work of the securitizing actors. The following tweets are complementary of the authorities. They all include a key signifier of securitization, namely 'safe' or 'safety' (No. trygg/trygghet).

> Excerpt 8. I feel very safe after the police chief of staff in Oslo was on the air at 14 #terrorthreat Today's most calm and well-spoken man. (24 July)
>
> Excerpt 9. Thumbs up for police director Humlegård. Seems very sturdy and exudes safety and credibility despite the circumstances. #terrorthreat. (25 July)
>
> Excerpt 10. Seems like a sturdy guy this Humlegård. Exudes safety. So does @AndersA-nundsen #terrorthreat #mediamanagement. (27 July)
>
> Excerpt 11. I feel safe that the police are on top of this to the extent they can now. One cannot protect oneself against all eventualities. #terrorthreat. (25 July)

The first example affords – with a high intensity marker – the police chief tenacious character traits ('Today's *most calm* and *well-spoken* man'), thus endorsing unambiguous positive judgement and attitude. This tweet also evaluates the author's own situation as 'very safe', where 'very' (like previously 'most') is upscaling the positive judgement. Furthermore, the reason for this positive state is attributed to the police chief in Oslo.

The next two tweets are almost identical in their attribution of tenacious characteristics to the director of the police ('sturdy', 'exudes safety'). Excerpt 9 uses more intensity in its positive judgement, opening with a cheerful idiom ('Thumbs up for police director Humlegård') and upscaling positive attitude ('*very* sturdy'). Excerpt 10 extends the positive evaluation to the minister of justice, addressing him directly through the @-character. Through the additional hashtag #mediamanagement, this user emphasizes the issue of how leaders deal with the media and addresses others who are interested in the question. Excerpt 11 gives a positive evaluation of the author's own situation ('I feel safe') and attributes this to the police by the use of a metaphor ('that the police are *on top of this*'). This tweet also includes a denial that all risks can be prevented, which down-scales the demands on the police.

Notably, it is only men who are constructed as these steady leaders who inspire feelings of security. The female head of PST, Marie Benedicte Bjørnland, is not mentioned in these terms in any tweet of my sample. Excerpt 8 presupposes that this type

DISCOURSE AND SOCIAL MEDIA

of crisis management leadership is a masculine task, and excludes women from the imagined competition ('Today's most calm and well-spoken *man*'). This indicates that gendered discourses operate as limitations on the attitudes expressed towards women and men as securitizing actors (Cohn 2009).

Certain critical attitudes are expressed towards the authorities' choice to alert the public despite giving vague information. These tweets therefore endorse the attitude that their communication is contradictory or possibly worse. The following three examples show common characteristics that will be examined in some detail:

> Excerpt 12. @PSTnorway holds press conf. about #Terrorthreatagainst Norway. Unspecif. sender, unspecif. goals and uspecif. content. Not an easy day for the media. (24 July)
>
> Excerpt 13. We do not know who is threatening us, what they threaten or completely when we are in danger. Nor do we know what we should do. Let's warn. #terrorthreat. (24 July)
>
> Excerpt 14. 'There is a concrete threat against Norway, but there is no information on who, how or what target' #terrorthreat. (24 July)

First, these tweets contain negatives (Halliday 2014) that endorse a perplexed, critical attitude. The signifiers 'unspecific', 'we do not know' and 'no information' signal the opposite of successful information dissemination and communications. Moreover, 'terror', 'threat' and 'danger' signify that it is in a time of high risk and heightened information need that the public is denied information, which of course worsens the image of the securitizing actors' communication. If they, on the contrary, would have been said to share knowledge, information and specific facts, positive alignment would be encouraged. Second, the communication is judged to be contradictory. Excerpt 13 ends with 'let's warn', although the previous sentence is leading in the opposite direction of action, which produces a popular, satirical effect. This tweet was retweeted 24 times. Moreover, a 'concrete' threat does not seem consistent with 'no information'. Third, these negative evaluations are intensified through repetition of the negative sounding 'unspecific' (see excerpt 12), and when the desire to be informed is denied, it pertains not only to the question of 'who', but to 'how', 'what' and 'when' as well (excerpt 14). Lastly, distancing formulations can also be important when alignment is created with specific attitudes. Through reported speech, the authors of tweet13 and 14 distance themselves from authorship of and responsibility for the statements. Yet naming the source is redundant given the minister of justice and the police held a press conference earlier the same day and figured everywhere in the media. The twitterers thus use several discursive techniques – negatives, intensification through repetition and distancing through reported speech – when articulating attitudes towards the securitizing actors' communications.

Attitudes toward the responsibilization of the public

After the police called on the public to be watchful (Norwegian Government 2014) and vigilant (TV2 2014), some tweets highlighted exactly this advice:

> Excerpt 15. How should today's press conference about the terrorist threat be interpreted? Should every one of us take over the role of watcher? #terrorthreat. (24 July)
>
> Excerpt 16. Can anyone answer what Anundsen means by saying that people should be more 'watchful'? #terrorthreat. (24 July)
>
> Excerpt 17. The minister of defence is urging: 'Citizens must be watchful in their affairs.' Hmmm… Okay. #terrorthreat. (24 July)

Excerpts 15 and 16 use rhetorical questions, the first of which endorses the strongest negative attitude while the second is a bit more open-ended. First off, the question is whether citizens should 'take over' the role of monitoring. To 'take over' is a strong statement in that it involves a change of roles between citizens and, presumably, the security police. This is an exaggeration of what Anundsen actually said at the press conference. So this tweet cues the reader to an inevitable answer: 'No'. While this tweet invites the reader to a dialogue, it also attempts to close the discursive space by presenting an unreasonable alternative. The tweet thus calls on the reader to assume a negative attitude to responsibilization. Excerpt 16 also contains a question that presupposes common attitude. The opening words ('can anyone answer') evaluates Anundsen's statement as obscure and illogical because it is assumed that *perhaps* someone in a large crowd can comprehend it. Thus, common sense is assumed to be to not understand and not agree with the proposition that citizens should monitor each other. Moreover, excerpt 17 uses reported speech and thus creates a distance to the putative proposition. It concludes with interjections ('Hmmm… okay'), which testify that the author is not very impressed.

A couple of tweets on this theme take the call from the securitizing actors literally, creating a humorous effect:

Excerpt 18. Now it would have been good to sleep, but PST asks everyone to be awake. #pst #terror #terrorthreat. (24 July)

Excerpt 19. Monitoring some suspicious girls sunbathing. No one is above suspicion. #terrorthreat. (24 July)

Excerpt 19 alludes to Anundsen's statement at the press conference that 'it is important that we, as citizens, do not condemn or react against particular groups in society' (Norwegian Government 2014). By casting suspicion over a seemingly harmless group ('sunbathing girls') this tweet stresses the absurdity of not taking specific groups of citizens under suspicion and instead, as a consequence, consider anybody a potential threat. Moreover, both these twitterers are deliberately portraying themselves as not interpreting and following the advice of the securitizing actors in the manner it was intended. The authors thus position themselves, as citizens, as unfit for responsibilization. These tweets rather call on readers to assume the attitude that ordinary people should stay ordinary and serious tasks, such as monitoring suspects, should stay with PST. Similar humorous and critical messages continued to be posted, especially after the newspaper VG reported that an innocent air traveller had been abducted by the police and strip-searched after another traveller suspected that he was a terrorist because of his dark complexion and tattoos.

There are some tweets, however, that attest that the authors perceive the threat as real and assume responsibilization. The following tweet both criticizes the way the authorities informed the public at the first press conference and testifies that serious action was taken.

Excerpt 20. This couldn't really have been more vague and diffuse and simultaneously frightening, I've done my part and frightened the young out of town #terrorthreat. (25 July)

Like tweets in the previous section, this one calls on the reader to adopt a negative attitude towards securitizing actors' communication, through evaluative adjectives such as 'vague', 'diffuse' and 'scary' Nevertheless, the tweet attests that the author takes the

DISCOURSE AND SOCIAL MEDIA

threat seriously and takes on a moral responsibility ('I have done my part') to protect 'the young', presumably her children.

Attitudes toward ethnicity and blame

Previous research has found that securitization discourse reproduces prejudice against ethnic minorities (Appleby 2010; Bhatia 2008). An exception is MacDonald et al. (2013) that found policy documents in the UK striving to avoid stereotyping and constructions of *us* and *them*. The present analysis shows that among the tweets analysed, twice as many take a stand against the blaming of minorities (*n* 10) versus those that reproduce or are less negative towards such discourse (*n* 5). The following tweets belong to the former category:

> Excerpt 21. Feeling actually with the many good Muslims who are constantly called out to "renounce" violence, threats and other idiocy #terrorthreat. (24 July)
>
> Excerpt 22. So Syrians in Norway should apologize to other Norwegians that other Norwegians with Syrian background threaten our common country? #SURR #terrorthreat. (25 July)
>
> Excerpt 23. The minister of justice asks people to be extra alert. "- It is also important that we do not judge anyone." Well said. Clever man. #terrorthreat. (24 July)
>
> Excerpt 24. Scary how the terrorist threat gives all racists whetted appetite. Radical forces are creepy, whatever origin. #terrorthreat #mylittlecountry. (25 July)

First, in excerpt 21, the author endorses a positive evaluation of Muslims ('all the *good* Muslims') and a negative evaluation of their becoming liable for the actions of others – by adding force ('*constantly* called out'), distancing through reported speech ('renounce') and additional intensification through repetition ('violence, threats and other idiocy'), which all signify excessive blaming. The next excerpt endorses the same critical attitude towards the blaming of Muslims. By positioning Syrians as part of the collective identity 'Norwegian', and by repeating 'Norway' and the 'Norwegians' three times, this tweet conveys that blaming an ethnic minority is absurd. Through this discursive move, and the rhetorical question, no other answer than 'no' is expected. The tweet thus attempts to compress a reader's interpretive options. The extra hashtag #SURR, an abbreviation of surreal, adds evaluative force and ties in with other tweets about surreal events. The two last excerpts also convey antiracist attitudes. Excerpt 23 does this by endorsing the minister of justice's antiprejudice statement through evaluative adjectives ('*Well* said. *Clever* man') and excerpt 24 by tying together lexemes that signal negative evaluation ('scary', 'racist', 'radical forces' and 'creepy'). Again, an extra hashtag, #mylittlecountry (No. #mittlilleland), adds evaluative information, in this case flagging collective self-pity and perhaps lost innocence.

Fewer Twitter messages endorse accepting attitudes toward the blaming of minorities. The following tweets position against antiprejudice views.

> Excerpt 25. Norwegians must stop complaining about everything #thepolice does! If they check foreigners extra carefully during #terrorthreat is that faulty as well?! #idiot. (29 July)
>
> Excerpt 26. Norwegian Muslims believe PST hurts the whole religion, but their distrust of PST really does more of this. http://www.nrk.no/ostlandssendingen/_-pst-gjor-muslimer-til-et-mal-1.11847954... #terrorthreat. (25 July)
>
> Excerpt 27. Wonder if Mads Gilbert, as in 2001, again possibly defends the
>
> Muslims'moral right to terrorism against the West. #MadsGilbert #terrorthreat. (26 July)

Excerpt 25 endorses a strong negative attitude, using intensifying modal choices ('*must* stop complain about *everything*'), and then a rhetorical question that ends with the hashtag #idiot. If the rhetorical question would be interpreted differently than intended, the hashtag proposes a final negative judgement.

The next excerpt attempts to align the reader with a negative attitude towards Muslims by first acknowledging ('Norwegian Muslims believe...') and then countering ('but their distrust of PST really does more of this'). Consequently, 'argumentative ground is given up initially [...]only for that ground to be retaken in the subsequent counter move' (Martin and White 2005, 124).'Muslims' in this case are the target without distinction.

Excerpt 27 proposes a negative evaluation of a physician and leftist politician who, in the aftermath of 9/11, expressed sympathy for the terrorists (Sarastuen 2001), which goes strongly against public opinion. By mentioning his name in a hashtag, it becomes clear that the person is subject to evaluation. Moreover, this tweet positions 'the Muslims', generally, without further explanation, as those who are inclined to engage in terrorism against the West, thus calling on readers to adopt a negative attitude towards Muslims. The Norwegian authorities have instead used the name 'extreme Islamism' (Norwegian Government 2014).

Conclusion

In order to contribute to knowledge about securitization as a dynamic, argumentative process where social media users are also involved, this study has analysed the articulation and variability of attitudes on Twitter in the wake of the Norwegian terror alert in July 2014. The public terror alert communication took off with a press conference held by the minister of justice together with the police and security police. This triggered numerous reactions on social media. Through an analysis of all twitter messages with the hashtag #terrorthreat (No. #terrortrussel) (*n*211), the study answers questions about how twitterers articulate, and call on readers to align with, specific attitudes towards the terror alert.

The study set out to delineate salient themes that twitterers emphasize. One theme concerns securitizing actors' communication. This is a vital aspect partly because successful securitization requires that a threat is conveyed and interpreted as 'real' (Buzan et al. 1998). Yet this is a very complicated task. Foucault and previous research on securitization have emphasized that security is a future-oriented control apparatus (Foucault 2009), and research on antiterrorism discourse has stated that such discourse is often vague and abstract (MacDonald et al. 2013; Stenvall 2003). Indeed, vagueness characterizes parts of the securitizing actors' communication in this Norwegian case, with statements about a 'possible terror threat' that is 'concrete but non-specific' (Bjørnland 2014). The study breaks new ground in that it analyses how Twitter users react to this characteristic. Twitterers recontextualize the actions of the authorities in ways that convey certain attitudes. One category of tweets attests that the vagueness raises uncertainty and fear, and they articulate more or less bluntly negative judgement of the authorities' communication in this regard. A sports journalist's message was retweeted the most in the whole sample. It was structured to emphasize the incongruity between expectations and what occurred – between the authorities' choice to announce the terror alert and yet offer little and vague information. Twitterers are thus asking for clear information, which communication research also recommend (Fischoff et al. 2003). Yet there is also a category of tweets that indeed attribute very positive traits to securitizing actors' communication, albeit to the men only. These tweets refer to them as very calm and sturdy despite a stressful situation. The absence of women – like PST's director Marie Benedicte Bjørnland – indicates in line with Cohn (2009) that male and female securitizing actors are viewed and judged differently. Yet the study also showed that the male minister of justice took the liberty to express with confidence that there was a threat, whereas the female chief of PST followed script and conveyed less certainty regarding the validity of the threat.

The second theme that twitterers emphasize is the securitizing actors' advice to the public to be watchful and vigilant. The study thus exemplifies how twitter users manage securitizing actors' attempts at 'responsibilizing' (Rose 1999) the general public into becoming overseers of terrorism risks. Already on 24 July, twitterers offer resistance to this attempted positioning. They call on readers to adopt a critical attitude to this advice using distancing, reported speech, rhetorical questions that assume a shared attitude towards peer surveillance and humorous exaggerations that portray ordinary people as unfit for such security work. On 25 July, a story about a wrongly suspected air passenger was published by the newspaper VG. His dark complexion and tattoos had made a fellow passenger so worried that she alerted the staff and police. Twitterers drew on this story and continued the criticism of peer surveillance.

This leads us to third point, namely issues of ethnicity and blame. Unlike studies of policy documents (Appleby 2010; Bhatia 2008) and news articles (Stenvall 2003), this study demonstrates that Twitter users offer a bag of more mixed and sometimes crude responses and attitudes regarding ethnicity and blame. A few tweets in the sample (*n* 5) endorse attitudes supporting police use of racial profiling, that Muslims themselves cause their own stigma in society and that 'Muslims', without distinction, carry out terrorist acts. However, more than twice as many tweets call on readers to adopt a critical attitude to stereotyping and blaming. These tweets position various ethnicities as belonging to the collective identity 'Norwegian', and thus attempt to counter constructions of us and them. They take sides with those minorities who feel forced to excuse themselves by publicly renouncing violence. They also give praise to the minister of justice who urged the public that no particular group should be judged.

Through a variety of evaluative lexical choices and grammatical means that signal mood and intensity, twitterers endorse particular attitudes regarding all of these themes. Some of them are:

(1) evaluative hashtags ('#*idiot*', '*#SURR*', '#*yolo*').
(2) adjectives ('vague', 'diffuse', 'frightening', 'clever', 'sturdy', 'scary', 'creepy').
(3) attitude verbs ('*Feeling* actually *with* the many good Muslims').
(4) negatives ('we do *not* know', '*no* information', '*un*specific').
(5) auxiliary verbs ('Norwegians *must* stop complaining').
(6) repetition ('*Unspecif.* sender, *unspecif.* Goals and *uspecif.* content').
(7) reported speech ('Nor do we know what we should do. Let's warn').
(8) rhetorical questions ('Should every one of us take over the role of watcher?').
(9) metaphors ('the police are *on top of this*').
(10) acknowledge and counter pairs ('Norwegian Muslims believe PST hurts the whole religion, *but* their distrust…').
(11) interjections ('Hmmm… okay').
(12) idioms ('*Thumbs up* for police director Humlegård').

By examining the attitude expressions through this kind of detailed analysis, this study has added to previous research and demonstrated how attitudes towards a terror alert are represented on social media. This is a novel addition to previous studies that have focused on official documents and edited news material.

Given that discourse psychology sees discourse as cocreator of the reality we perceive, the messages on twitter are understood here as a potential force in shaping securitization. However, the study shows that Twitter is not used by the authorities to enable an argumentative process involving individual Twitter users. The securitizing actors never responded to others' tweets when they were addressed through the @-character or when they were given feedback on their own tweets. Thus, propositions and questions addressed to them were unchallenged and had no apparent effect. Furthermore, through a nationwide telephone poll, published by mid-August, declaring that 85% of the population thought the authorities made the right decision to go public with terror warning, their communication was legitimized (Hind 2014). The securitization process got a stamp of approval. Yet, the Twitter communication, even if it does not reach the authorities in any visible way, provides a wide group of Norwegians the opportunity to express unfiltered views on securitization and form opinion. The messages that endorse perplexed or critical attitudes to securitization and its actors are a democratic expression of the view that securitization is not an all-good exercise of public authority (Buzan et al. 1998). They flag concerns regarding peer surveillance, excessive suspiciousness, increased insecurity and ethnic discrimination. They also critique the authorities' way of communicating. At the same time, other messages reinforce the securitizing actors' power and agenda. Regardless of the particular positioning, the study has demonstrated how twitterers, through seemingly 'microscopic' discursive means, create rich meaning-making regarding securitization. In particular, through the unfiltered modes of expression, they spell out good and bad characteristics of securitizing actors and events, adding emotional colouring that certainly contributes to public engagement in issues of security.

The study has explored three salient themes that entails certain eclecticism. Future studies may instead examine each of these themes separately and in-depth. Another worthwhile direction for future research would be to examine visual content posted on social media in times of securitization. Extensive visual material was inserted and linked on Twitter, but fell outside the scope of the present study.

Disclosure statement

No potential conflict of interest was reported by the author.

Funding

This research was financed by The Research Council of Norway and its programme Societal Security (SAMRISK II).

Notes on contributor

Joel Rasmussen is currently working as a postdoctoral fellow at the University of Oslo, and was before that head of media and communication studies in Örebro, Sweden. His research focuses on how risk and risk responsibility are understood and managed in organizational communication and in communication in society at large. In his recent work, he focuses on how social media affects risk and crisis communication. Rasmussen has published articles in edited volumes and journals such as Human Relations and Discourse & Communication.

References

Allan, S. 2014. Witnessing in crisis: Photo-reportage of terror attacks in Boston and London. *Media, War & Conflict* 7, no.2: 133–151.

Altheide, D.L. 2007. The mass media and terrorism. *Discourse & Communication* 1, no.3: 287–308.

Appleby, N. 2010. Labelling the innocent: how government counter-terrorism advice creates labels that contribute to the problem. *Critical Studies on Terrorism* 3, no.3: 421–436.

Baden, C., and N. Springer. 2014. Com(ple)menting the news on the financial crisis: The contribution of news users' commentary to the diversity of viewpoints in the public debate. *European Journal of Communication* 29, no.5: 529–548.

Baker-Beall, C. 2014. The evolution of the European Union's 'fight against terrorism' discourse: Constructing the terrorist 'other'. *Cooperation and Conflict* 49, no.2: 212–238.

Bartolucci, V. 2012. Terrorism rhetoric under the Bush Administration: Discourses and effects. *Journal of Language & Politics* 11, no.4: 562–582.

Bennett, D. 2013. Exploring the impact of an evolving war and terror blogosphere on traditional media coverage of conflict. *Media, War & Conflict* 6, no.1: 37–53.

Bhatia, A. 2008. Discursive illusions in the American National Strategy for Combating Terrorism. *Journal of Language & Politics* 7, no. 2: 201–227.

Bigo, D. 2002. Security and immigration: Toward a critique of the governmentality of unease. *Alternatives: Global, Local, Political* 27, no.1: 63–92.

Billig, M. 1996/1987. *Arguing and thinking: A rhetorical approach to social psychology.* Cambridge: Cambridge Univ. Press.

Bjørnland, B. 2014. *Mulig terrortrussel mot Norge* [Possible terror threat against Norway]. http://www.pst.no/media/pressemeldinger/mulig-terrortrussel-mot-norge/.

Buzan, B., O. Waever, and J. de Wilde. 1998. *Security: A new framework for analysis.* Boulder, CO: Lynne Rienner.

Cammaerts, B. 2008. Critiques on the participatory potentials of Web 2.0. *Communication, Culture & Critique* 1, no.4: 358–377.

Cohn, C. 2009. International security, language and gender. In *Language and power: The implications of language for peace and development*, eds. B. Brock-Utne and G. Garbo, 33–47. Dar es Salaam: Mkuki na Nyota Publishers Ltd.

Fischoff, B., R.M. Gonzalez, D.A. Small, and J.S. Lerner. 2003. Evaluating the success of terror risk communications. *Biosecurity and Bioterrorism: Biodefence Strategy, Practice, and Science* 1, no.4: 1–4.

Foucault, M. 2009. *Security, territory, population: Lectures at the Collège de France 1977-1978.* New York: Picador.

Gillmor, D. 2006. *We the media: Grassroots journalism by the people, for the people.* 2nd edition. Sebastopol, CA: O'Reilly Media.

Halliday, M.A.K. 2014. *Halliday's introduction to functional grammar.* 4th edition (revised by C.M. I.M. Matthiessen). London: Routledge.

Hind, R. 2014. *Politiets håndtering av terrortrusselen i månedsskiftet juli – august 2014* [The police's handling of the terrorist threat in late July-August 2014]. Oslo: TNS.

Hodges, A., and C. Nilep, eds. 2007. *Discourse, war and terrorism.* Amsterdam: John Benjamins.

Hogan, B., and A. Quan-Haase. 2010. Persistence and change in social media. *Bulletin of Science, Technology & Society* 30, no.5: 309–315.

Holland, J. 2013. *Selling the war on terror: Foreign policy discourse after 9/11.* Abingdon and New York: Routledge.

Kelley, P.G., M. Sleeper, and J. Cranshaw. 2013. Conducting research on Twitter: A call for guidelines and metrics. Paper presented at CSCW Measuring Networked Social Privacy Workshop, February 23–27, in San Antonio, TX, USA.

Kettell, S. 2013. Dilemmas of discourse: Legitimising Britain's war on terror. *The British Journal of Politics & International Relations* 15, no.2: 263–279.

Larsson, A.O., and H. Moe. 2014. Triumph of the underdogs? Comparing Twitter use by political actors during two Norwegian election campaigns. *Sage Open* 4, no.4: 1–13.

Lorenzo-Dus, N., and S. Marsh. 2012. Bridging the gap: Interdisciplinary insights into the securitization of poverty. *Discourse & Society* 23, no.3: 274–296.

MacDonald, M.N., D. Hunter, and J.P. O'Regan. 2013. Citizenship, community, and counter-terrorism: UK security discourse, 2001-2011. *Journal of Language & Politics* 12, no.3: 445–473.

DISCOURSE AND SOCIAL MEDIA

Martin, J.R., and P.R. White. 2005. *Language of evaluation: Appraisal in English*. London: Palgrave Macmillan.

McInnes, C., and S. Rushton. 2013. HIV/AIDS and securitization theory. *European Journal of International Relations* 19, no.1: 115–138.

Metronet. 2014. *Statistikk sosiale medier 2014* [Statistics social media 2014]. https://metronet.no/statistikk-sosiale-medier-2014/.

Mythen, G., and S. Walklate. 2006. Communicating the terrorist risk: Harnessing a culture of fear? *Crime, Media, Culture* 2, no.2: 123–142.

Norwegian Government. 2014. *Pressekonferanse om mulig trussel* [Press conference about possible threat]. https://www.regjeringen.no/nb/aktuelt/dep/jd/nett-tv/Pressekonferanse-om-mulig-terror trussel/id765442/?regj_oss=10.

Norwegian Police. 2014. *Råd fra politiet* [Advice from the police]. https://www.politi.no.

NOU. 2012. 14. *Rapport fra 22. juli-kommisjonen* [Report from the 22 July Commission]. Oslo: Departementenes servicesenter, Informasjonsforvaltning.

O'Malley, P. 1996. Risk and responsibility. In *Foucault and political reason*, eds. A. Barry, T. Osborne, and N. Rose, 189–208. Chicago: The Univ. of Chicago Press.

Obdradovic, L. 2014. *Gender integration in NATO military forces: Cross-national analysis*. Farnham: Ashgate.

Potter, J. 1998. Discursive social psychology: From attitudes to evaluative practices. *European Review of Social Psychology* 9, no.1: 233–266.

Potter, J., and D. Edwards. 1992. *Discursive psychology*. London: Sage.

Potter, J., and M. Wetherell. 1987. *Discourse and social psychology: Beyond attitudes and behaviour*. London: Sage.

Rose, N. 1999. *Powers of freedom: Reframing political thought*. Cambridge: Cambridge Univ. Press.

Sarastuen, K. 2001. Forsvarer angrepet på USA [Defends the attack on USA]. *Dagbladet*, September 30, News section.

Shi-xu. 2015. Cultural discourse studies. In *International encyclopedia of language and social interaction*, eds. K., Tracy, C. Ilie, and T. Sandel, 1–9. Boston, MA: Wiley-Blackwell.

Stenvall, M. 2003. An actor or an undefined threat? *Journal of Language & Politics* 2, no.2: 361–404.

'Terrorism'. n.d. *Oxford English Dictionary*. http://www.oed.com.db.ub.oru.se/view/Entry/199608.

Thompson, J.B. 1996. *The media and modernity: A social theory of the media*. Cambridge: Polity Press.

TV2. 2014. *Dette er siste nytt fra politiet om terrortrusselen* [This is the latest news from the police regarding the terror threat]. http://www.tv2.no/a/5842123.

Waever, O. 1995. Securitization and desecuritization. In *On security*, ed, R. Lipschultz, 46–86. New York: Columbia Univ. Press.

Waever, O. 1997. *Concepts of security*. Copenhagen: Univ. of Copenhagen.

Yin, R.K. 1984. *Case study research: Design and methods*. Beverly Hills, CA: Sage.

Zappavigna, M. 2011. Ambient affiliation: A linguistic perspective on Twitter. *New Media & Society* 13, no.5: 788–806.

Zappavigna, M. 2012. *Discourse of Twitter and social media: How we use language to create affiliation on the web*. New York: Continuum.

Radicalist discourse: a study of the stances of Nigeria's *Boko Haram* and Somalia's *Al Shabaab* on Twitter

Innocent Chiluwa

Department of Languages, Covenant University

This study examines the features of stance in tweets downloaded from the English Twitter accounts of *Boko Haram* and *Al Shabaab*, referred to as 'radicalist discourse'. Stance, referred to as 'positioning' or point of views of tweeters, is defined in terms of features such as hedges, boosters, attitude markers, self-mention and threats. These express commitment, attitude and judgement of writers on the issues being discussed. Applying mostly qualitative analysis, the study shows that self-mention and attitude markers are the most prevalent features of stance in radicalist discourse. Thus, stance is used to express triumph, satisfaction, anger and hate by the radical groups under study. The various expressions of attitude and self-mention in the data portray positive construction of in-group and negative evaluation of others (i.e. governments and institutions) referred to as *infidels* and *apostates*.

1. Introduction

Stance refers to the ways writers present themselves and convey their judgements, opinions and commitments in their writings. Thus, authors express 'a textual voice or community recognized personality ...' as well as 'stamp their personal authority onto their arguments or step back and disguise their involvement' (Hyland 2005, 175). The study of stance-taking in discourse takes a cue from the understanding that a speaker's or writer's internal thoughts, opinions and attitudes about a topic being conveyed can be expressed implicitly or explicitly through certain words or grammatical forms the writer chooses (Biber 2006). Hence, Biber and Finegan (1989, 124) define stance as 'the lexical and grammatical expression of attitudes, feelings, judgements, or commitment concerning the propositional content of a message'.

Stance in computer-mediated discourse (CMD), which is of particular interest to the current study, not only manifests in terms of vocabulary (i.e. lexical stance) and grammar (i.e. grammatical stance) but also paralinguistically (see Biber et al. 1999). Paralinguistic devices such as pitch, degree of loudness, duration of sound in verbal or synchronous online communications are often depicted in CMD through signs and some typographical conventions (Park 2007). *Affect* (or emotion), for example, is often depicted by *emoticons* showing either sadness or joy (see Gales 2010, 58–59). The current study however focuses on lexical and grammatical stances since online discourse produced by radical groups does not reflect non-linguistic devices probably because the writers' stances are expressed more through the written word than paralinguistic signs. Unfortunately there was none at all in the data for this study.

Some studies on religious violence, particularly the Boko Haram insurgency in Nigeria, have examined its historical and political implications (See Loimeier 2012; Okemi 2013; Burchard 2014). However, stance-taking in discourse, especially of radical and terrorist groups in Africa in the context of computer-mediated communication (CMC) and their broader political implications, is almost non-existent. Hence, certain questions about online behaviours of radicalist (or terrorist) groups in Nigeria, Mali, Somalia or Sudan have not really been answered. For example, how have these groups utilized the Internet or social media to spread their ideologies in an attempt to solicit for supports of or radicalize other Internet users? What stance do they take and how do they position themselves in CMD that they produce given the overwhelming influence of information technology in modern (political) communication?

This study shows that online discourses associated with rebel groups and radical movements not only reflect total commitment to some particular positions and viewpoints in texts, but also express emotional commitment to those viewpoints (Chiluwa, in press). This study further attempts to provide answers to the following questions: (1) How do radicalist groups in Nigeria and Mali express their viewpoints and emotional commitment through stance markers (e.g. boosters and hedges)? (2) How do they express ideology through attitude markers, self-mention and threats? The three aspects of stance identified by Hyland (2005) namely evidentiality, affect and presence expressed as *hedges*, *boosters*, *attitude markers* and *self-mention* (and I add *threats*) are applied in the analysis.

2. Social media in political communication

Social media have provided a medium for individuals and groups to make their voices heard. Although they started off as a digital platform for networking among friends, social media have since turned into a dynamic resource for sociopolitical and civil engagements. Popular responses through digital social networks have been the radical rejection of erstwhile oppressive regimes and the demand for sociopolitical change. Radical and rebel groups also utilize the opportunities and affordances provided by digital communication resources to advance their positions and activities. Studies on the use of social media for civil and political purposes have established that *Twitter* in particular is the fastest and most critical campaign tool for reaching and mobilizing people; for gathering data and responding to public reactions (Vergeer and Hermans 2013; Parker 2012). Individuals and social groups who are concerned about social developments and events in their various countries have also mobilized protests using social media (web 2.0, i.e. social networking sites, blogs, wikis, etc.). In the Tunisian Revolution for example, social media acted as an important resource for popular mobilization against the government by allowing digital media practitioners to break the national media restriction to make information available for the mainstream media. Social media also provided the basis for intergroup collaboration that facilitated mass participation; thus overcame the collective action problem through reporting the magnitude of events that raised the perception of success for the protesters (Breuer et al. 2012, 1). Direct reporting of events with supporting photographs added 'emotional mobilization' through 'depicting the worst atrocities associated with the government's response' to the protests (2).

Most of the individual and group communications/protests that take place on digital media platforms consist of 'positioning' of individual or group arguments, or point of view of speakers and writers. As highlighted above, this point of view generally expresses the writer's attitude, commitment and opinion towards the proposition or the subject matter in question. This positioning or point of view is referred to as *stance* (Hyland 2005).

Political and cultural discourses often highlight group relations, conflicts and resistances and involve debates that are often publicized by the mass media and the Internet. And generally, stances reflect the kind of social and cultural positions, assumptions and identities people take in relations to other members of the society. Ideologies expressed through stance-taking generally recognize the main ideological and cultural assumptions of certain groups as well as other groups, and when people feel that their identities, cultures and social rights are infringed upon, they resist and conflict results. This nature of ideologies characterizes political groups, social movements or rebel/terrorist groups (van Dijk 2005). Hence, having proper understanding of people's cultural and social uniqueness as expressed in the kind of discourses they produce, as well as proper respect for such cultural and ideological positions and stances, will achieve social harmony. Like Shi-xu (in press) rightly observes, being conscious of people's cultural differences and adopting critically minded approaches to communication towards them will foster cultural coexistence, harmony and prosperity. In the study of the stances of the rebel/terrorist groups on Twitter, which highlights their positions (in terms of why they do what do they; what cultural assumptions they espouse and what they wish to be known for), this study recognizes that human discourses are culturally differentiated and competitive in terms of groups' worldviews, identities, interests, values or representations (see Shi-xu 2009); therefore, having the right understanding of and proper attitude towards the rebels groups in question, in terms of their uniqueness; and they in turn, having respect to the society's expectations of them, will likely foster peace and social harmony.

3. Boko Haram

Boko Haram was founded in 2002 by a Muslim cleric, known as *Mohammed Yusuf* in Maiduguri, Northeastern Nigeria. *Boko Haram*, (in *Hausa*) stands for 'western education is sacrilegious', and the group claims to reject everything Western, including education and social lifestyle, and has carried out attacks on schools, beer halls and pubs. The radical Islamic group insists on a strict adoption of *Sharia* in all parts of Nigeria particularly the north eastern part of Nigeria, and have attacked some northern governors accused of compromising Islamic standards. 'Sharia' refers to the moral code and religious law of a prophetic religion (e.g. Islam); Sharia law is a major source of legislation in various Muslim countries (see Bearman et al. 2014). In June 2009 for instance, Boko Haram, embarked on an armed uprising, which according to them was aimed at fighting corruption and to Islamize the entire northern states. The uprising was confronted by the Nigerian military, resulting in the death of over 700 sect members. For the group, this has meant a greater reason to pursue its objectives (see Chiluwa and Adegoke 2013).

Boko Haram, which has since formally confirmed its link with al-Qaeda in the Islamic Maghreb and the Somalia-based *Al Shabaab*, operates also in Mali and probably Somalia (Blair 2012; Olagunju 2012), and members call themselves the 'Nigerian Taliban'. The group is also said to have split into three factions operating in Cameroon, Chad and Niger with some possible links to some terrorist groups in North Africa (Onuah and Eboh 2011). Several bombings at beer pubs, banks and police stations for which Boko Haram claimed responsibility have resulted in several deaths. On 26 August 2011 for instance, the radicals bombed the United Nations Headquarters at Abuja killing over

20 people and wounded 116 others. A bomb attack on St. Theresa's Catholic Church in Madalla (a town in Niger state) on the 25 December 2011 resulted in the death of over 35 worshippers. Since, its formation, the group is said to be responsible for the death of over 3000 people (Christians and Muslims alike) in northern Nigeria. Due to frequent series of violent attacks that destroyed government buildings and killing of officials and civilians in the northern states, the Nigeria Government in May 2013 declared a state of emergency in Adamawa, Borno and Yobe states and ordered more military troops to be deployed in the affected states (see *BBC News*, May 15, 2013). This state of emergency, however, does not seem to have deterred the militants. On 8 July 2013, Boko Haram attacked a boarding school at Mamudo in Yobe state, killing over 30 students and a teacher when their dormitory was doused in fuel and set on fire. Some who tried to escape were shot dead (*Amnesty International*, July 8, 2013). In a similar attack (29 September 2013), the sect in spite of the state of emergency, again killed over 40 students at a College of Agriculture at Gubja in Yobe state. On the 25 February 2014, the group attacked a Federal Government Secondary School at Buni Yadi in Yobe state and murdered 59 students while they slept in their dormitories (*Premium Times*, February 26, 2014). On 14 April 2014, *Boko Haram* again bombed a bus station at *Nyanya* in the Nigerian federal capital (Abuja) killing 75 people and injuring over 200. The following day, the Islamist militants kidnapped 276 girls at a government school in Chibok (Borno state) and burnt down the school; 43 of the girls escaped, and as at the time of this research, over 200 girls were still missing. Several attacks and sacking of whole villages in the northeast have continued up till the early parts of 2015. Some villages have even been taken over by them.

4. Al Shabaab

Al Shabaab which in Arabic means 'the youth,' was founded in 2006 as a radical arm of the Union of Islamic Courts in Mogadishu and is estimated to control over 7000 fighters (see Calamur 2013). Their leader *Aden Hashi Ayro* was killed in a US air strike in May 2008 and was replaced by *Ahmed Abdi Godane* (or Abu *Zubayr*) as their top commander (Ungerleider 2013). Al Shabaab operates from the Southern and Central Somalia with a mission to create a fundamentalist Islamic state in Somalia. It enforces a harsh interpretation of the Sharia and like the Boko Haram, prohibits Western lifestyle and entertainment. Hence, it condemns Western education, music, movies, haircut, etc., and had kidnapped and conscripted schoolchildren to fight in battles. They attack non-Muslims, including Christians and are a major threat to humanitarian and other international workers. For instance, the group was said to be responsible for the assassination of Somali peace activists, international aid workers, journalists and numerous civil society personnel, and was blamed for blocking the delivery of aid from some Western relief agencies during the 2011 famine that killed thousands of Somalis (see Masters 2013).

Members of *Al Shabaab* are said to be drawn from different clans and regional sub-clans and their militant groups. They also exert influences and recruit radicalized youths from elsewhere in the African sub-regions. Some radicalized American youths from the Somali-American Diaspora are also said to have been recruited. According to Gentleman (2011), educated Westerners work for Al Shabaab and several Somali-Americans have killed themselves as suicide bombers. Some non-Somali Westerners (including a man from Alabama) is also said to serve as battlefield commanders.

DISCOURSE AND SOCIAL MEDIA

As an affiliate of *Al-Qaeda*, *Al Shabaab* has resisted and fought against the Transitional Federal Government (TFG) of Somalia and its allies, including the African Union Mission in Somalia peacekeepers, and non-governmental aid organizations. The group is said to be more interested in their nationalistic battle against the TFG and hopes to regain control of Southern and Central regions of Somalia, which it had attacked and took over in 2006 but was overthrown by the Somali Government with the help of Ethiopian forces. The in-fighting and military pressure from the Somali Government and its allies has continued to liberate key towns from Al Shabaab. However, the group had continued to threaten neighbouring African countries and Western interests in Africa. Al Shabaab had claimed responsibility for several bombing attacks including suicide bombings in Mogadishu and in central and northern Somalia. The attacks had targeted Somali Government officials and their allies. They have also carried out some five coordinated suicide car bombings in October 2008 that simultaneously hit targets in two cities in northern Somalia killing about 26 people and injuring 29 others. Al Shabaab also claimed responsibility for the twin suicide bombings in Kampala (Uganda) on 11 July 2010 that killed over 70 people who gathered to watch the world cup. The USA designated this group as foreign terrorist organization and their leader as a global terrorist in 2008 (see *http://www.cfr.org/somalia/al-shabaab/p18650*).

5. Tweets in radicalist discourse

I shall define 'radicalist discourse' broadly as language use by radical movements and rebel groups, either written or spoken. This genre of discourse shares similar features with protest discourse such as language use in a direct rejection of perceived victimization, denial of rights, marginalization or human rights violations by national or regional governments. Literature on discourse by radical/terrorist groups is not common. Gales (2010) describes the ideology of 'threatening communication', which does not specify particular threats by rebel groups: anyone can issue a threat, and threats are only one feature of radicalist discourse.

Radicalist discourse is associated with sociopolitical activism as well as calls for actions in form of riots and protests. Such calls generally involve the expression of radical ideas and opinions through strong language that oppose/resist existing sociopolitical structures. Radical/terrorist groups like the Boko Haram of Nigeria and the Somalia's Al Shabaab, for example, have used *Twitter* to enunciate not only their ideological orientations but also to attack national governments, as well as enhance their own reputation and prestige. Unlike the discourse of resistance (Chiluwa 2012b) in organized rebellions like those being witnessed in the Arab spring or occupy movements, language use by radical groups combines highly organized resistance with threats and verbal war. Ungerleider (2013), calls this verbal war 'hate speech'. Al Shabaab's *Twitter* accounts have been closed down at different times for using the Twitter platform to spread 'linguistic violence' (Gay 1999).

Discourse of radicalism is highly ideological and generally characterized by the assertion of group identity; radical demands for social justice; rejection of religious tolerance and demand for the restoration of individual or group rights/privileges that are assumed to have been denied by governments or institutions. The structure of ideological discourse by rebel groups includes the enunciation of 'we' in-group in the establishment of religious or cultural identity and the definition of membership; they also identify and define their friends and enemies; establish their goals and group ideology as the basis for their activities (see van Dijk 2005). In most cases radicalized members of this group denounce the 'other' often referred to as 'infidels' or 'apostates'. Boko Haram and Al Shabaab have one thing in common, i.e., the fact that both groups espouse Islamic religious ideology and claim to defend Islam from corruption by Western enemies. They also advocate strict adherence to Sharia laws and apply violence to enforce Jihadism; thus, reject Western and 'un-Islamic' influences. But they have also been criticized by other Muslims for their extreme violent approach in the pursuit of Jihad. In some cases, liberal Muslims have been attacked and killed by Boko Haram in northern Nigeria, and some liberal Muslim clerics have also been persecuted by Al Shabaab.

Twitter has also been used not only to champion revolutionary approaches through activism but also to recruit as well as radicalize protesters and militants (see Gonzalez-Bailon et al. 2012). Gonzalez-Bailon (2011) had earlier explained that when activists make calls to action from different online sources (including Twitter), their effects were amplified, resulting in 'recruitment bursts', which is responsible for the recruitment of many users who were responding to the collective behaviour of others (1). Because the messages of tweets are usually brief, users can send several tweets and respond to others within a very short time. 'Tweeters' report and respond to ongoing events and contribute to discussions. Except in some rare cases (i.e. cases of spreading of verbal attacks by rebel groups), 'tweeting' is usually unrestricted. And with the added advantage of 'retweeting' (an equivalent of email forwarding where users post messages originally posted to others) (see Boyd et al. 2010), *Twitter* enables users to coordinate events and disseminate news and information on some specific trendy topics.

As noted above, the use of *Twitter* by Islamist militant groups (e.g. Al Shabaab and Boko Haram) has often been characterized by linguistic violence or 'twitter terrorism' (Gentleman 2011) against institutions and governments accused of undermining their rights to exist. Boko Haram, for example, has used Twitter to project their ideological stance and accuse northern Nigerian governors of compromising Islamic teachings. They have also applied their tweets to assert their identity and goals as well as mobilize supporters (see Chiluwa and Adegoke 2013). According to Gentleman (2011), terrorist organizations utilize the Internet to recruit individuals, fundraise and distribute propaganda more efficiently than they had done in time past. Some radicalize young people (e.g. Americans) and other recruits from elsewhere have gone ahead to become social media 'stars' and use the English language Twitter feeds to serve as a link between their organizations and the outside world. Thus, their forms of activism have involved the use of Twitter to manage their public diplomacy and taunt regional enemies (Gentleman 2011). The sample below is an example of tweets by *Al Shabaab* to the Kenyan army:

Your inexperienced boys flee from confrontation & flinck in the face of death. (@HSMPress)

The real identity and locations of the tweeters are uncertain. For Boko Haram, it is possible that the tweeters are radicalized Muslim youths in northern Nigeria with evidence that some of the tweets end with Hausa slogans (users of this type of slogans are likely Muslims; see an example below). The tweets may also have been written by some southern youths who support Boko Haram's mission and tactics.

@_BokoHaram @_Boko_Haram
As drops of water we are firing Arewa and infidel Nigeria.
Yaro dan is cene.

Since the tweets are written in English, the audience is not necessarily Muslims or Hausa speaking northerners/Fulanis but all Africans, and may also have aimed at reaching outsiders, especially radicalized Muslims from other countries in Europe and the USA. The tweets have the potential to radicalize Muslims from other parts of the Africa where they are less likely to speak Hausa (See Chiluwa and Ajiboye 2014).

6. Linguistic features of tweets

In terms of style and structure, CMD combines features of spoken and written language (e.g. English). Honeycutt and Herring (2009), for instance, identify the conversational patterns of language use in Twitter that is characteristic of person to person exchanges. And tweets have also been described as an 'electronic word of mouth', due to their often informal manifestations (Jansen et al. 2009). In many instances, Internet language (including Twitter) departs from grammatical norms that are associated with Standard (English) writing. According to Crystal (2011), lexical and grammatical forms of online communication are characteristic of short forms, sentence fragments and lengthy coordinated sentences. It is also not uncommon to find multiple instances of subordination, and elaborately balanced syntactic patterns and items of vocabulary that are never spoken. Interestingly, there is also evidence of 'nonsense vocabulary', obscenity and slang in online writing (including Twitter; 18). Crystal further observes that grammatical complexity also exists in tweets, which is reflective to higher levels of discourse organization (47). This means that online communication combines evidence of standard and non-standard writings.

Since *Twitter* is constrained by space, tweeters are forced to restrict their writings to the available space (not more than 140 characters); this often results in sentence fragments or minor sentences. But in most cases, points of view of writers (like radical groups) are usually not in any way endangered, except in cases of complete incoherence arising from typing errors. This is consistent with the original purpose and use of social media as a tool for networking among young people, who are easily amenable to linguistic creativity and play. However, tweets that are posted on the Twitter accounts of radical/rebel groups lack the playful nature of digital communication; thus, do not contain any form of linguistic creativity; short forms are generally rare or completely absent. Thus, Twitter language of Boko Haram and Al Shabaab falls within the generic category described by Hu et al. (2013) as 'surprisingly formal' with evidence of the use of grammatical intensifiers and personal pronouns and could well be described as 'conservative and less informal than SMS and online chat' (1).

But Twitter constrains its users to some contextual features such as linguistic/typographic markers like the *hashtag* (#) or @ sign (e.g. @boko haram). The latter brings other tweeters into a conversation, republishing other tweets and flagging topics that may be adopted by multiple users (Zappavigna 2011). Prefixing an item with a *hashtag* (i.e. #) indicates that some posts have been grouped under a semantic topic such as #government or #bokophilosophy. This is to enable others to follow conversations that centre on a particular topic.

Zappavigna (2011) observes that tweets perform both ideational and interpersonal functions following the systemic functional theory. Within the context of interpersonal meaning is 'evaluation', where 'language is used to build power and solidarity by adopting stances and referring to other texts' (794). To analyse evaluative meaning draws on a theory of appraisal (Martin and White 2005), which views linguistic patterning in a text as a meaning potential for emotional language. This emotional language is expressed in a*ttitude* (making evaluations), *engagement* (bringing other voices into the text and *graduation* (scaling up or down evaluation; Zappavigna 2011). The analysis of stance in the present study relies mainly on the evaluative character of stance to reflect attitude and judgement.

7. Stance in discourse

Several scholars and authors adopt different terminologies for stance and focus on different aspects of positioning in various genres of discourse. For instance, Biber's and Finnegan's (1989) study was based on recorded written and spoken texts, while Ochs (1990) focused on the analysis of conversational interactions. Hyland (2005) was concerned with academic discourse of published research articles. These are among several other approaches to stance studies applied to different genres of language use.

As pointed out in the Introduction, the present study adopts Hyland's (2005) approach to the study of stance. Here, stance is defined as 'positioning' or 'adopting a point of view in relation to both the issues discussed in the text and to others who hold points of view on those issues'. 'In claiming the right to be heard and their work taken seriously ... stance takers express a textual "voice" or community recognized personality ...' (175). And this can be seen as an attitudinal dimension and includes features which refer to the ways writers present themselves and convey their judgements, opinions and commitments.

According to Hyland, stance consists of evidentiality, affect and presence, which are expressed in a text as *hedges, boosters, attitude markers* and *self-mention*. *Evidentiality* is the author's position or his expressed commitment to his topic and the credibility of his/her claims, as well as his possible impact on the reader; *affect* reflects the writer's communication of attitude and feeling in his proposition and *presence* is how the writer chooses to project himself/herself (Hyland 2005, 178). 'Hedges' in discourse is a point where the writer withholds commitment to a proposition, leaving the information he/she presents as an opinion rather than a fact. This implies that a statement is based on plausible reasoning rather than certain knowledge (Hyland 2005). Hedges manifests in grammar as *adverbs* (e.g. probably, possibly, perhaps, may be, etc.), *modals* (may, might), *prepositional phrases* (kind of, sort of), etc.

Unlike hedges, boosters such as *certainly, clearly, obviously, surely, without/no doubt,* etc. are used to express the writer's certainty of a proposition (or findings) and also to mark the level of commitment and involvement with the topic and solidarity with his/her audience. Boosters also function to stress shared information, group membership and engagement with readers (Hyland 1999, 2005).

Attitude markers express the writer's affect (i.e. emotions and feelings) towards a topic or proposition. Attitude markers may express surprise, importance, frustration, agreement, etc. rather than commitment (Hyland 2005). 'Self-mention' is the use of personal pronoun 'I' or 'we' (and 'us'), and the possessive adjective 'our' to indicate proposition, affect and interpersonal information (Hyland 2001, 2005). This is not common in scientific writings (Hyland 2005) but the presence or absence of a definite reference indicates the type of authorial identity the writer wishes to adopt in his/her work. Thus, Hyland (2005) version of stance is viewed as the most appropriate in the analysis of stance in radicalist online discourse as it provides the right framework for examining points of view, and emotional commitment of the writers.

8. Methodology

Data for this study comprise mainly tweets downloaded from the Boko Haram English Language Twitter profile and that of *Al Shabaab* between 2012 and 2014. As at the time of this research, there were only 148 tweets (of 3090 words) and retweets (with 565 followers and 8 following) on the Boko Haram account (i.e. @Boko Haram) posted between 2011 and 2012. Surprisingly, the Boko Haram Twitter account appears dormant since 2012. The reasons for this inactivity in the account are not immediately known. Possible reasons could be that those who operated the account suddenly withdrew their supports for the group; second, Boko Haram deliberately abandoned their English language account for whatever reason. When the sect first came on Twitter, they operated two separate accounts namely: @Boko Haram (republic of Arewa) and @Boko Haram (Chadian border). The latter account was shut down not long afterwards, probably for using it to spread linguistic violence. The former account (i.e. @Boko Haram, republic of Arewa) was left, where I obtained the data for this study. Al Shabaab's English language account was closed down by Twitter shortly after the attack on Nairobi Westgate Shopping Mall for breaking Twitter's terms of service, (i.e. Twitter prohibits the use of Twitter for making threats of violence; see *AP 24 September 2013*). Al Shabaab had live-tweeted the Mall attack and posted tweets that defended the mass killings and threatened more bloodshed (see Ortiz 2013). An example below is a live tweet by Al Shabaab during the Westgate attack:

*SHAB*7. MSM Press Office @HSM_PR

The Mujahideen entered #Westgate Mall today at around noon and are still inside the mall, fighting the #Kenyan Kuffar inside their own turf

Al Shabaab Twitter feed (i.e. @HSMPress) carries a self-identify description (i.e. 'Harakat Al Shabaab Al Mujahideen is an Islamic movement that governs South & Central Somalia and part of the global struggle towards the revival of Islamic Khilaafa'). The Boko Haram account on the other hand carries a slogan: 'I hate School', which appears as a logo. It also carries an explanation such as 'to hate is human, to bomb is divine'. 'We hate western inventions including Twitter: however, we feel the necessity to use it to reach out to our fans'. The first tweet by Al Shabaab is in the name of God with the following words: 'In the name of God, the most gracious, the most merciful'.

The data rely on tweets that were posted by Al Shabaab (already about 20 tweets that attracted 3016 followers) before the Twitter account was shut down. A few other tweets posted from 2011 are included totally 34 tweets (of 800 words). Altogether this study examines 182 tweets, which I think is enough for a study of groups that do less talk and more (violent) actions. Although this number is very small, being what was available at the time of research, they give sufficient insight to the discursive character of radicalist discourse in the social media. The analysis is mainly qualitative involving textual/ discourse analysis of the tweet samples showing the functions of the stance markers being studied. A small amount of quantitative analysis is also adopted in order to account for the frequencies of the stance markers in the data.

9. Analysis and discussion

Analysis examines the expression of stance following the Hyland's model discussed above, where stance is viewed in terms of evidentiality, affect and presence manifesting as hedges, boosters, attitude markers and self-mention. First, evidentiality or point of view is discussed independently in order to fully examine the position of the radicalist groups under study.

9.1. Evidentiality in radicalist discourse

In projecting their positions in texts, writers (including tweeters) are usually aware that their readers also have points of view on the issues they discuss. Hence their goal is to persuade and possibly convince their readers to adopt their own point of view. Every written discourse therefore anticipates a response from the reader as the discourse itself belongs to a community whose members already hold certain forms of argument or position on the issues being discussed (Hyland 2005). 'Evidentiality' in the context of this study stands for tweet authors' positions, which explain the reasons why the radical groups under study have carried out series of attacks in Nigeria and Somalia, and how they have engaged the readers in their argument, while negotiating solidarity.

Radicalist discourse is characterized by features that suggest group reaction to perceived injustice. Some radical groups lay claim to their right to resistance against institutional victimization, persecution by national/regional governments, ethnic/religious marginalization or racial discrimination (see Chiluwa 2011). The overall position of the Islamic tweeters in the radicalist discourse of tweets has been the creation of the Islamic state of Northern Nigeria strictly governed by the *Sharia* law (for the Boko Haram), and the control of Southern and Central regions of Somalia as a Sovereign Islamic state by the Al Shabaab. Tweets in this context are mainly used as propaganda against government actions, or to mobilize support and followership. Boko Haram claims responsibility to protect Islam through violence from compromise and total collapse in northern Nigeria, where some Muslim governors (according to them) have compromised Muslim standards and adopted Western lifestyle. The entire northern Nigeria is viewed as polluted by Western influence and the violation of Sharia laws. Hence, the sect members seek not only to secure a separate government in the north but also claim to liberate the people and defend sociocultural and moral ideals (Chiluwa and Ajiboye 2014). This type of argument in a predominant Muslim north and in a fairly populated Muslim south is most likely to attract support, even among the liberal Muslims who have criticized the sect's violent method of achieving Jihad in northern Nigeria. However, Boko Haram is not alone in their agitation for a separate state in Nigeria: the Biafra campaign groups have consistently made similar demands for an independent state of the Igbos (see Chiluwa 2012b). Thus, Boko Haram is not only making a sentimental appeal but also appeals to the shared knowledge between them and the reader, as a form of engaging the reader's positioning in constructing similar line of reasoning since they share same sociopolitical and cultural context.

It is therefore clear that the Radicalist groups under study seek both political and religious independence from their national and regional governments. They have also made this position clear in their tweets. Below is an example from *Al Shabaab* Twitter account:

SHAB2. MSM Press Office @HSM_PR

The attack at Westgate Mall is just a very tiny fraction of what Muslims in Somalia experience at the hands of Kenyan invaders.

SHAB5.HSMPRESS @HSMPRESS1

The Mujahideen strive to liberate Muslim lands & lift the oppression from Muslims who are forced to live under the heel of Kafir Invasion.

The point of view expressed in the above tweets is simply that the writers view their activities as a revenge mission for some perceived injustice meted to Somali Muslims by the Kenyan authorities. Attacks on the Westgate mall were viewed as an action to 'liberate' Muslims from the assumed oppression. Thus, Al Shabaab take the position of liberators. But as serious as the above allegations may sound, there are no obvious documented proofs that Muslims have been oppressed by the Somali governments (a far as I know). It is, however, possible that the Somali Government's battle with Al Shabaab may have resulted in the death of civilians. In which case, any group in Somalia that represents Islamic interests has the right to seek legal action against the government if there is indeed evidence of oppression against Muslims in Somalia, rather than direct attacks on civilians at a shopping mall.

Nigeria's Boko Haram have also made similar mission statements in the past. However, in the examples from the data below, the Islamic fundamentalists appear to be committed to 'liberating' not only the northern states but also the entire country from the corrupt leadership of the 'infidel government of Nigeria'. This argument is expressed in the examples below. (It is important to mention here that the tweets being analysed are those written by *Boko Haram* and not their supporters. Those written by their supporters appear in the data as retweets.)

BOK2. BOKO HARAM @BOKO_HARAMM

We love Nigerians, it's only the nigerian polis, nigerian army, drunkards, prostitutes, politicians, usurers, teachers, touts we can't stand.

BOK3. BOKO HARAM @BOKO_HARAMM

2 fools: Obasanjo and Babangida (plus one infidel dunce in aso rock) taking 150 million people for fools. Join Arewa Boko republic.

BOK4. BOKO HARAM @BOKO_HARAMM

We have left Nigeria. We are in Boko Republic of Arewa. The infidel nig. govt and kafiri army should leave us.

In expressing stance as positioning and point of view, Boko Haram in the above tweets also claim to be liberators of Nigerians, again assuming the position of 'lovers of Nigeria'. By implication, their activities are not to be viewed as antisocial, rather as 'freedom fighting'. In *BOK4* above, they take the position of non-Nigerians, who are fighting for the creation of the so-called 'Republic of Arewa'.

Apart from building on some shared background knowledge, thus constructing solidarity with the reader, tweeters attempt to convince their readers by making calls to them to adopt a particular viewpoint. In *BOK3* above, the tweet calls on the reader to 'join Arewa Boko republic'. This form of engagement involves rhetorically pulling the reader to 'critical points, predicting possible objections, and guiding them to particular interpretations' of the issues at hand (Hyland 2005, 182). For example, Nigerians are called upon to see Boko Haram as friends rather than enemies.

The Boko Haram tweeters have actually taken the advantage of the common knowledge of the history of Nigeria's underdevelopment usually attributed to government corruption, ineptitude and incompetence. Already, several voices in the Nigerian society are demanding for a social revolution, similar to those currently being witnessed in North Africa (Chiluwa 2012a). Hence, the Boko Haram tweeters adopt this persuasive engagement of the reader in assigning to the Nigerian reading public a role (who are already tired of corruption in Nigeria) in creating the argument and assuming their solidarity.

Having established the conventional position and textual voice of Boko Haram and Al Shabaab on Twitter in their struggle to establish dominant Islamic enclaves in their separate Africa sub-regions, I now examine how they express their commitment, attitude, emotion or feelings through hedges, boosters, attitude markers, self-mention and threats in the discourse of sociopolitical and religious freedom.

9.2. Hedges

According to Hyland (1998), hedges (e.g. probably, possibly, etc.) enable the writer to involve the reader as participant in the argument, conveying modesty or respect for the view of others. So hedging does not make specific claims in terms of reality or factuality. Interestingly, radicalist discourse makes claims most of the time. In the entire data of the Al Shabaab tweets, only four instances of grammatical hedging are evident, where hedges are used to express mere disbelief in a perpetual closure of the Al Shabaab Twitter account and to give an unconfirmed number of deaths the group claimed responsibility for. Here are the examples:

> *SHAB14. HSMPRESS @HSMPRESS1*
>
> Freedom of speech is but a meaningless rhetoric. So long @HSMPress! *You might* be gone, but your legacy lives on.
>
> *SHAB15. HSMPRESS @HSMPRESS1*
>
> And it is *arguable* that the closure of the account is a clear indication of the effectiveness of the message emanating from the 'other side'.
>
> *SHAB16. HSMPRESS @HSMPRESS1*
>
> The Mujahideen have last night carried out a large offensive against the #Ethiopian invaders in Bidoa, killing *at least* 24 of the invaders.

Hedges in the above samples are certainly not intended to express deference or modesty to the opinion of readers. This is not surprising considering the general nature of radicalist discourse. In many cases, radicalist discourse has been characterized by claim-making (sometimes unconfirmed claims), assertive statements and accusations, all of which do not require the use of hedges. This explains why there are so few occurrences of hedges in the data. In *SHAB14* above, 'you might be gone' is rather used in defence of the existence of their Twitter account (i.e. *@HSMPress*) that was closed down for violating Twitter's operational guidelines. Al Shabaab views this closure as an infringement on their freedom speech. Here, hedging is used as rhetorical strategy to 'mourn' the demise of @HSMPress and to indirectly maintain that it has not really died. This is confirmed by the fact that the account was reopened after a short while before the Westgate attack. The closure following the Westgate attack was about the fifth time in two year and the second time in 2013 (see *Associated Press,* 23 September 2013). Even after the English language account was suspended, the Arabic language accounts continued to operate and were used to denounce the suspension as media censorship and infringement on their rights to freedom of speech (see *http://www.news24.com/Technology/News/Insurgents-Twitter-account-suspended-20130125*). This message is both explicitly and implicitly conveyed in the samples above.

In the Boko Haram data, again only four instances of hedging were used (e.g. 'we are *not sure* this is ...'), which of course is less frequent in comparison with that of Al Shabaab. This is expected because, as highlighted above, tweets and statements by rebel groups seem to hardly consider the point of view of reader. In the samples below, the verb phrase 'thinking of' is used to indicate *undecidedness* rather than opinion. The use of hedges like 'we think' indicates that a statement is not based on empirical findings, rather on the author's evaluative judgement. But in the Boko Haram's case, they had simply not made up their mind to carry out the activities expressed in the tweets.

BOK10. BOKO HARAM @BOKO_HARAMM

We are *thinking of* banning jeans, Tshirt and Tmlewin shirts … jelabia is more suitable to the Maiduguri sun and for banks #1STEPAHEAD.

BOK11. BOKO HARAM @BOKO_HARAMM

Boko Haramm *thinking of* replacing cigarettes with sheesha … healthier and with more vitamins #PROGRESS.

In their effort to Islamize the north and carry out their intended sociocultural revolution, Boko Haram intends to ban Western lifestyle. Western lifestyle includes fashion and the use of clothing items associated with the West such as jeans and T-shirts and replace them with local wears (e.g. 'jelabia' – a locally made *long gown*). They also intend to ban smoking and replace it with a local stuff (e.g. 'sheesha'; see Chiluwa and Adegoke 2013). Since this way of 'thinking' will eventually amount to a mandatory infringement on peoples' rights to socialization and choice of a lifestyle, it becomes more like threats. It is therefore right to conclude that hedges defined in terms of holding backing commitment to a proposition (as they appear in academic discourse) do not really exist in radicalist discourse.

9.3. Boosters

Boosters, such as *certainly, clearly, obviously, surely*, etc., enable writers to present their work with assurance while achieving interpersonal solidarity (Hyland 2005). In the Al Shabaab tweets below, the writers attempt to sound convincing by introducing some forms of boosters such as 'a clear', to argue against the illegality of the closure of their Twitter account, which they (Al Shabaab) attribute to Twitter's fear of the effectiveness of their (Al Shabaab's) message often viewed by the public as coming from the 'other side' (i.e. terrorists). They also use 'everything practically possible' to appeal to the understanding of the reader in their explanation that women and children were not targeted in the Westgate attack.

SHAB15. HSMPRESS @HSMPRESS1

…the closure of the account is *a clear* indication of the effectiveness of the message emanating from the 'other side.

SHAB4. MSM Press Office @HSM_PR

Mujahideen have no desire to kill women & children and have done *everything practically possible* to evacuate them before attacking.

While it is possible that the authors of the above tweets may have anticipated the readers' solidarity with the 'clarity' of the propositions, it is also doubtful that readers (i.e. non-supporters of Al Shabaab) agree that the Al Shabaab's Twitter account was ethically effective. Al Shabaab's argument in *SHAB4* is also hardly convincing since reports confirmed that both women and children were injured in the Westgate attack, some even lost their lives. So they could not have 'done everything practically possible' to evacuate

DISCOURSE AND SOCIAL MEDIA

them before the attack (See *www.theguardian.com/world/2013/gunmen-kenyan-shopping-centre-nairobi*).

In the same vein, the Boko Haram attempt to appeal to the readers' solidarity when they argue for the rightness of their actions. They are aware that some sections of southern (Nigerian) youths are indeed in support of their bombing attacks in Nigeria and have asked that the Boko Haram should rather bomb Abuja (the seat of power) and dismiss the current government (see Chiluwa and Adegoke 2013). Nigerians that anticipate a revolution like those of Tunisia and Libya have also tweeted their views and shared them in online forums (e.g. Balya, jokolo. @HeyItsBalya @BOKO_HARAMM *I love you guys*!! *God bless you*. Retweeted by BOKO HARAM). In *BOK20* below the writer applies some boosters 'sure', and 'surely', first to argue the legitimacy of the activities of Boko Haram, and it appears he takes the support of the reader for granted, when he say 'I'm sure you know …'; the Nigerian Government is referred to as 'the infidel in 'Aso Rock' (Aso Rock is Nigeria's seat of power equivalent to the US' White House). The writer of tweet in *BOK21* also uses 'surely' to express his conviction of the certainty of the success of the Boko Haram insurgency.

> *BOK20*. BOKO HARAM @BOKO_HARAMM
> *I'm sure* you know we were right all along. We suspected this. The infidel in Aso rock has no clue. #joinboko.
>
> *BOK21*. BOKO HARAM @BOKO_HARAMM
> We are happy to announce the closure of 3 universities: UNIMAID, UI, UNIBEN. Slowly but *surely* we shall overcome #UPBOKO.

In *BOK21*, Boko Haram announce the closure of some Nigerian universities (i.e. University of Maiduguri, University of Ibadan and University of Benin); but this appears much like a propaganda since it was never confirmed that these Universities were at anytime shut down by Boko Haram. I am aware that Nigerian universities were shut down for about four months in 2013 due to disputes between the Academic Staff Union of Universities and the Nigerian federal government due to disputes associated with university funding. There were no cases of university closure in 2011 or 2012 arising from Boko Haram's attacks. The emphatic 'surely' in the above tweet, which also indicates a firm commitment and assurance of the writer in the closure of Nigerian universities, does not of course, represent the view of most Nigerians who strongly believe in the importance of Western education.

In radicalist discourse, writers simply make assertive statements and claims, and in most cases are confident of the certainty of these claims. This is the reason why boosters occur more often in the data than hedges (see Table 1). Some of the assertions and claims appear as accusations levelled against some institutions and governments. The examples below represent some common boosters in radicalist discourse:

> *BOK22*. BOKO HARAM @BOKO_HARAMM
> *The truth is* it's the army killing innocent people … #askodipeople #askgoodluck. The army is a mad dog. We are for you.
>
> *BOK23*. BOKO HARAM @BOKO_HARAMM
> *Fact:* federal govt of Nigeria has killed more people thru incompetence this year than Boko Haram, armed robbers, kidnapaz and MEND.#GASKIYA

Some of the claimed 'truth' and 'fact' in the above tweets are followed by verbs 'killing' and 'killed' that indicate actions of the accused agents. In other words, the Nigerian Government and security agents are accused of killing innocent citizens and this is referred to as 'truth'. Again, the readers' position is hardly taken into account. In this case the reader is viewed as a student who should unquestionably accept the (supposed) factual information provided by his tutor. The Boko Haram here attempts to influence the view of the Nigerian public and possibly win their sympathy. Some forms of emotional appeal using stance markers to the reading public are strategic in the process of radicalization of young people, who might be reading the tweets.

9.4. Attitude markers

Attitude markers express the writer's affect or emotions. They are usually expressed by *nouns* (e.g. infidel, terrorist, coward, fool, etc.), *adjectives* (e.g. good, happy, foolish, ludicrous, etc.), *verbs* (e.g. love, win, plead, massacre, etc.) and *adverbs* (e.g. unfortunately, absolutely, practically. etc; see Biber et al. 1999; Gales 2010). In the radicalist discourse under study, attitude markers generally express triumph, satisfaction, pride, hate and anger, involving the use of labels and name-calling for governments and institutions. These attitude markers represent several negative evaluations of the 'other', which occurs frequently in the two sets of data for the study. The Government of Nigeria and security agents are constantly referred to as 'infidels' or 'terrorists' by the Boko Haram, while the Somali Government and security agents are called 'apostates'. Adjectives, such as *ludicrous, bad, lazy, flagrant, ragtag,* etc., exhibiting anger and hate are also used to describe the governments and their actions. Below are a few examples:

SHAB20. MSM Press Office @HSM_PR

It is *absolutely ludicrous* how the Kenyans seem to disregard their military's *flagrant massacre* of Muslims in Somalia and cry about #Westgate.

SHAB21. HSMPRESS @HSMPRESS1

HSM forces *overran apostate* checkpoints in the city during initial phase of the *multipronged assault*, killing dozens of *inebriated apostates*.

BOK30. BOKO HARAM @BOKO_HARAMM

Even Boko Haramm would not sit by and allow a *gang rape*. The *infidel government* of Nigeria has done enuf #absu #evil5.

BOK31. BOKO HARAM @BOKO_HARAMM

We didn't kill Aikhomu. *Bad* healthcare *unleashed* by *Terrorist infidel Government* did.

The above samples exemplify some forms of lexical and grammatical stance markers in the data. These consist of accusations and other forms of linguistic violence against the governments of Nigeria and Somalia. The writers probably believe that strong or offensive language actually does some harm such as discrediting the accused before the public or inciting a mass action against them. The expression of hate in the expression

Table 1.   Stance features in the activist discourse data.

Stance	Boko Haram = 3060		Al Shabaab = 800	
	words	Total (%)	words	Total (%)
Self-mention	131	4.28	04	0.50
Attitude markers	59	1.93	13	1.63
Boosters	06	0.20	04	0.50
Hedges	04	0.13	04	0.50
Threats	03	0.10	02	0.25

'absolutely ludicrous' and the claim 'flagrant massacre' in SHAB20 are subtle stance markers that appeal to emotions of the reader. For instance, a report that Muslims are flagrantly massacre in Somalia by the Kenyan military has the tendency to incite some forms of mob action or protest against the government and possibly radicalize those who are already sympathetic of Al Shabaab's activities. In *BOK31*, *Boko Haram* blames the death of Augustus Aikhomu (a former Vice President of Nigeria, during Babangida's Government) on the federal government's health care policy. (Aikhomu died in Lagos on 17 August 2011 after a long illness.) The meaning and tone of the verb 'unleashed' in the tweet is sequel to the character of the 'terrorist' that is used to describe the Nigerian Government. Again, this type of claim by Boko Haram is a subtle way of appealing to public sympathy and to win support. A direct reference to the poor health care policy of the government, which is a sensitive issue, is the writer's persuasive attempt to persuade the reader as well as win public approval and support.

9.5. Self mention

Self-mention is the use of personal pronoun 'I' or 'we' (and 'us'), and the possessive adjective 'our' to indicate proposition, affect and interpersonal information (Hyland 2001, 2005). The presence or absence of a definite reference indicates the type of authorial identity the writer wishes to adopt in his/her work. In radicalist discourse, the identification of 'we' in-group and the ideological positive self-evaluation that follows is almost highly mandatory. In the two data for this study, the discourse of the tweets reflects the positive representation of 'we' in-group, which aligns with van Dijk's ideological square, namely: (1) emphasize our good properties/actions; (2) emphasize their bad properties/actions; (3) mitigate our bad properties/actions; (4) mitigate their good properties/actions (van Dijk 1998, 33). In the Nigerian context, Boko Haram represent 'We' and 'Us', while the Nigerian Government and security agents represent 'They' and 'Them'. In the Somali context, the TFG of Somalia are 'They' and 'Them', while Al Shabaab represent 'We' and 'Us'. Both radical groups claim to fight for the people (e.g. Muslims) against their national governments. In the data, instances of 'We', 'Us' and 'Our' with their attributing positive qualities are frequent. A few examples from the data below illustrate the positive actions of the 'us' and the negative actions of 'them'.

BOK40. BOKO HARAM @BOKO_HARAMM

Jonathan, Abati, Omokri *are a threat* to Nigeria *not Boko Haramm*. *We* fight for your liberation even though you are not grateful #LONGTERM.

BOK41. BOKO HARAM @BOKO_HARAMM

Nigeria is a joke. Polis, army & govt are jokers. *They* kill more innocent pple evryday than Boko has done in a year.

BOK42. BOKO HARAM @BOKO_HARAMM another's

We have left Nigeria. *We* are in Boko Republic of Arewa. The infidel nig. govt and kafiri army should leave *us*.

BOK43. BOKO HARAM @BOKO_HARAMM

@admutebo. thanks for recognising *our good work*. One man's terrorist is freedom fighter. No retreat no surrender.

SHAB22. MSM Press Office @HSM_PR

Your eccentric battle strategy has got animal rights groups quite concerned, Major.

SHAB23. MSM Press Office @HSM_PR

Your inexperienced boys flee from confrontation & flinck in the face of death.

In *BOK40* above negative actions are attributed to 'Jonathan' (i.e. President Goodluck Jonathan), 'Abati' (i.e. Reuben Abati, Special Adviser to President Jonathan on Media and Policy) and 'Omokri' (i.e. Reno Omokri, Special Assistant to President Jonathan on New Media); they are also described as 'threats'. On the other hand 'we' (Boko Haram) is said to fight for the liberation of the Nigerian people. The Nigerian Government and security forces (i.e. 'they') are also accused of killing innocent people (*BOK42*). Positive evaluation of the in-group generally involves the conscious enunciation of positive property or 'our good work', sometimes with some claimed proofs (e.g. *BOK45*; *BOK46* below) or with a comparison between 'us' and other militant groups (*BOK47*). In *BOK47*, Boko Haram claims to be after 'ideals', while MEND (another ethnic militia group) is said to be 'after money' (see Chiluwa and Ajiboye 2014). In other words, 'they' are bad but 'we' are good. Hence, they (Boko Haram) appeal to Nigerians to join in their fight (e.g. *BOK48*).

In the Al Shabaab tweets above, the tweeter is answering back to the Somali military commander; the latter representing the Somali Government. He represents the 'They' whose battle is referred to as 'your battle' and soldiers as 'your boys'. Here, the 'Other' naturally attracts negative evaluation of the Al Shabaab tweeter.

> *BOK45*. BOKO HARAM @BOKO_HARAMM
>
> Wives and children now see their husbands in the night in Abuja and Maiduguri. Countless marriages have been saved #COLLATERALEFFECT.
>
> *BOK46*. BOKO HARAM @BOKO_HARAMM
>
> Rate of alcoholism has reduced in Abuja and Maiduguri because of *our good work* #COLLATERALEFFECT.
>
> *BOK47*. BOKO HARAM @BOKO_HARAMM
>
> *MEND is after money, we are after ideals*. Ideas that come at the right time flourishes. MEND VS. BOKO HARAM PT.2 #DEADIDEALS
>
> *BOK48*. BOKO HARAM @BOKO_HARAMM
>
> I wonder how many years of bombing the infidel in aso rock can survive. *We* plead with Nigerians to join us in *our* fight.

Self-mention in radicalist discourse also usually involves the negotiation of group identity often perceived as endangered by dominant government and institutional forces. Arguably, Al Shabaab's activities are rooted in both political and cultural struggle that is hoped to redefine a new identity for Muslims in Somalia. Unfortunately, they have consistently applied unethical methods in the pursuit of this objective. In *BOK42* above, the Boko Haram explicitly states that they are no longer Nigerians; thus implying that although still identified in a physical geopolitical space with Nigeria, they are psychological and spiritually out of Nigeria and ask to be left alone. Self-mention in radicalist discourse therefore goes beyond the authorial reference that merely identifies a writer and his personal role in a research work or his academic authority and achievement. Since radicalist (protest) writing is not to be viewed as an academic endeavour, its style, focus and audience also defer. Hence, self-mention in radicalist discourse projects groups identities, actions and goals that revolve round a group who construct themselves in terms of their rights to sociopolitical and cultural privileges.

9.6. Threats

According to Fraser (1998, cited in Gales 2010, 6), threats are intentional acts that use language to send a (special type of) message (*addition mine*). They are just like any other type of speech act that depends on the illocutionary force or the intent of the message with which they are uttered (Gales 2010). However, threats are different in terms of force, from the act of promise or invitation, for example, because they are usually made to express anger, or instil fear. In radicalist discourse, they are mainly used to express hate, give warning and challenge authority; they are also used to show intent of purpose, and to attract media attention. In the data, the Boko Haram and Al Shabaab issue several threats to the Nigerian and Kenyan armies in order to warn them against impending attacks. For instance *SHAB24* below is a response to the Kenyan Government's failure to heed a threat before the Westgate attack.

SHAB24. MSM Press Office @HSM_PR

The Kenyan government however, turned a deaf ear to our *repeated warnings* and continued to massacre innocent Muslims in Somalia #Westgate.

While the attack was still going on at Westgate shopping mall, the Al Shabaab were still issuing threats, with photos of attackers parading the mall. *SHAB25* below is an example. This type of threat is generally issued in order to instil fear and probably disorganize the Kenyan armed forces. The 'big surprise' in *SHAB25* below probably refers to the high number of casualties and the battle that lasted for two whole days.

SHAB25. MSM Press Office @HSM_PR

The Kenyan govt and FM haven't the faintest idea of what's going on inside #Westgate mail. Rest assured. *Kenyans are in for a big surprise*!

In the Boko Haram data, threats also occur. While some of them appear like mere information, they actually function as threats in disguise as in *BOK50* and *BOK51* below.

BOK50. BOKO HARAM @BOKO_HARAMM

Full list of legitimate targets should be out soon. To be advertised in the national dailies #NOWAYOUT.

BOK51. BOKO HARAM @BOKO_HARAMM

Boom, boom, boom, Boko Haram bomb, do you have *any target*, yessah yessah, 1 are the *infidels in Maidug, 2 the ones in Abuja* #BOKOWORKOUTRHYMES.

BOK52. BOKO HARAM @BOKO_HARAMM

We wonder if the polis in Nigeria is still at his job, take a cue from the met polis and resign. *We'll mess you up again* #INCOMPETENCE.

In the Boko Haram threats in *BOK50–52*, the words 'target' occurs twice (50 and 51), each of them announcing an intended attack. BOK51 tweet goes further to apply some form of rhetoric (play on words) to express their intention (this also sounds like a mockery of the Nigerian military). The threat in *BOK52*, 'we'll mess you up again', directed to the Nigerian Police, suggests that they had mess the Police before. As a matter of fact, Boko Haram is indeed not only messing up the Nigeria security system, but also the Nigerian Government in the various successes they have recorded in the last three years.

Threats occur as a significant feature of radicalist discourse and from the reports and experiences of terrorized places, threat from terrorists and radicalist movements should not be taken lightly by governments and security agencies. If the Kenyan Government

DISCOURSE AND SOCIAL MEDIA

had taken some oversight actions to protect the Westgate mall, even after Al Shabaab had warned them, the impact might not have been that devastating.

Table 1 shows the occurrence of stance markers in the data; it highlights the prevalence of certain stance markers above the others and to further shade some light on the feature of radicalist discourse. For instance, as already mentioned in the discussion above, certain stance markers (e.g. self-mention and attitude markers) are bound to occur frequently in the discourse of radical movements giving the ideological nature of their arguments, attitudes and points of view. In most cases, their arguments almost lack modesty; in other words, they hardly withhold commitment and leave certain claims as an opinion with the use of hedges and show some respect to the reader's viewpoint; rather, they present their arguments as facts and show a great deal of emotional commitment to them. Emotional words are used to appeal to the emotions of the reader, which is a strategy to attempt to attract sympathy or even radicalize the reader. Although boosters reflecting certainty of propositions occur far less than self-mention in the data, they are still more than hedges.

Wordsmith is used to calculate the frequencies of the stance markers. (Wordsmith is computer software often used by corpus linguists for a quantitative method of linguistic analysis. Wordsmith is capable of counting and analysing features of language use being studied. For instance, Wordsmith can calculate how frequent certain lexical items occur in a text giving an insight to the language forms or choices made by speakers or writers in a text. Frequencies can be given as a raw figure or in percentage.) The Boko Haram data comprise 3060 words and Al Shabaab 800 (as shown on the Table 1), and are converted to a computer-readable format (i.e. plain text) and analysed using *Wordsmith* (2010). Since the data are very small, the frequency of words being sought in the data was simply counted manually from the concordance. (A *concordance* is a list of all the occurrences of a particular word or search term in a corpus and the context in which they occur.) Figure 1, for example, is a concordance of 'Infidel' (attitude marker) from the data.

Stance features in each of the data were obtained and counted manually. The total sum of the occurrences of words reflecting self-mention (e.g. we, us, our, etc.) in the

N	Concordance	Set Tag Word #	t. #	os.	a. #	os.	d. #	os.	t. #	os.	File	%
1	SEE THE INNOCENT PEOPLE THE INFIDEL GOVERNMENT IS KILLING	1,470 190	6%	0	1%		0	1%	earch corpus.txt		34%
2	out...Aso rock is bombing down infidel politicians build it up with looted	1,567 203	7%	0	3%		0	3%	earch corpus.txt		36%
3	TAN IS NT UR FRIEND INFIDEL! BOKO HARAM	1,350 177	0%	0	9%		0	9%	earch corpus.txt		31%
4	2 Aug 11 @melifew213 INFIDEL YOU ARE ALREADY OUR	1,193 159	5%	0	5%		0	5%	earch corpus.txt		27%
5	2 Aug 11 Imagine this infidel saying MEND has a legitimate	1,238 163	4%	0	6%		0	6%	earch corpus.txt		28%
6	ALONG. WE SUSPECTED THIS. THE INFIDEL IN ASO ROCK HAS NO CLUE.	1,703 214	3%	0	6%		0	6%	earch corpus.txt		39%
7	@DRDAMAGES. WE ASSUME HE IS INFIDEL AND HIS WORDS DONT	2,698 319	5%	0	7%		0	7%	earch corpus.txt		62%
8	of Sharia in Nigeria and ensure that the infidel does not go unpunished. 4) We	4,361 414	0%	0	2%		0	2%	earch corpus.txt		93%
9	wonder how many years of bombing the infidel in aso rock can survive. We plead	2,498 289	7%	0	3%		0	3%	earch corpus.txt		57%
10	we conciliate &adjudicate wt decadent infidel pestiferous rulers of nig, we then r	1,781 221	8%	0	8%		0	8%	earch corpus.txt		40%
11	26 Jul 11 REASON THE INFIDEL RULERS LIKE NIGERIA: IT IS	1,875 225	5%	0	0%		0	0%	earch corpus.txt		43%
12	We are in Boko Republic of Arewa. The infidel nig. govt and kafiri army should	1,156 156	3%	0	4%		0	4%	earch corpus.txt		26%
13	?@BOKO_HARAMM If we tell the infidel govt to vote for Palestine and they	473 69	9%	0	0%		0	0%	earch corpus.txt		11%
14	not sit by and allow a gang rape. The infidel government of Nigeria has done	556 81	3%	0	2%		0	2%	earch corpus.txt		13%
15	day of bombs...hope this is not an infidel song. BOKO HARAM	378 51	5%	0	8%		0	8%	earch corpus.txt		9%
16	A drop of water we are firing Arewa and infidel Nigeria. Yaro dan is ce ne BOKO	284 43	2%	0	6%		0	6%	earch corpus.txt		7%
17	bitch, Jesus in one sentence, you are infidel #ASSWIPE BOKO HARAM	312 45	8%	0	7%		0	7%	earch corpus.txt		7%
18	?@BOKO_HARAMM 17 Sep 11 INFIDEL OBJ DISTURBING THE PEACE	782 109	9%	0	7%		0	7%	earch corpus.txt		18%
19	Bad healthcare unleashed by Terrorist infidel Government did. BOKO HARAM	1,089 146	8%	0	3%		0	3%	earch corpus.txt		25%
20	we have been causing havoc and bad. Infidel federal government still clueless	1,108 149	5%	0	3%		0	3%	earch corpus.txt		25%
21	Obasanjo and Babangida (plus one infidel dunce in aso rock) taking 150	1,005 136	5%	0	1%		0	1%	earch corpus.txt		23%
22	?@BOKO_HARAMM Wonder how that infidel sleeps at night. Oh we know.	902 124	3%	0	9%		0	9%	earch corpus.txt		21%
23	?@BOKO_HARAMM Heard the infidel goyyim at Aso rock got himself	920 128	7%	0	9%		0	9%	earch corpus.txt		21%

Figure 1.   Concordance of 'Infidel' from the Boko Haram data.

Boko Haram data is 131 as shown above (only 04 instances are shown in the Al Shabaab data due to the size of data). The same goes for *attitude markers*. From Table 1, it is quite clear that words reflecting ideological positive self-evaluation and words reflecting attitude markers (or emotional commitment) are the most prevalent in radicalist discourse. This shows that discourses of radical groups or terrorist are highly ideological as this study shows. Hence, the study of stance in discourse is one fruitful method of studying the nature of language features as well as their functions in a wider social context.

10. Conclusion

The present study highlights the various subtle ways stance functions in online discourse of radical groups, showing how authors reflect their positions, commitments and attitudes in the social media. This attempt is therefore likely to open up reactions and possible further research endeavours in discourses produced by activist/terrorist groups. The study also shows that the roles and functions of Twitter in providing a platform for individuals and groups to express themselves, their viewpoints and attitudes on issues affecting them is very important. This research also shows that attitude markers and self-mention the most prevalent features of stance in activist discourse and in most cases are used to express ideological propositions.

Disclosure statement

No potential conflict of interest was reported by the authors.

Notes on contributor

Innocent Chiluwa (Ph.D.) is Associate Professor (Language and Communication) in the Department of Languages, Covenant University, Ota (Nigeria). His research interest focuses on pragmatics and discourse studies, particularly the investigation of social crisis/conflict, ideology, identity and activism in (New) Media and CMCs, as well as in social, political and religious discourses. He has published scholarly articles in *Discourse and Society, Discourse Studies, Discourse and Communication, Journal of Multicultural Discourses, Journal of Language and Politics, Africa Today,* etc.

References

Bearman, P., Th. Bianquis, C. Bosworth, E. van Donzel, and W. Heinrichs. 2014. *Encyclopedia of Islam.* 2nd ed. Brill Online.

Biber, D. 2006. *University language: A corpus-based study of spoken and written registers.* Amsterdam: John Benjamins.

Biber, D., and R. Finnegan. 1989. Styles of stance in English: Lexical and grammatical marking of evidentiality and affect. *Text* 9: 93–124.

Biber, D., S. Johansson, G. Leech, S. Conrad, and E. Finegan. 1999. *Longman grammar of spoken and written English.* Harlow: Longman.

Blair, D. 2012. Al-Qaeda's hands in Boko Haram's deadly Nigerian attacks. *The Telegraph,* February 5. http://www.telegraph.co.uk/news/worldnews/al-qaeda/9062825/Al-Qaedas-hand-in-Boko-Harams-deadly-Nigerian-attacks.html, accessed on 23 August 2012.

Boyd, D., G. Scott, and L. Gilad. 2010. Tweet, tweet, retweet: Conversational aspects of retweeting on Twitter. HICSS-43. Kauai, HI: IEEE, January 6.

Breuer, A., T. Landman, and D. Farguhar. 2012. Social media and protest mobilization: Evidence from the Tunisian revolution. Paper prepared for the European Communication Conference, October 24–27, in Istanbul, Turkey.

Burchard, S.M. 2014. Boko Haram and the 2015 Nigerian elections. *Africa Watch,* April 4, 2011. http://www.ida.org/upload/africawatch/africawatch-apr-11-2014-vol4.pdf.

DISCOURSE AND SOCIAL MEDIA

Calamur, K. 2013. *Somalia's Al-Shabaab: 4 things to know*. http://www.npr.org.

Chiluwa, I. 2011. *Labeling and ideology in the press: a corpus-based critical discourse study of the Niger Delta Crisis*. Frankfurt: Peter Lang.

Chiluwa, I. 2012a. Citizenship, participation and CMD: The case of Nigeria. *Pragmatics and Society* 3, no.1: 61–88. doi:10.1075/ps.3.1.03chi

Chiluwa, I. 2012b. Social media networks and the discourse of resistance: a sociolinguistic CDA of *Biafra* online discourses. *Discourse & Society* 23, no.3: 217–244. doi:10.1177/0957926511433478

Chiluwa, I. in press. Digital discourse of radical movements: Exploring stance and positioning in Nigerian militant groups' online discourses. In *Exploring democracy in Nigeria @15: Papers on language and politics*, ed. T. Opeibi, S. Awonusi, J. Schmied, and P. Ifukor. Gottingen: Cuvillier Verlang.

Chiluwa, I., and A. Adegoke. 2013. Twittering the Boko Haram uprising in Nigeria: Investigating pragmatic acts in the social media. *Africa Today* 59, no.3: 83–102. doi:10.2979/africatoday.59.3.83

Chiluwa, I., and E. Ajiboye. 2014. 'We are after ideals': A critical study of ideology in the tweets by Boko Haram. *Global Media Journal, African Edition* 8, no.2: 318–346.

Crystal, D. 2011. *Internet linguistics*. London: Routledge.

Gales, A. 2010. Ideologies of violence: A corpus and discourse analytic approach to stance in threatening communications. An unpublished Doctoral thesis. University of California.

Gay, W. 1999. The language of war and peace. In *Encyclopedia of violence, peace, and conflict*, ed. L. Kurtz, vol. 2, 303–312. San Diego: Academic Press.

Gentleman, J. 2011. Somalia's insurgents embrace Twitter as a weapon. *The New York Times*, December 14. http://www.nytimes.com/2011/12/15/world/africa/som.

Gonzalez-Bailon, S. 2011. *The role of the social media in protests*. Oxford: University of Oxford. http://www.ox.ac.uk/media/news_stories/2011/111612.I.

Gonzalez-Bailon, S., J. Borge-Holthoefer, A. Rivero, and Y. Moreno. 2012. *The dynamics of protest recruitment through an online network*. Oxford: Oxford Internet Institute, University of Oxford.

Honeycutt, C., and S. Herring. 2009. Beyond microblogging: Conversation and collaboration via Twitter. Proceedings of the Forty-Second Hawaii International Conference on System Sciences (HICSS-42). Los Alamitos, CA: IEEE Press.

Hu, Y., K. Talamadupula, and S. Kambhampati. 2013. 'Dude, srsly?': The surprising formal nature of Twitter's language. *Association for the Advancement of Artificial Intelligence*. www.aaai.org.

Hyland, K. 1998. *Hedging in scientific research articles*. Amsterdam: John Benjamins.

Hyland, K. 1999. Disciplinary discourses: writer stance in research articles. In *Writing: Texts: processes and practices*, ed. C. Candlin and K. Hyland, 99–121. London: Longman.

Hyland, K. 2001. Bringing in the reader: Addressee features in academic articles. *Written Communication* 18, no.4:549–574. doi:10.1177/0741088301018004005

Hyland, K. 2005. Stance and engagement: a model of interaction in academic discourse. *Discourse Studies* 7, no.2: 173–192. doi:10.1177/1461445605050365

Jansen, B.J., M. Zhang, K. Sobel, and A. Chowdury. 2009. Twitter power: Tweets as electronic word of mouth. *Journal of the American Society for Information Science and Technology* 60, no.11: 2169–2188. doi:10.1002/asi.21149

Loimeier, R. 2012. Boko Haram: The development of a militant religious movement in Nigeria. *African Spectrum* 47, no.2–3: 137–155.

Martin, J., and P. White. 2005. *The language of evaluation: Appraisal in English*. New York: Palgrave Macmillan.

Ochs, E.. 1990. Cultural universals in the acquisition of language: Keynote address. Papers and reports on child language development, Stanford University, 29:1–19.

Masters, J. 2013. Al Shabaab. *Council on Foreign Relations,* September, 23. http://www.cfr.org/somalia/al-shabaab/p18650, accessed on 23 October 2013.

Okemi, M. 2013. Boko Haram: A religious sect or terrorist organization. *Global Journal of Politics and Law Research* 1, no.1: 1–9.

Olagunju, L. 2012. Boko Haram confirms Al-Qaeda link. *The Tribune,* January 29. http://tribune.com.ng/sun/front-page-articles/6254-boko-haram-confirms-al-qaeda-link-as-cameroun-stations-soldiers-at-nigerias-borders, accessed on 23 August 2012.

Onuah, F., and C. Eboh. 2011. Boko Haram explodes five bombs in Nigeria. *Mail & Guardian Online*, December 25.

DISCOURSE AND SOCIAL MEDIA

Ortiz, E. 2013. *Al Shabaab's alleged Twitter account taunts Kenyan officials following mall rampage.* http://www.nydailynews.com/news/world/terrorists-tweeting-new-account-claims-kenyan-mall-militants-article-1.1465961.

Park, J.-r. 2007. Interpersonal and affective communication in synchronous online discourse. *The Library Quarterly* 77, no.2: 133–155. doi:10.1086/517841

Parker, A. 2012. In nonstop whirlwind of campaigns: Twitter is a critical tool. *New York Times*, January 28. http://www.nytimes.com/2012/01/29/us/politics/twitter-is-a-critical-tool-in-republican-campaigns.html?pagewanted=all, accessed 16 August 2012.

Shi-xu. 2009. Reconstructing eastern paradigms of discourse studies. *Journal of Multicultural Discourses* 4, no.1: 29–48. doi:10.1080/17447140802651637

Shi-xu. in press. Cultural discourse studies. In *International encyclopedia of language and social interaction*, ed. C. Tracy, C. Ilie, and T. Sandel. Boston, MA: Wiley-Blackwell.

Ungerleider, N. 2013. *How Al-Shabaab uses the internet to recruit Americans.* http://www.fastcompany.com/3018339/how-al-shabaab-uses-the-internet-to-recruit-americans.

Van Dijk, T. 1998. *Ideology: A multidisciplinary approach.* London: Sage.

Van Dijk, T. 2005. Opinions and ideologies in the press. In *Approaches to media discourse*, ed. A. Bell and P. Garret, 21–63. Malden, MA: Blackwell.

Vergeer, M., and L. Hermans. 2013. Campaigning on Twitter: Microblogging and online social networking as campaign tools in the 2010 general elections in the Netherlands. *Journal of Computer-Mediated Communication* 18, no.4: 399–419. doi:10.1111/jcc4.12023

Zappavigna, M. 2011. Ambient affiliation: A linguistic perspective on Twitter. *New Media & Society* 13, no.5: 788–806. doi:10.1177/1461444810385097

Visual forms of address in social media discourse: the case of a science communication website

Yiqiong Zhang[a], David Machin[b] and Tao Song[c]

[a]*Center for Linguistics and Applied Linguistics, Guangdong University of Foreign Studies;* [b]*Örebro Universitet;* [c]*School of English for International Business, Guangdong University of Foreign Studies*

> This paper shows how a multimodal discourse analysis of the changing visual designs of a science news website between 2009 and 2013 can reveal fundamental changes in visual forms of address, which must be acknowledged alongside shifts being observed at the level of linguistic address. Designers deploy design features in a shift from presenting science as official, formal, and authoritative, where communicative style is a monolog, to one which must suggest a sense of a conversation, of accessibility, of engagement, with a reader presumed to have opinions and needs. This is shift from a culture of transmission of information to a culture which rather formulates, channels, and retrieves information and which is dominated by scan-and-go media use. The analysis describes the changes of design details. It places these observations within the scholarly debate about the consequences of the Internet and social media for science communication.

Introduction

The rise of what has been called Web 2.0, 'a second generation of the Web that allows people to produce and debate information online' (Brossard and Scheufele 2013, 41), has brought sweeping changes to the landscape of communication with new features of hypertextuality, multimodality, interactivity, and accessibility (Deuze 2003). Science communication has been included in this shift ushering in the era of 'Science 2.0' (Lievrouw 2010). Like Web 2.0, Science 2.0 is a sphere where science information is partly user-generated content and is shared by users via social media dialogs, with the need for the scientific community to connect with the public in new ways. Science communication is no longer a matter of transmitting authoritative knowledge from the science community to an uninformed public, but includes dialogs that involve different levels of specialists, institutions, and organizations via platforms such as *YouTube*, *Facebook*, and *Twitter* (Brossard 2013). There has, Lievrouw (2010) suggests, been a shift from 'big science' dominated by information provided by wealthy institutions, mass-marketed on a global scale to 'little science', which is something much more localized, specialized, and personalized. However, little is known about this process and there is urgency for scholarly attention (Allan 2009; Brossard and Scheufele 2013; Lievrouw 2010).

What is of specific interest to us in this paper is the visual communication that characterizes these shifts in relations performed through social media, a ubiquitous discourse phenomenon and yet seemingly neglected by discourse analysts. In this paper, taking the case of an online science magazine *Futurity*, and how it has changed over time, we investigate the way that these shifts in social relations, from one where authoritative experts presented information to a passive public to one of engagement, of participation, of niche communities of users and of seeking and sharing of information, a shift to a realm where everything is seen as opinion rather than fact, must on the part of such magazines be realized visually as well as in terms of linguistic forms of address and through kinds of contents. We show how this must be done through very specific and identifiable visual semiotic features. These both increasingly take forms appropriate for the social media environment but must signify ideas, values, and identities, which correspond with this. These point to the broader shifting discourses about the nature and status of knowledge, expertise, kinds of authority, and use of visual communication that can be found realized across contemporary, social media–rich societies.

While scholars have begun to explore how social media have transformed business communication (Aral, Dellarocas, and Godes 2013), and to a much lesser extent changes in science communication (Lievrouw 2010), we need to know more about the way that visual design plays an important role in these shifts. Visual communication is not mere addressing, but itself communicates discourses about the identity of a site and its social relations with and between users, the meanings of the forms of interactions that take place there and the nature of the very content itself – in this case what science is. We show how our analysis helps to consider these shifts in respect to the consequences of these for science communication itself and reflect on what happens when it becomes integrated with social media genre and formats.

This study offers insights into how social media, in and through the discourse of public science communication, is changing the power relationships between official institutions and the public, reshaping the culture of communication both within and outside the science community, and ultimately has the potential to shift the very nature of cultural notions of knowledge themselves, across organizations and across different societies. It contributes to the scholarship of cultural discourse studies (Carbaugh 2007; Shi-xu, forthcoming) by expanding the coverage of discourse to the seemingly neglected area of science communication and by demonstrating the power of multimodal analysis in revealing the discursive dynamics of discourse being reshaped by social media.

Science communication in Web 2.0

Science information was formerly delivered to the public by the mass media in the form of news and magazines. On the one hand this was seen as one part of the expository phase of scientific practice, which is vital to the scientific enterprise (Gregory and Miller 1998) and an integral component of the knowledge production (Whitley 1985). On the other hand, science news has tended to be judged rather negatively by the scientific community (Lewenstein 2001; Nelkin 1995) since such representations differ greatly from traditions established in the textualization of scientific knowledge in research articles. As a result, science news is generally considered by the science community as being simplistic, inaccurate, sensational, and biased (Lewenstein 2001).

It has been considered, however, that the 'authority-to-public' model has been turned 'inside-out' as the Internet and social media have shifted the boundaries between previously separated spheres of communication (Trench 2008). Science news is no longer consumed in isolation as it used to be, but instead is now contextualized by cues such as *Facebook* likes, readers' comments, or *Twitter* mentions (Brossard and Scheufele 2013). As well as shifts in the way that people find, seek out, and obtain science information, it has also meant that scientific institutions are able to bypass traditional mainstream media outlets, which is considered as a significant developmental stage in science communication (Brossard 2013; de Semir 2010; Trench 2007, 2008).

The bypassing of traditional forms of media outlets is also driven by the social force of marketization. To attract funding from governments and nongovernmental organizations which is crucial to maintain and expand the expensive scientific enterprise, institutions have increasingly sought to 'sell' the importance of science to the public (Nelkin 1995). Institutions include science news on their websites to publicize their research achievements and demonstrate their excellence (de Semir 2010). This process has also seen individual institutions themselves adopt a journalistic model of communication, applied even when the information is passed from professional sources to professional audiences (Trench 2008). Hired journalists provide accessible summaries of research findings and other achievements. Science presented as 'science news' is thus becoming a standard feature of such institutional websites.

Scholars have expressed some concerns about this impact of new media on science journalism. Allan (2009) calls for scholar attention to 'how, and to what extent, the internet is changing the characteristics of science news' as 'it promises to dramatically recast science journalism's familiar norms and values in unanticipated ways' (162). It has been suggested that, science news, especially that disseminated by institutions, have been found to be transformed from the 'logic of journalism' which 'investigates scientific issues via credible sources and developing subject expertise and a critical response' to the 'logic of corporate communication' for 'promoting corporate interests and noncritical public relations' (Bauer and Gregory 2007, 45). How the shift has been manifested at the level of discourse remains unexplored.

Web 2.0, social media, and representational practices

The new media environment has brought dramatic changes not only to the intermediation of science news but also to the representational practices. Science news in the Web 2.0 era combines visual, audio, and verbal resources to translate science knowledge for novice audiences and to arrange all this information in an array of interlinked web pages and social media networks, while enabling the readers to navigate and create their own pathways through this virtual 'universe' of science and other related information. Science news is now very often embedded in the discourses of new media platforms, including the video sharing platform of *YouTube* and social networking platform of *Facebook*.

It has also been argued that social media, along with other shifts in the nature of design and branding culture, have had huge impacts on representational practices in a broader sense (Tsimonis and Dimitriadis 2014). From a study comprising interviews with leading web and news designers from the around the world, Machin and Polzer (2015) show that visual designs have had to increasingly come to speak to more specified niche markets, but that this has shifted from more traditional information styles where information was provided in an authoritative and more formal manner to one where they speak on a equal footing and need to address a reader who sees themselves as already well informed, who has strong opinions and wants to feel they are making choices. These are a newer generation of readers accustomed to social media with its sense of community engagement, interactivity, and a vast range of choices of sources of information. Designers spoke of the way that the Web need to visually communicate these new kinds of social relations had also transformed print design, due to changing viewer expectations and design culture.

These changes can be seen also as part of an overall cultural shift with social media at its heart (Julier 2006). Visual design, in a culture of the voice of authority, was formerly about pure representation, narrative, and about conveying messages. This has changed as culture has changed its relationship to information. In a culture which formulates, channels, and retrieves information, design has become 'about the structuring of systems of encounter within the visual and material world' (Julier 2006, 67), and information consumers have the expectation to be active participants in media (Hanna, Rohm, and Crittenden 2011). The new forms of media are not simply replacements for the old but have to communicate a sense of choice, show that they reach out to people, create intimacy, and engage with them (Hanna et al. 2011). Myers (2010), writing on the kind of language styles that characterize successful blogs, points to the way this must not be in the form of monolog, but must give a sense of a conversation, of accessibility on behalf of the speaker and of engagement with a reader presumed to have opinions and needs. For Machin and Polzer (2015), the difference between older and newer forms of visual design can be thought about as part of a similar shift away from monolog to engagement and participation and also one which assumes readers will have scan-and-go attitude.

Theorists such as Dean (2010) draw attention to the way that social media must be placed in a cultural shift – what Žižek (1998) would describe as the death of the 'big other', in other words the waning of there being a sense of consensual central, institutional body of knowledge which includes rather fixed ideas, values and identities. In place, Dean (2010) suggests, we have a culture of 'communicative capitalism', which offers constantly new and varied ways to imagine ourselves, of course where the concept of choice to do so is very powerful. We can see this in social media as we find a rise of more specialist online spaces. But Dean suggests this also leads to an increase in skepticism where everything is treated as opinion rather than as information, where we tend to easily fall back on to what is comfortable. Couldry (2012) asked what the wider consequences of these kinds of shifts in media practice are and how they shift our basic assumptions and expectations for everyday life – the knock-on effects of concepts like 'user community', the high value of 'connectivity', the routinization of presenting what 'other people bought', 'what other users read', but where there is always a 'scan-and-go' attitude and an ability to simply click in and out of an online discussion. It is clear that we need to know much more about these kinds of shifts as the realized new forms of discourse practices. In this paper, we show these shifts as they must be acknowledged in visual forms of address and their consequences for the nature of knowledge can be explored through the case of a science magazine website.

Visual design and the case of *Futurity* science magazine

In this paper we choose one example of this shift in visual forms of address in the case of science communication. We look at a website called *Futurity* (http://www.futurity.org/), which was launched in 2009 to aggregate research news from partner universities. It was initiated by the members of the *Association of American Universities in America and Canada* and then was expanded to include leading universities from across the world. We analyze the original designs of the home page and a news page and then their redesigns in 2010 and 2013, doing so by starting with an analysis of *Facebook* posts to show how the influence of these can be seen across the design. Across all the examples, we find visual cues used to communicate discourses about what science is and about what reading about and sharing science means. It also relates interpersonal information about the identity of the website itself, its values and attitudes, and about the identity of the user and community of users. As part of this research, we investigated a range of science communication websites and there are differences across those that are more commercially driven to those that are funded through universities. Such differences will be the topic of a different paper since here it is the fundamental shifts in forms of visual address in social media that are our specific focus where *Futurity* serves as one highly illustrative case study.

Theory and methods

Design is realized through forms (often referred to as design patterns by designers), the relationship of which can be discussed with the construct of genre (Müller 2011). Genre is concerned with properties of text types shaped by social practices or socially recognized communicative practices and serves specific functions (Lemke 2005). The formal features of a genre as realizations of the communicative action's purpose provide workable tools for discourse analysts to address patterns in web page design, in this case to understand *Futurity* through its changing designs.

Genres found on the Web are different from print pages in that they can not only be read as traditional print texts but also act like portals to related texts with hyperlinks. Given the dual functionality of web pages, meanings are constructed via two dimensions: the reading dimension and the navigational dimension (Askehave and Nielsen 2005). In the reading dimension, verbal and visual resources (e.g. color, image, and layout) interact to construct a text to be read as it stands; while in the navigational dimension, meanings are construed via what contents hyperlinks on the page direct to (i.e. navigation content) and how they are directed to (i.e. navigation style) (Zhang and O'Halloran 2012). The two-dimensional model sheds light on the generic properties of web pages in terms of the traditional text perspective and the hypermedia one (Bateman 2008) and provides a way to unpack the multimodality and hypertextuality of web page discourse. Meaning construed in both dimensions can be related to higher level cultural and ideological meanings (Zhang and O'Halloran 2012, 2013). We adopt the model to investigate how the evolving discourse practices of *Futurity* home page and news page are 'shaped by' and 'shaping' the changing social context of science communication. We focus mainly on the reading dimension due to the scope of the paper.

The analysis of the case of *Futurity* is also done using tools from Multimodal Discourse Analysis (MDA), an approach informed by Systemic Functional Linguistics (Halliday 1994; Halliday and Mathiessen 2004) and the more social semiotic tradition of MDA (Halliday 1978; Hodge and Kress 1988). This provides tools for analyzing meaning potentials of semiotic choices and the discourse they realize. From the perspective of MDA, a web page is examined as a complex of visual signs which include language (Knox 2009) and has been increasingly applied to critical investigation of the hypermodality of online discourse (e.g. Lemke 2002; Zhang and O'Halloran 2012). This analysis draws attention to the way that visual semiotic resources are able to fulfill specific communicative functions, to communicate quite specific ideas and attitudes as well as be used textually to create links and hierarchies between elements (Kress and van

DISCOURSE AND SOCIAL MEDIA

Leeuwen 2006). In this way they are able to signify wider discourses about things like identities, values, and social relations.

Analysis

We carry out an analysis first of *Facebook* posts. This is important as we shall show that many of the generic features of these posts are transferred to the wider design of later redesigns of the home page and news pages. We then analyze the home page and news page redesigns in turn.

Facebook post of Futurity

Facebook and *Facebook* posts have been increasingly significant as a source for the design of the *Futurity* home page and news page. The design of social media 'creates the socio-technical foundation on which the strategies, management and value derived from social media are built' (Aral et al. 2013). We therefore first analyze the design of *Facebook* post by discussing its generic components.

A *Facebook* post, as any type of communicative event via social media, is with a design that enables and constrains its use to achieve goals of maintaining social relationship. In general, the components of a *Facebook* post remain stable along the years, including the following generic components:

> *Event attribution*: the top part of a post revealing the *Facebook* identity of the person who posts the message, and the time for the posting
>
> *Event comment*: comments made by the poster towards the message being shared, explaining why the message is shared
>
> *Event focus*: the image and verbiage about an event as the focus to orient readers to the hyperlinked event
>
> *Action panel*: buttons of 'comment', 'like', and 'share' for readers of the post to take action towards the event message; readers' feedback will be automatically recorded and displayed in the post

In the 2009 *Facebook* post of *Futurity* news items, *Event comments* are mainly put in a form of question to engage readers for further reading. In the first post of Figure 1, for instance, the question of 'What's the greenest way to ski?' is to engage readers into *Futurity* news item about research on a green way to build ski runs. The original news title from *Futurity* is kept in the *Event focus* with the *Futurity* icon. The post in 2009 takes a form of 'news in the post', with majority of the information remained to be represented as it is in the original news. The institutional identity of *Futurity* has been a crucial element of the post to present the information. The format is continued to 2013 but images are gradually used to replace the *Futurity* icon in the *Event focus*. As manifested in the post as of 2011, an image of an avocado is used in the news titled 'Add avocado to holiday meals'. We will say more about this use of stock images shortly.

These generic components of *Facebook* posts have been increasingly incorporated into the design of *Futurity* home page and news page, as we shall demonstrate in the next section of analysis. For *Futurity* news post on *Facebook*, both of the *Event comment* and *Event focus* function ideationally, interpersonally, and textually to foster further engagement.

93

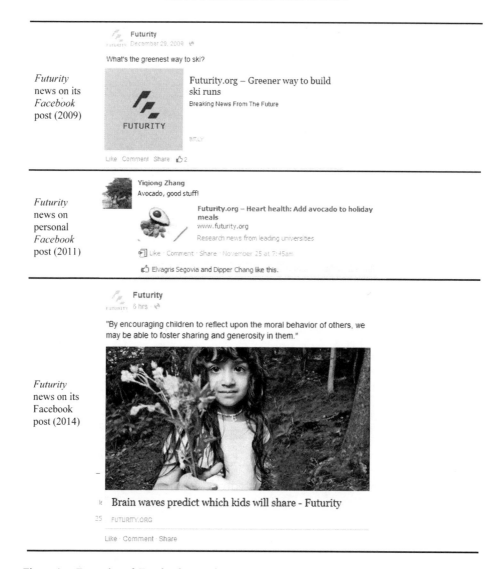

Figure 1. Examples of *Facebook* post about *Futurity* news.

The changing Futurity home page

We analyze the redesigns of the *Futurity* home page by looking closely at the visual design (the reading dimension). As the reading dimension is not isolated from the navigational dimension, we address the navigation purpose of the design whenever necessary. The three versions of *Futurity* home page are displayed in Figure 2. In what follows, we analyze the elements of image, color, font, and composition in turn.

Image

One of the most obvious changes across the three versions of home page is found in the use of images. Here we find a shift from more literal and decorative use of images to the image as a design feature and its more deliberate and playful symbolic use.

DISCOURSE AND SOCIAL MEDIA

2009 version	2010 version	2013 version

Figure 2. *Futurity* home page in 2009, 2010, and 2013.
Note: Only two thirds of the 2013 version from the top is presented here due to space constraint.

In the 2009 version (left of Figure 2), the main image of the expert, is literal and old-style portrait. It is the face of an approachable scientist, set in a realistic work-type setting. The other three images closely related to the reported event are used in the fashion of bullet points. The one on the left is the logo of the conference reported in the news, the middle with a shot of a doctor giving an injection on a patient as a demonstration of reported flu shot, and the right with an image of molecules and bacteria to illustrate the findings of the research event. Ideationally, these images represent typical science-type subjects and help to construe science as distant, lofty, and specialist (Nelkin 1995). Interpersonally, there is a sense of engaging the reader more informally with the use of the close shots, and the main image engages readers with the scientist's direct gaze. Textually, the images are used in a way that is un-integrated with the identity of the overall design.

In the 2010 version (middle of Figure 2) more stock images are used. The main image is a stock image showing a friendly mature woman used to symbolize the subject group reported in the scientific findings that people get happier when they get old. Interpersonally, the pose and closer shot also create a sense of playfulness and increased approachability. It is de-contextualized as regards the background and brings brightness and optimism to the image along with the higher key lighting. The image does not document a particular person or scientific issue, but serves to engage the reader.

We still find the image for molecules, although this time it is brightly colored and more lively. We also find a much more conceptual use of these images, as in that showing a woman sitting at a table accompanying the story on abortion rates and anorexic women (the third one to the last). This is a highly stylized, attractive, extremely de-contextualized image, where the empty plate connotes 'diet' as the cropped person appears to sit in contemplation. In the carousel bar below the main image, a pile of computer keys are used for a story on spelling errors and a de-contextualized image of an attractive young black woman holding up a headphone socket plug (the third from the left) signifies black youth plugging into politics. Such images are a step toward more creativity and playfulness with representation. Ideationally, these images, such as of the black woman and the empty plate, have the effect of de-contextualizing science. The complexity of political engagement, racial inequalities and the marginalization of black youths, and tragedies of anorexia are concealed behind the playful images. As such images textually link as part of the design, they become seamlessly contained by the brand as positive-thinking 'science' alongside molecules and bacteria. At the bottom of the page we do still find one realistic image for the climate change story, though such images are later eliminated. Interpersonally, such stock images can also at the same time be as symbolizing a particular thing can 'evoke (other) moods and concepts' (Machin 2004, 330) such as pleasure, beauty, and glamour. Science here is infused with 'positive thinking'.

In the 2013 design (right of Figure 2), there are no longer any literal images. Here all images are not only placed into the design but also the basic feature of the design itself, carrying colors that link them textually across the composition. Modality here is low as they have been altered for color in order to make them brighter and to link across the composition. The symbolic use of the images has also taken on a new dimension. A de-contextualized image of dental floss (middle of the second row) illustrates gum disease; a 'welcome' door mat (middle of the third row) illustrates a racially mixed neighborhood. In place of the older typical image of 'molecules' for the top story, we find the cut-out of the burger to make a basic montage with the words 'eat, sleep, repeat' placed instead of the burger filling. This is a highly playful use of the symbolizing potentials of these images. This use in itself is important in setting up the interpersonal relationship between the site and its community of users, signaled by the salient POPULAR STORIES ON FUTURITY text box (right of the second row).

What we saw on the 2010 version as regards the simplification and linking of stories with complex backgrounds shifts to a new level. The stock images allow the 'welcome' mat to represent the complexities and huge range of opinions regarding the nature of living in multicultural cities. This can be placed as the same order of science as the study of molecules, influenza vaccines or a map of the United States to show its racial profile, although the ideology of making such a profile is hidden by the connotations of science and discovery that the page communicates.

Most importantly, overall these changes represent a shift away from more fixed and literal or indexical uses of images, to one where the ideational is much more playful, and where the interpersonal and textual role is much more important. This shift from visualizing the science world literally (i.e. present researchers, fieldwork and diagram about findings) to visualizing with stock images what science is concerned about (i.e. study objects or social phenomenon) and how science is related to our everyday life (i.e. the social significance of the findings) indicates a shift from hierarchical institutional discourse to social media discourse in the sense that the visualized science world is about 'us' rather than 'others' who produce the knowledge. And crucially these 'images-as-stories' can be transferred easily to create playful *Facebook* posts (see the third post in Figure 1).

Color

The changing use of color, in terms of ideational, interpersonal, and textual function is also important for shaping the way the stories and how they are to be used are presented. Floch (1995) stressed the importance of considering not only representation itself, in terms of the kinds of iconography we find images, but also the way this meaning shifts through how the images are then integrated into designs.

In the 2009 version, we find a clear intention to try to represent *Futurity* more as a magazine than a colder official news and information site. Science has tended to be more associated with cool and rational blues, but here the choice was for a brighter orange. In European history, orange has been used to connote enthusiasm, fascination, creativity determination, and stimulation (Gage 1993). It has become more common to find orange, along with yellows and brighter greens used in contemporary newspaper designs shifting away from reds and blues. Designers explain this as a shift away from formality and authority as part of more magazine look where news merges with interest items and lifestyle (Machin and Polzer 2015) and where readers will no longer relate to media that claim to present authoritative facts in isolation without engagement with the reader. Such expectations have been fostered by wider blurring of genre, by the culture of branding in the Internet and social media environment where a reader's interests, favored pastimes, and consumer behavior should naturally appear in one place.

The 2009 and 2010 versions also use black for box fills, which is later eliminated. Black can bring connotations of seriousness and when used with white alone it can mean measure, restraint, and subtlety as opposed to the fun or garishness of the wider color palette that is found on the later version. But black together with yellow is associated with danger. So in the 2010 and 2013 version, dark grey has replaced black. The design here has cleverly maintained the high contrast, but through muting the black to a grey the hazard association has been completely taken out and instead a notion of sleekness has been introduced. Muted blacks are also associated with elegance and urban chic and also with the whole field of online media. We find lots of white space on the page. White space is used systematically by contemporary designers to create open borders between sections of text, to spread out lines of text, and to provide space between text boxes and images. Contemporary designs may have large bands of space simply to suggest both lightness of the reading experience. It also creates a sense of 'room to think' of 'contemplation'. An older style newspaper design is filled with dense text in contrast and communicates the opposite, that it is providing comprehensive amounts of detailed information fulfilling its role as an informer. In the social media environment, designers are clear that the market for this is vanishing (Machin and Polzer 2015).

It is in 2013 that we see more systematic and deliberate use of color. First we find a greatly increased color palette. We find yellows, greens, and light blues. These communicate ideas and moods of optimism through their hue but the increase in palette itself indicates more lively moods, away from the relative restraint of 2009. This fulfils an important interpersonal function as regards the way that it addresses the reader not as a serious viewer seeking to be informed and learn, but who wants to be engaged at a lighter level of seek and dismiss, described by commentators on web-viewing behavior.

Also important as regards the shift in color choice is that in the 2013 design they are all neon fused. This connotes modernity, energy, and emotional vibrancy. Perhaps the most important change on the 2013 version has been the sophisticated textual use of color. Images, text boxes, borders, and fonts textually link and rhyme through color across the design. We find purple being used to link the words TWORK and REPEAT, in the background to the flu tablets, and in the background in the bee image. The 'bee' image (middle of the second row from the bottom) also links with the yellow in the top story text box, in the gum disease image, and in one of the objects in the background for the credit card and junk food images.

This textual use of color allows the brand to 'contain' contents as well as to communicate a particular kind of identity and user experience. This is not so much information but a branded entertainment package. These stories and what they are about, is re-contextualized through the use of the stock images. The textual linking of color also serves to ring them into the same category of thing as part of the brand.

So here, for example, the complexities of multicultural neighborhoods are represented by an image of a 'welcome' door mat. This has an ideological quality as we have established above. But the design element here then presents this as part of an interlinked design, where it shares features with bacterial research and further controls its nature, with each mutually confirming the other. What kind of science this is has not been so much overtly stated but has been communicated visually, which also points to the social relations between the site and its users.

Font and composition

Fonts too are used much more systematically in the later design. There is a much more restricted palette of fonts that are used to create rhyming and hierarchies across the page. While the increased color palette and the playful use of images suggests something less formal and serious, this more systematic use of fonts helps to create a sense of order. This is accompanied by attention to alignment and framing. In 2009, we find signals of formality and tradition though the use of vertical columns with discrete slim vertical borders as in older style newspapers. But we also find poor alignment of elements and use of symmetry. For example, the columns do not align well with the main image and the elements in the right-hand column do not align well with the elements in the left-hand part of the page.

In 2010, we find a shift to horizontal composition. Machin and Polzer (2015) show that designers explain this shift as one away from the kinds of compositions produced by older forms of print setting, regimented into columns, to one that looks more like a list and a set of choices. In the 2013 redesign, we find a shift to a grid look made of tiles, each of which can be used in a *Facebook* post and which in itself provides a textual link for visitors to the social media nature of the site. Here, apart from the headline, elements are for the most part placed into equally sized tiles. For example, POPULAR STORIES ON FUTURITY has become more equal to other contents raising the salience of the community of users. This look is also more akin to use in tablet and mobile devices where the tiles could be swiped across to see more. On the one hand, it signals clearly that there is user community which is engaged. On the other hand, this suggests not any order or hierarchy of reading, but a set of choices presented in neat, 'scan-and-go' packages. Again this form of organization allows contents to be textually linked as choices of the same order as tiles of the same size also create textual linking or rhyming, alongside that accomplished by color and fonts. On this particular page, therefore, the story on racial neighborhood relations is of the same order as children's diet, which is very much the case of social media posts, although we could argue this is problematic.

It is important here, however, that the basic grid is used 'playfully'. The tile of POPULAR STORIES ON FUTURITY and others are allowed to break the rules to some extent. In this new design some elements are able to leave their frames and even overlap into others. van Leeuwen (2005) explains this having the meaning potential of overlapping or bleeding of meanings. In tabloid newspapers, it is common to find extensive and even chaotic overlapping and bleeding to communicate, lack of formality, playfulness, and unrestraint/overstepping of boundaries. In contemporary designs aimed at upper middle class readers, it is common to combine careful design with some chosen and more subtle overlaps and bleeding. This is also important to signify openness and 'creative' without becoming bawdy and chaotic.

So, in sum, science shifts to be able to incorporate any kind of 'research', which is textually linked into the whole helped by color, font, and frames and by the low modality of the stock images. We find images that suggest more interesting and involved viewing points. Then items are presented as teasers and invite comment and opinion linguistically. This all builds to be more in harmony with social media rather than authoritative information.

The redesign of the Futurity news page

While the home page of *Futurity* has been redesigned, radical changes are taking place in its news pages. This is driven across news sites by the simple fact that individual stories and pages will as likely be accessed through web searches and through social media sharing as much as, if not more, through the portal of the home page (Machin and Polzer 2015).

In the earlier version, *Futurity* news pages adopted traditional news presentation practices where verbal texts play the dominant role and where images play a distinctive role as bearing witness where the contents are organized around vertical columns. The redesigns of the news page involve a shift to more images and their symbolic use, but it also crucially involves changes in the layout, which leads to changes of functions of images and image–text relationships (Feez, Iedema, and White 2008). And it is here where we see a gradual change culminating in the tile-look of the 2013 redesign.

In the 2009 news page, we find four major components in the page: the headline, the image, the verbal story and the comments. The layout suggests that the headline, the image with its caption, and the verbal story are three relatively independent semantic units, and the verbal story is presented as a continuous text unit. In this kind of composition, the image plays a role of providing literal visual evidence.

In the 2010 version of the news page, there is a shift to a Head-Tail layout (middle of Figure 3). The Head created by the white space and the positioning of the image and texts form a 'hypermodal nucleus'. To the whole news page, the nucleus form a unit, as the 'Head' of a Head-Tail page structure where the 'first screen' of the page is set apart from the remainder of the page with 'the information valued as of the most immediate relevance and importance' being placed 'above the fold' (Knox 2007, 38). The tail of the news page includes the remaining part of the verbal story, links to the original research article, and comments. And notably it is here where we do still find the more literal use of a photograph to shape a new genre of a 'hypermodal nucleus' (Zhang and O'Halloran 2014), which includes components of a headline, a university attribution, a verbal lead, an image, a caption for the image, and access to social media sharing. This emerging representational practice fulfills the information sharing demands of social media sites such as *Facebook* and *Twitter*. And of course it signals a discourse of engagement and sharing.

Particularly noteworthy components in the nucleus are the tools for social media sharing. As shown in Figure 3, below the verbal lead and on the left of the image, there

Figure 3. *Futurity* news page in 2009, 2010, and 2013.

are three buttons available for sharing the news in social networking sites: *Twitter*, *Facebook*, and *Google+*. The number of times the item is shared is auto-recorded and displayed, providing contextual cues of the popularity of the news as they are in Facebook posts.

In the 2013 version, the hypermodal nucleus evolves even more toward the design of a *Facebook* post, including the following components: (1) an image, (2) social media sharing tools, and (3) a verbal commentary. These components of the hypermodal nucleus take the form of a *Facebook* post and proceed before the news title. The nucleus is then followed with the news title and the news story. With the design, the news itself is read as if it is from a *Facebook* post to the news. The 'traversals' between the spheres of social media and science communication (Lemke 2005) are semiotically realized with the design of the news page.

Conclusion

The analysis of the visual design of the changing versions of *Futurity* home page and news page allows us to make a number of key observations, both as regards broader shifts in design brought about in the reader requirements in the social media environment and as

DISCOURSE AND SOCIAL MEDIA

regards the cultural shift in the nature of knowledge provision which has very specific consequences for the communication of science.

As regards shifting design, we have shown how visually such news sites need to communicate as engaging with a community of users, playfully, knowingly, and in dialog, rather than simply providing formal information. Here we find basic shifts in the way that design elements are deployed, which works as part of the integration of such sites into social media platforms. Design, however, is a complex social process concerning with issues of culture, esthetics, social structure, technology affordances, and many other factors. Adopting a discourse analysis approach, what we have achieved in this paper, unsurprisingly, is to reveal a small part of the story. To unpack the complexity, interviews with designers could bring out different stories about the design from interpretations by us as discourse analysts, as the book by Machin and Polzer (2015) reveals. Though in the current study, we were not able to present insights from designers and the administrators of the website, we believe such a direction would be worthy for further deepening our understanding about the complexity of design.

As regards the consequences for knowledge provision and science communication, we find that *Futurity* has changed from a kind of news sheet to what we call 'scifopost': the integration of science information into the design of social media post. Here, working in harmony with the design changes, there is a move from presenting scientific findings to, in the first place, building an intimate relationship with the users. Scholars have pointed to shifts in science communication to engage with the personal relevance of members of the public (Nisbet and Scheufele 2009). This shift to a 'scifopost' format, created with a social media mindset, 'facilitates social media sharing of the news and increases the happen-stance encountering of science information' (Horrigan 2006). Our analysis points to the way that science communication becomes part of the wider 'scan-and-go' culture of social media and the Web.

On the one hand, this raises questions as to whether it is a further challenge to the validity and ethics of the scientific community (Bauer and Gregory 2007) and where institutions must, in times of market pressures, gear up to this kind of dissemination of findings and the more playful scan-and-go sharing friendly subjects and formulations that are now favored. The 'social properties' afforded by social media (e.g. openness, flexibility, editability, and transparency) are noticeably different in nature from the established norms and routines of the science community (Osama 2013). The science community is often characterized by 'tendencies to control knowledge and work practices, top-down hierarchic structures, formal relationships, rigid, hierarchic structures, formal relationships, rigid information flows, etc.', while the social media is characterized by 'informal relationships among people, open and transparent interactions, flexible and participatory production of knowledge, etc.' (Osama 2013, 3).

On the other hand, could these 'scifoposts' rather draw a wider public into engagement with deeper encounters with science (Burns, O'Connor, and Stocklmayer 2003)? What we can say for certain is that these changes in communication practices, here observed at the level of visual design, are part of a dramatic shift in power relationships between official institutions and the public, the real consequences of which we may yet see. We live in a world of constant flows of communication, asking us to click and making attempts then to make us stay, extract a small slice of any remaining attention span that we have left, but where we have finite time. In this world the standards of visual design and its sophistication in the use of different semiotic modes will likely increase. But, put simply, this shift will surely have huge consequences on how contents can be presented. Dean (2012) has suggested that these processes may ultimately decrease the utility of ideas. But then this too should be placed in the broader context of the rise of global neo-liberalism and the shift in how societies are to produce, use, and make money from knowledge and education. As Dean suggests, societies in the age of global capitalism may no longer have a need to an educated middle class anyway: such needs too can be outsourced.

Acknowledgements

The authors thank Dr. Gwen Bouvier and the anonymous reviewer for their helpful comments on earlier versions of this paper. They also thank the website of *Futurity* (www.futurity.org) for granting permission to reprint screenshots of its web pages in the paper.

Disclosure statement

No potential conflict of interest was reported by the authors.

Funding

The study is supported by the National Social Science Foundation of China [grant number 14CYY061] and the China Postdoctoral Science Foundation [grant number 2014M550430].

Notes on contributors

Yiqiong Zhang is Associate Professor of Applied Linguistics at the Center for Linguistics & Applied Linguistics in Guangdong University of Foreign Studies, China. She obtained her PhD degree from the National University of Singapore in 2013 with a thesis titled 'Representing science: A multimodal study of science popularization on institutional and mass media websites'. Her research mainly focuses on MDA of web data. Her publications appear in *Semiotica*, *Critical Discourse Studies*, etc.

David Machin is Professor of Media and Communication at Orebro University, Sweden. He has published mainly in the areas of critical discourse analysis with a particular interest in multimodality. His more recent research is specifically about design in news. His books include *Analyzing Popular Music* (2010), *The Language of Crime and Deviance* (2012), *The Language of War Monuments* (2013), and *Visual Journalism* (2015). He is co-editor of two peer-reviewed journals: *Social Semiotics* and *Journal of Language and Politics*.

Tao Song is Lecturer of English at the School of English for International Business in Guangdong University of Foreign Studies, China. His research interests include English for specific purposes, discourse analysis, and translation studies. He is an experienced translator of science communication.

References

Allan, S. 2009. Making science newsworthy: Exploring the conventions of science journalism. In *Investigating science communication in the information age: implications for public engagement and popular media*, ed. R. Holliman, E. Whitelegg, E. Scanlon, S. Smidt, and J. Thomas, 149–165. Oxford: Oxford University Press.

Aral, S., C. Dellarocas, and R. Godes. 2013. Social media and business transformation: a framework for research. *Information Systems Research* 24, no.1: 3–13.

Askehave, I., and A. Nielsen. 2005. Digital genres: a challenge to traditional genre theory. *Information Technology & People* 18, no.2: 120–141.

Bateman, J.A. 2008. *Multimodality and genre*. New York: Palgrave Macmillan.

Bauer, M.W., and J. Gregory. 2007. From journalism to corporate communication in post-war Britain. In *Journalism, science and society: science communication between news and public relations*, ed. M.W. Bauer and M. Bucchi, 53–70. New York: Routledge.

Brossard, D. 2013. New media landscapes and the science information consumer. *Proceedings of the National Academy of Sciences* 110, Supplement 3: 14096–14101.

Brossard, D., and D.A. Scheufele. 2013. Science, new media, and the public. *Science* 339, no.6115: 40–41.

Burns, T.W., D.J. O'Connor, and S.M. Stocklmayer. 2003. Science communication: a contemporary definition. *Public Understanding of Science* 12, no.2: 183–202.

Carbaugh, D. 2007. Cultural discourse analysis: communication practices and intercultural encounters. *Journal of Intercultural Communication Research* 36, no.3: 167–182.

Couldry, N. 2012. *Media, society, world: social theory and digital media practice*. London: Polity.

de Semir, V. 2010. Science communication and science journalism. Media for Science Forum. http://www.mediaforscience.com/Resources/documentos/booklet_en.pdf.

Dean, J. 2010. *Blog theory: feedback and capture in the circuits of drive*. London: Polity.

Dean, J. 2012. *Communist horizon*. London: Verso.

Deuze, M. 2003. The Web and its journalisms: considering the consequences of different types of newsmedia online. *New Media and Society* 5, no.2: 203–230.

Feez, S., R. Iedema, and P.R. White. 2008. *Media literacy*. Sydney: NSW Adult Migrant Education Service.

Floch, J.M. 1995. *Visual identities*. New York: Continuum.

Gage, J. 1993. *Color and culture: practice and meaning from antiquity to abstraction*. Boston: Bulfinch Press.

Gregory, J., and S. Miller. 1998. *Science in public: communication, culture and credibility*. New York: Plenum Trade.

Halliday, M.A.K. 1978. *Language as social semiotic: the social interpretation of language and meaning*. London: Arnold.

Halliday, M.A.K. 1994. *An introduction to functional grammar* (2nd ed.). London: Edward Arnold.

Halliday, M.A.K., and C.M.I.M. Mathiessen. 2004. *An introduction to functional grammar* (3rd ed.). London: Arnold.

Hanna, R., A. Rohm, and V.L. Crittenden. 2011. We're all connected: the power of the social media ecosystem. *Business Horizons* 54, no.3: 265–273.

Hodge, R., and G. Kress. 1988. *Social semiotics*. Cambridge: Polity.

Horrigan, J.B. 2006. The Internet as a resource for news and information about science. Pew Internet Website. http://www.pewinternet.org/Reports/2006/The-Internet-as-a-Resource-for-News-and-Information-about-Science.aspx.

Julier, G. 2006. From visual culture to design culture. *Design Issues* 22, no.1: 64–76.

Knox, J. 2007. Visual-verbal communication on online newspaper home pages. *Visual Communication* 6, no.1: 19–53.

Knox, J. 2009. Multimodal discourse on online newspaper home pages: a social-semiotic perspective. PhD diss., University of Sydney.

Kress, G., and T. van Leeuwen. 2006. *Reading images: the grammar of visual design* (2nd ed.). London: Routledge.

Lemke, J.L. 2002. Travels in hypermodality. *Visual Communication* 1, no.3: 299–325.

Lemke, J.L. 2005. Multimedia genre and traversals. *Folia Linguistica* XXXIX, no.1–2: 45–56.

Lewenstein, B.V. 2001. Science and the media. In *International encyclopedia of the social & behavioral sciences*, ed. N.J. Smelser and P. Baltes, 13654–13657. Oxford: Pergamon.

Lievrouw, L.A. 2010. Social media and the production of knowledge: a return to little science? *Social Epistemology* 24, no.3: 219–237.

Machin, D. 2004. Building the world's visual language: the increasing global importance of image banks in corporate media. *Visual Communication* 3, no.3: 316–336.

Machin, D., and L. Polzer. 2015. *Visual journalism*. London: Palgrave.

Müller, K. 2011. Genre in the design space. *Computers and Composition* 28: 186–194.

Myers, G. 2010. *The discourse of blogs and wikis*. London: Continuum.

Nelkin, D. 1995. *Selling science: how the press covers science and technology* (2nd ed.). New York: W.H. Freeman and Company.

Nisbet, M.C., and D.A. Scheufele. 2009. What's next for science communication? Promising directions and lingering distractions. *American Journal of Botany* 96, no.10: 1767–1778.

Osama, M. 2013. The bureaucracy of social media: an empirical account in organizations. PhD diss., Linnaeus University.

Shi-xu. forthcoming. Cultural discourse studies. In *International encyclopedia of language and social interaction*, ed. K. Tracy, C. Ilie, and T. Sandel. Boston, MA: Wiley-Blackwell.

Trench, B. 2007. How the Internet changed science journalism. In *Journalism, science and society: science communication between news and public relations*, ed. M.W. Bauer and M. Bucchi, 133–141. New York: Routledge.

Trench, B. 2008. Internet: Turning science communication inside-out? In *Handbook of public communication of science and technology*, ed. M. Bucchi and B. Trench, 185–198. London: Routledge.

Tsimonis, G., and S. Dimitriadis. 2014. Brand strategies in social media. *Marketing Intelligence & Planning* 32, no.3: 328–344.

van Leeuwen, T. 2005. *Introducing social semiotics*. London: Routledge.

Whitley, R. 1985. Knowledge producers and knowledge acquirers: popularisation as a relation between scientific fields and their publics. In *Expository science: forms and functions of popularisation*, ed. T. Shinn and R. Whitley, 3–30. Dordrecht: D. Reidel Publishing Company.

Zhang, Y., and K.L. O'Halloran. 2012. The gate of the gateway: a hypermodal approach to university homepages. *Semiotica* 2012, no.190: 87–109.

Zhang, Y., and K.L. O'Halloran. 2013. 'Toward a global knowledge enterprise': university websites as portals to the ongoing marketization of higher education. *Critical Discourse Studies* 10, no.4: 468–485.

Zhang, Y., and K.L. O'Halloran. 2014. From popularization to marketization: the hypermodal nucleus in institutional science news. In *Critical multimodal studies of popular discourse*, ed. E. Djonov and S. Zhao, 160–177. New York: Routledge.

Žižek, S. 1998. *The interpassive subject*. Paris: Traverses.

Food fight: conflicting language ideologies in English and French news and social media

Rachelle Vessey

School of Education, Communication and Language Sciences, Newcastle University

Although social media provide new opportunities for minority language use and communication, the extent to which they differ from mainstream news media requires more investigation. This paper addresses this issue by comparing French and English language ideologies in Canadian news media and on Twitter. These ideologies are investigated using a specific case study where an Italian restaurant owner in French-speaking Canada was challenged for using Italian words on a menu. This generated extensive media coverage and Twitter activity. A corpus-assisted discourse study sheds insight on the complex dynamics of language politics and how they play out on different media platforms. It also indicates that minoritised groups are under growing pressure to translate linguistic cultures into English and globalised, market-driven contexts.

1. Introduction

In a recent report, the Canadian Standing Senate Committee on Official Languages acknowledged that social media pose new challenges for language rights. While the Committee's (2012) report observed the need for greater presence of French online, arguably of equal importance are the representations of languages online. Language representations can be used as a barometer, indicating the evolving ideological and discursive ecologies in which policies exist and to which they must adjust. Furthermore, although social media provide new opportunities for language use and for communication more generally, it is unclear the extent to which they differ from more traditional news media. Canadian news media have traditionally existed along parallel lines in English and French and these divisions could indeed be reproduced in Canadian social media, with concomitant divisions in terms of the language ideologies embedded in these media. Furthermore, as English continues to be the international language of communication, interactions between international English language media and Canadian national English-language media should not be underestimated. Thus, the aim of this paper is to compare trends in news and social media representations, English-medium and French-medium representations and national and international language ideologies. With this basis, the aim is also to gauge the 'barometer' capacity of social media, i.e. their status as indicators of new and evolving language policy contexts. To examine these issues, data are examined from media focusing on a specific 'language ideological debate' (Blommaert 1999) in Quebec known as 'Pastagate'.

In February 2013, inspectors from the *Office québécois de la langue française* (OQLF) sent a warning letter to the owner of the Buonanotte restaurant in Montreal for its use of Italian words such as 'pasta' and 'bottiglia' on its menus. When the owner tweeted a photo of the letter to his followers, it was picked up by local journalists and activist groups, which shared links to the story over social media several thousand times within the first day of the story breaking. The story was picked up by international news media and reported in as many as 14 countries and in a variety of different languages (Wyatt 2013). The negativity of international news and social media has been argued to have contributed to the resignation of the OQLF head Louise Marchand, the revision of OQLF complaint procedures and the abandonment of Bill 14, which proposed changes to Quebec's Charter of the French Language. With relation to this context, the following research questions are addressed:

- How are languages represented in news articles, news commentary and retweets of the news stories focusing on 'Pastagate'?
- Do representations differ according to the country of origin (Canada, USA, UK, France)?
- Do representations differ across languages (English, French)?

This paper proceeds as follows: Section 2 outlines the theoretical concepts of language ideologies and moral panics in the media; Section 3 presents the news and social data under investigation and the methods used for analysis; Section 4 outlines the principle findings; and Section 5 summarises the conclusions.

2. Context

The fact that 'Pastagate' had rather sudden and direct effects on Quebec's language policy demonstrates that language policies do not exist in isolation. Policies may be taken up to varying degrees depending on what Schiffman (2006) has called 'linguistic culture'. Linguistic culture refers to the 'sum totality of ideas, values, beliefs, attitudes, prejudices, myths, religious strictures, and all the other cultural "baggage" that speakers bring to their dealings with language from their culture' (Schiffman 2006, 112). Linguistic culture does not imply that culture resides *in* language (e.g. in grammar) but rather than language tends to be used as a vehicle to communicate the beliefs of linguistic communities (i.e. communities delineated by language use; Schiffman 2006, 121). In other words, policies may be understood and taken up to different extents if languages themselves are understood differently within communities, and especially if these communities tend not to share a common language. In order to effect change in understandings about languages, it has been suggested (Lo Bianco 2005) that concomitant with status, corpus and acquisition planning should be discourse planning: the planning of discursive constructions of languages in public discourse (Hult 2010, 158). The need for such planning is that uptake of policy depends on discourses on the ground, which require at least some degree of language management.

In Canada, the coexistence of official language policies (i.e. the Charter of Rights and Freedoms (Constitution Act 1982, s. 33) and the Official Languages Act [R.S.C. 1985, c. 31 (4th Supp.), which institute the official status of English and French] and multiculturalism policies [i.e. the Canadian Multiculturalism Act, R.S.C. 1985, c. 24 (4th

Supp.)] explicitly denaturalises one-to-one relationships between languages and cultures. Nevertheless, the notion of 'two solitudes' has been used to describe a Canadian divide based not only on language, but also on culture (e.g. Heller 1999, 143). Thus, it is possible that Canada's language policies are implemented within distinct 'linguistic cultures'. Indeed, the distinction between English speakers and French speakers is arguably reinforced by the fact that the majority of Canada's population claims to have English as a first language (57%), whereas only 21.2% claim to speak French as a first language and 87% of this population lives in the province of Quebec. In Quebec, the population is governed by an additional language policy, the *Charter of the French Language* (R.S.Q. c. C-11; henceforth, 'Charter'), which is known in English as 'Bill 101'; this is in place to protect and promote French in the province. Within these arguably distinct populations, beliefs and understandings about languages (i.e. 'language ideologies') may circulate through different mediums (i.e. English and French) and may affect the uptake of language policies.

3. Theoretical framework

Beliefs and understandings about languages have been widely studied in news media (Johnson and Ensslin 2007, Johnson and Milani 2010), although to a much lesser extent in the Canadian context. News media are understood to be a particularly valuable site for the study of language ideologies because they are places where public figures contribute to metalinguistic arguments about language and as literal texts they embody a particular ideology of orthography, syntax and usage (Di Giacomo 1999, 105). Also, news media are the product of the news producing community, where ideologies of language are part of journalistic practice (see Cotter 2010). The news media have also been credited with the creation of 'moral panics' (e.g. Cohen 1972) in society – and in particular moral panics focusing on language issues (e.g. Cameron 1995; Johnson 1999). Moral panics have been described as 'supposedly emanating from the ever-increasing moral laxity within our society' and they tend to involve the following successive stages: (1) something or someone is defined as a threat to values or interests; (2) this threat is depicted in an easily recognisable form by the media; (3) there is a rapid build-up of public concern; (4) there is a response from authorities or opinion-makers; and (5) the panic recedes or results in social changes (Johnson 1999, 2).

Moral panics in the news relate to what Fowler (1994, 91) has called 'hysteria': 'behaviour which attains autonomy, which sustains itself as an expressive performance, independent of its causes'. In other words, these are 'pseudo-events' – events that are only real in so far as they become topics within the media (Boorstin cited in Cotter 2010, 111) that become real 'discursive events' (Fairclough 2010, 94). When such discursive events focus on language and evolve into moral panics, these are forms of 'language ideological debates' (Blommaert 1999, 1). In other words, the media become sites and platforms for individuals to voice their language ideologies; i.e. make explicit beliefs and understandings about languages that more often tend to be taken for granted and understood as common sense (Woolard 1998, 27).

When moral panics about language evolve, they often involve metaphoric arguments about language and society that draw on language ideologies (Cameron 1995; Johnson 1999). However, according to a constructivist approach, the extent to which ideologies can evolve into moral panics depends on the interests of a particular group in promoting a problem, the resources available to them, the ownership that they secure over the issue and the degree to which their analyses of the issue are accepted as authoritative (Jenkins

1992, 3 cited in Johnson 1999, 21–22). Thus, the creation of a moral panic may be contingent on the extent to which branches of the media grant particular groups the time and space to air their views to specific audiences. Furthermore, in order for an issue to develop into a moral panic, a common language is arguably required to communicate the story to a wider audience.

In a globalised world, online transnational forums offer new and unprecedented opportunities for communication, interaction and the development of minoritised and even endangered languages (see e.g. Leppänen and Häkkinen 2012, 18). Nevertheless, the English language continues to have an important role as a medium of communication in international media. Also, English is also one of the official languages of Canada alongside French, and historically Canadian media developed along parallel lines in English and French (Raboy 1991). Web 2.0 provides affordances to minoritised languages and indeed more opportunities for Canadian English and French speakers to bridge the previously established 'two solitudes' gap that has been reinforced by the news media. However, it remains unclear if these affordances and opportunities are being drawn on by users. It also remains unclear the extent to which new and social media differ from traditional news media and whether these are simply being used to further the divide to a wider audience. Indeed, the fact that English Canadian media have ready access to an international English-speaking media audience suggests that English Canadians have greater capacity to propagate a 'moral panic'. To explore the extent of this capacity, comparisons of national and international, news and social and English and French media are required.

4. Data and methods

Online news articles were collected for analysis according to language (English and French), their place of publication (Canada, the USA, Britain and France), the scope of their readership (e.g. national and international news) and their focus on the 'Pastagate' story. More specifically, the *Globe and Mail* and the *National Post* newspapers are Canada's only two English-language national (i.e. national market) newspapers and both have some of Canada's highest average weekday circulation figures (*National Post:* 163,063; *Globe and Mail:* 346,485; Newspapers Canada 2013). In the USA, FoxNews.com is an English-language online news source linked to the Fox News cable and satellite news television network and is the sixth most frequently visited news website internationally (eBizMBA 2014). *National Public Radio* (henceforth *NPR*) is a national syndicator of public radio stations in the USA and ranks 669 on the Alexa Global Rank of most-visited websites in 2014 (alexa.com). The *Guardian* is a British newspaper and its website is the 10th most popular news site internationally (ebizmba.com). Finally, the *Economist* is a news magazine based in London; its website had an average of 7,860,671 unique monthly visits in 2012 (Audited Media 2012). In French, *La Presse* is the most widely read French newspaper in Canada, with an average weekday circulation of 241,659 (Canadian Newspapers 2013). *Le Devoir* is an elite Quebec newspaper with an average weekday readership of only 35,158 (Canadian Newspapers 2013). *Le Huffington Post Québec* is the French branch of the online news website of Huffington Post. *Radio Canada* is the French arm of the Canadian national public broadcaster. Finally, the *Nouvel Observateur* is a weekly French newsmagazine and the third most frequently consulted website for French information with 6,911,000 website hits in April 2014 (Mediaobs 2014). One article focusing on Pastagate was selected from each of these sites (see Table 1).

DISCOURSE AND SOCIAL MEDIA

Table 1. Selection of international news articles.

	Author	News source	Country	Date of publication	Web source
English data	Canadian Press	*Globe and Mail*	Canada	8 March 2013	http://www.theglobeandmail.com/news/national/quebecs-language-watchdog-head-steps-down-after-pastagate/article9513486/
	Nelson Wyatt	*National Post*	Canada	26 February 2013	http://news.nationalpost.com/2013/02/26/quebecs-pastagate-pr-nightmare-story-gets-60-times-more-coverage-outside-province-than-marois-investment-trip/
	Bill Chappell	*NPR*	USA	26 February 2013	http://www.npr.org/blogs/thetwo-way/2013/02/26/172982758/pastagate-quebec-agency-criticized-for-targeting-foreign-words-on-menus
	(No author)	*Fox News*	USA	22 February 2013	http://www.foxnews.com/leisure/2013/02/22/canadian-restaurant-told-pasta-should-be-in-french/
	(No author)	The *Economist*	UK	11 March 2013	http://www.economist.com/blogs/johnson/2013/03/language-policy
	Allan Woods	The *Guardian*	UK	1 March 2013	http://www.theguardian.com/world/2013/mar/01/quebec-language-police-ban-pasta
French data	(No author)	*Huffington Post*	Canada	18 October 2013	http://quebec.huffingtonpost.ca/2013/10/18/oqlf-modernise-pratiques-plaintes_n_4122643.html
	Émilie Bilodeau	*La Presse*	Canada	20 February 2013	http://www.lapresse.ca/actualites/montreal/201302/20/01-4623777-le-mot-pasta-cause-un-exces-de-zele.php
	Guillaume Bourgault-Côté	*Le Devoir*	Canada	8 March 2013	http://www.ledevoir.com/politique/quebec/372805/presidence-de-l-oqlf-louise-marchand-quitte-son-poste
	(No author)	*Radio Canada*	Canada	21 February 2013	http://www.radio-canada.ca/nouvelles/societe/2013/02/21/002-oqlf-buonanotte-plainte.shtml
	Daniel Girard	*Nouvel Observateur*	France	26 February 2013	http://leplus.nouvelobs.com/contribution/789937-francophonie-quand-le-gouvernement-quebecois-fait-dans-l-exces-de-zele.html

DISCOURSE AND SOCIAL MEDIA

Table 2.   International English-language news articles, comments, Tweets and word counts.

Article	Number	Word count	Comments	Commentary word count	Tweets	Twitter word count
Globe and Mail	1	732	92	3741	31	583
National Post	1	679	525	14,794	25	490
NPR	1	612	40	1795	99	1775
Fox News	1	262	4	81	9	192
The *Economist*	1	618	295	19,860	140	2627
The *Guardian*	1	764	539	14,525	247	4814
Totals	6	3667	1495	54,796	551	10,481

In addition, all publically available online comments on these articles were collected from the news websites. Also, the headlines generated by news websites through retweeting (i.e. the headline generated when the reader clicks the Twitter icon on a news story web page to retweet) were entered into Twitter and all publically available Tweets citing these articles were collected for analysis (see Tables 2 and 3).

Data were analysed using a form of cross-linguistic corpus-assisted discourse analysis (Vessey 2013) adapted for the different languages and genres within the data-set. For the corpus component of the analysis, data were analysed according to frequency and concordances. Words of high and low frequency are understood to indicate topics that are particularly salient (or not) within a data-set (Stubbs 2001, 166). A high frequency of references to 'French', for example, could suggest that this language is topical within a data-set, especially if this frequency is compared with that of another word (e.g. 'Italian'). Also, words that tend to 'collocate' (or co-locate in proximity to one another) are understood to indicate semantic relationships between words and may suggest the broader contexts in which a topic is being discussed. Semi-fixed phrases in the form of 'clusters' also indicate how these semantic relationships become fixed in labels or representations.

Since tweets consist of a maximum of only 140 characters and they tend to be highly repetitive (Zappavigna 2012), the Twitter data were studied primarily in terms of non-verbatim retweeting (e.g. original user content) and hashtags. Hashtags play a particularly important role in Twitter as user-generated searchable tags that have predominantly evaluative functions (Zappavigna 2012); these were analysed according to frequency and ostensible topicality.

Finally, the discourse analysis began by establishing which categories of lexical items dominated each article with the aim of identifying lexical chains (e.g. hyponyms,

Table 3.   International French-language news articles, comments, Tweets and word counts.

Article	Number	Word count	Comments	Commentary word count	Tweets	Twitter word count
Huffington Post	1	450	24	553	11	248
La Presse	1	394	0	0	44	1005
Le Devoir	1	577	16	1051	21	484
Radio Canada	1	551	160	7349	12	247
Nouvel Observateur	1	843	10	1015	10	220
Totals	5	2815	210	9968	98	2204

synonyms, metonyms) that contributed to the cohesion of articles (Halliday and Hasan 1976). In addition, representations of languages were studied in both articles and comments and analyses focused on the extent to which languages were represented as descriptors of people, institutions or locations, on the one hand, or stand-alone objects with or without agentive power, on the other. Above all, all analyses are comparative in terms of language (English/French), source country and genre (news/social media). The next section first outlines findings from the news articles, then the commentary and finally the Twitter data. Section 5 outlines the findings in relation to the research questions.

5. Findings

5.1. News article findings

The analysis, which began with the discourse analysis of English articles, indicated that the themes of control, negativity, international contexts and business permeate these data. For example, the *Globe and Mail* article uses adjectives such as *embarrassing, undesired, bitter, damning, [not] proud, aggressive* and *dwindling* and nouns such as *ridicule, symptom, controversy, incidents, headache, problem, difficulty* and *consequences*. The article also thematises control by repeatedly referring to the OQLF as the 'language watchdog' (four instances), which 'enforce[s] Quebec's language law'. The OQLF is imbued with the more general themes of negativity and control, as in Example 1.

> Example 1 (*Globe and Mail*)
> The head of Quebec's language watchdog agency has resigned after a series of controversies that created embarrassing headlines at home and abroad.

Similarly, the *Fox News* article evokes a highly monitored society through the use of words such as *strict, rules, forced, enforces* and *police;* these dimensions of control are mocked throughout the article, as in: 'All this ribbing caused the language police to eat their words'. The *Guardian* article also focuses on the controlling nature of Quebec, mentioning powerful social actors (e.g. *inspectors, police, transgressors, spy agency, top-court judge*), controlling actions (*protect, deploy, rein in, take on, conduct spot checks, break the law, force, undercut, order, wield the power, crackdown*) and general negativity (*scrutiny, complaints, picking a fight, outrage, unleash, tempest, outcry, frustrations, sinister, plot, perfect storm, failed, threatened, cacophony, severe*). The theme of control permeates *The Economist*, too, which uses negative adjectives (e.g. *[not] good, ridiculous, serious, not easy, bad*) and negative nouns (e.g. *ridicule, warning, violation, fine, incident, issue, distraction*) to thematise controlling actions (e.g. *forced, instructed, tussled, barraged, preserving, needed, toughen*). Finally, in *NPR*, the theme of control is again salient, with words such as *enforce, rules, guard, allowed, stricken, infractions, allowed* and *police*. The negative depiction of such control becomes clear with nouns such as *criticism, disbelief, outrage, barrage, complaints, problem, flap* and *debate* and adjectives such as *serious, sad, depressed* and *wrong*.

The juxtaposition of local and international contexts is also an undercurrent in these articles. For example, the Buonanotte restaurant is represented as 'trendy' (*National Post*) and popular with internationally renown celebrities (e.g. Leonardo DiCaprio, Robert De Niro, Bono, Rihanna, Jerry Seinfeld, cited in *Fox News* and the *Guardian*). More generally, the OQLF – and Quebec more generally – tend to be juxtaposed with an international, English-speaking context, as in Example 1. Journalists from the *Globe and*

Mail, NPR and *National Post* all stress the impact of international reporting of this story. In fact, the *National Post* article focuses on this topic and repeats the international media figures three times. First, the figures are cited in the headline (see Example 2).

Example 2 (*National Post*)
Quebec's 'pastagate' PR nightmare: Story gets 60 times more coverage outside province than Marois investment trip.

Then, the figures are mentioned twice in the article. Also, the *National Post* reinforces the importance of the international context (e.g. 'outside the province', 'trip', 'foreign', 'out-of-province', '14 countries' and '160 countries'), naming specific international destinations (e.g. New York, Australia) and using lexical and numerical quantification that stress the impact of news reporting(e.g. *multiplied, 60 times, significantly, 350, all, 12, 160, a period of, few months*).

Against such an influential international context, Quebec and its language laws seem rather marginalised. Indeed, the *Economist* seems to underscore this status, describing Quebec as 'barraged with English from *the rest of Canada* and from *the United States*' (emphasis added). Quebec is depicted as marginalised not only within 'a world where English is the language of business' but also within the country: 'Quebec [is] a former French colony conquered by Britain before it became part of Canada'. Similarly, the *Guardian* article seems to marginalise Quebec by indirectly contrasting the '*regional* Quebec government' with '*big* corporate transgressors' and '*celebrity* clientele'. More specifically, the journalist discursively amalgamates 'anglophones', 'ethnic communities' and 'English-speaking entrepreneurs and businesses' in Quebec with 'English voices in North America' more generally and contrasts this diverse and widespread group with 'French-language advocates and Quebec separatists'.

Alongside these other themes, there is also an emphasis on the importance of business. Although a focus on the Buonanotte restaurant and other restaurants, too, is unsurprising given the immediate context of Pastagate, most articles mention business more generally (e.g. 'other businesses', 'a business', 'companies', 'business owners', 'business partner', 'entrepreneurs and businesses', 'small companies', 'corporate transgressors'). Additionally, both the *Globe and Mail* and the *National Post* cite De Courcy's statement about the negative impact of the story on 'businesses, the Office personnel, the public and Quebec in general'. The *Economist* and *National Post* mention the Quebec Premier's (unsuccessful) efforts to drum up 'investor interest' and while the *Economist* notes that 'English is the language of business', the *National Post* suggests that the international media coverage could have an impact on 'business decisions'.

In contrast, *control, negativity, international contexts* and *business* are not dominant themes in the French news articles. The *Radio Canada* article discusses control to some extent, describing the use of foreign words on menus as 'allowed' (*permis*) but they 'must not' be dominant or replace the French (*ne doivent pas être prédominants ni remplacer les descriptions et explications en français*). Nevertheless, the majority of the article focuses on corrections and clarifications – that is, changes – being made to the OQLF procedures. For example, it is noted that the OQLF published a statement to 'clarify' (*clarifier*) its position and to 'admit' (*constater*) that the inspectors had been 'over-zealous'. It also includes a statement from De Courcy, the Minister responsible for the Charter of the French Language, who stresses that 'judgement and moderation' (*jugement et moderation*) must be what guide the OQLF and she is 'confident' in the expertise and work of the institution (*j'ai raison de faire confiance à l'expertise et à la qualité du travail réalisé*).

Similarly, *Le Devoir* explains that the Marois Government 'changed tack' (*a donné coup de barre*) on the OQLF following the departure of Marchand, who left her post following the Pastagate controversy. The article continues to note 'change' (*changement*) and 'review' (*révision*) and the 'creation' (*création*) of a new post dealing with OQLF service and quality. In *La Presse*, the actions of the OQLF are represented negatively as an 'error' (*erreur*), but the focus of the article is mainly on subsequent changes to OQLF procedures. Similarly, *Huffington Post* thematises change, using verb tenses (e.g. past and future) and temporal markers (e.g. 'until now'/*jusqu'ici*, 'now'/*maintenant,* 'from now on'/*à compter d'aujourd'hui*) to note developments in the OQLF. There is not, however, a contrast between negativity in the past and positivity for the future, because it is noted that historically the OQLF treated complaints 'consistently and equally in the same way' (*de manière égale et uniforme*) and now out of a 'concern for efficiency' (*souci d'efficacité*) the OQLF is developing a personal follow-up approach (*faire un suivi personnalisé auprès des personnes touchées*), addressing general and collective interests (*l'intérêt general ou collectif*) and improving the quality of services (*l'amélioration de la qualité de services*).

In contrast, the *Nouvel Observateur* is much more negative in its representation of events and it also thematises the international context. For example, the author notes that whereas the Pastagate scandal was a source of 'amusement' and 'derision' (*dérision*) for the international public, such issues 'often preoccupy' francophones overseas (see Example 3).

Example 3 (*Nouvel Observateur*)

Dérive ou vrai débat? Retour sur ces petites affaires qui animent beaucoup certains francophones outre-atlantique.

[Downward spiral or real debate? Returning to these little affairs that often preoccupy some francophones overseas.]

The contrast between a marginalised 'overseas' group and the international public represents francophones as isolated internationally. Furthermore, the journalist negatively evaluates the Quebec Government as 'poorly adapted' and 'narrow-minded' within an international context of globalisation and migration (see Example 4).

Example 4 (*Nouvel Observateur*)

Ces pratiques bureaucratiques absurdes donnent plutôt l'image d'un gouvernement étroit d'esprit et inadapté à la mondialisation. Elles découragent l'intégration des immigrants plutôt que de la faciliter.

[These absurd bureaucratic practices instead give an image of a narrow-minded government that is poorly adapted for globalisation. They discourage immigrant integration rather than facilitating it.]

The theme of control also figures in the journalist's account of a restaurant owner being required (*a dû*) to cover the English on his telephone and the PQ Government believing it 'must' (*il faut*) act to 'brake' (*freiner*) the growth of English and 'reinforce' (*renforcer*) the Charter of the French language. Thus, this article is rather distinct from the other French-language articles in its thematisation of control, internationalisation and negativity.

DISCOURSE AND SOCIAL MEDIA

Table 4. References to languages in English articles.

	French (*French/ francophone/s*)	*Langue française/e française/e*	English (*English, anglophone/s*)	Language (*language/s, linguistic/s*)	Italian	Other
National Post	2	2	1	7	3	0
The *Guardian*	9	1	10	9	5	0
The *Economist*	9	1	6	7	2	0
National Public Radio	10	0	2	8	2	0
Fox News	2	2	0	2	5	0
Globe and Mail	5	1	4	10	1	0
Totals	37	7	23	43	18	0

The second step in the analysis was to establish how languages were being represented within the articles. In the English articles, the French language is discussed most frequently, whereas English and Italian occur less frequently. Language more generally, though, tends to be the topic of discussion (see Table 4).

In most cases (18 instances), 'Italian' is used to describe the Buonanotte restaurant or the words or terms used on the menu (i.e. the words that were objected to by the OQLF). Thus, there is no mention of Italian outside of restaurants and Italian speakers do not figure in the articles. The English language, which is discussed more frequently (23 occurrences), is represented as a humanised language. For example, there are six references to 'anglophone/s' (in the *Guardian, Globe and Mail* and *National Post*) and references to 'English-speakers', 'English-speaking' entrepreneurs and populations and 'English voices'. Other references to 'English' suggest the diverse contexts in which English is used [e.g. it is an international language: 'in a world where English is the language of business' (*Economist*)].

The English language articles discuss French speakers less frequently than English speakers: there are only five references to 'francophones' and no references to 'French speakers' or 'French voices'. There are two instances where people are described as 'being' French (meaning, in these cases, French-speaking), but these in fact come from a restaurateur whose restaurant was targeted in OQLF investigations similar to those of Pastagate (see Example 5, emphasis added).

Example 5 (NPR)

'I love Quebec … but it's not getting any easier,' David McMillan, owner of Montreal's Joe Beef, tells *National Post*. McMillan speaks both English and French. '*My wife is French*, *my business partner is French*, my children go to French school, but I just get so sad and depressed and wonder, what's wrong with *these people?*'

Although the restaurateur humanises the French language by using it as a descriptor of his wife and business partner, he then distinguishes them from other French speakers ('these people'), who reportedly have something 'wrong' with them. In other words, the French language is not humanised in the same way as the English language is in the English articles.

Finally, references to LANGUAGE tend to be used to refer to language policies or institutions rather than to human or individual issues, and these tend to be negatively evaluated. The negative evaluation takes shape at the most basic level with the labelling

114

employed by journalists: the *Globe and Mail* refers to the OQLF as the 'language watchdog' (four instances) and all other articles use the label 'language police' (eight instances). The *Economist* explains that OQLF inspectors are 'known in English' as the 'language police', but later the journalist uses the term 'language police' without reference to the fact that this label is only meaningful to one linguistic community. Thus, the journalist (perhaps) unwittingly aligns with an English-speaking readership and perpetuates the negative representation of the OQLF as the 'language police'. All other uses of the label 'language police' fail to indicate that this is a term used (predominantly) by English speakers (i.e. not French speakers). Indeed, the *Guardian* journalist uses the passive voice to contend that '[t]hey are known as the language police', without indicating *by whom* they are known. The negative connotations associated with this label are reinforced by depictions of their aggressive military-style actions (e.g. 'deploys', 'rein in', 'take on', 'conduct spot checks'). The *Guardian* also describes OQLF inspectors as 'zealots', and the negative fanaticism associated with this label is in keeping with representations in other articles. For example, *NPR* discusses 'the government's efforts to *cleanse* [restaurants] of languages other than French' (emphasis added). Since 'cleansing' pertains to purification, this description implies that other languages are perceived to be impure and even dirty by the government; indeed, in addition to cleaning and beauty regimes, 'cleansing' also tends to be used within discussions of genocide (e.g. 'ethnic cleansing'), thus, *NPR*'s use of 'cleanse' is arguably part of an overall depiction of Quebec's language policy as extremist.

In the French articles, the languages most under discussion are French, Italian and English, respectively (see Table 5). The Italian language is the second-most frequently discussed language, but most references to *italien* refer to the Buonanotte restaurant (e.g. *restaurant italien*) and 'Italian words' (e.g. *mots italiens*) or the 'use of Italian' (*l'usage de l'Italien*) on menus. As with the English articles, then, the language itself is not really represented outside of restaurants nor are speakers discussed. Similarly, there are notably few references to the English language in the articles. For example, the *La Presse* and *Radio Canada* articles do not contain any references to 'English' or 'anglophones' and the *Le Devoir* article only contains one reference; this refers to the fact that the original complaint that sparked the OQLF investigations into Buonanotte pertained to the use of English – not Italian – on the restaurant menu. The relevance of this point is that it is English, and not Italian, that is seen as relevant to discussions of French.

Finally, most references to both *langue* and *française* tend to refer to the Office Québécois de la *languefrançaise* and the Charte de la *langue française* (Quebec's *Charter*

Table 5. Frequencies of references to language(s).

	French (*français/e/s, francophone/s, franciser/ francisation*)	English (*anglais/e/s, anglophone/s, angliciser/ anglicisation*)	Language (*langue/s, linguistique/s*)	Italian (*italien/ ne/s*)	Other (*grec*)
Nouvel Observateur	16	6	6	6	0
La Presse	4	0	4	4	0
Radio Canada	10	0	7	4	2
Huffington Post	3	2	2	2	0
Le Devoir	3	1	5	2	0
Totals	36	9	24	18	2

of the French language). In fact, 47% (or 17 instances) of *français/e/s* and 75% (or 19 instances) of *langue* refer to the Charter or the OQLF. Also, there are few references to francophones in the articles. Thus, similar to the English articles, there is a strong emphasis on Quebec language policy and less focus on French speakers. Nevertheless, there are also references to *francisation* ('to make more French'), which occur in the *Nouvel Observateur* and the *Le Devoir* articles. For example, the *Nouvel Observateur* discusses cases where restaurants were required to 'become more French' through changes to menus and signage. Thus, the 'objective of making more French', which is part and parcel of Quebec's language policy more generally, underpins descriptions of the actions and intentions of the OQLF and its requirements from the public. In other words, language policy seems to permeate the French articles not only in explicit ways (e.g. through references to the OQLF and the Charter), but also through the vocabulary used – and the fact that the act of 'making things more French' (i.e. *franciser, francisation*) is used so unproblematically by the journalists in question.

5.2. News commentary findings

Following the analysis of the news articles, the news commentary was examined in order to determine if the journalists' representations were corroborated by reader comments. Notably, in English the articles that received the most comments were international publications: the *Guardian* (539 comments) and the *Economist* (19,860 words; see Table 2). The high number of comments could be the result of the wider (and more active) readerships of these publications (see e.g. Marchi 2013), but the involvement of these audiences nevertheless indicates the international interest in and dissemination of the story.

The English commentary corpus contained 650 references to FRENCH and FRANCO* (FRANCOPHONE, 43, FRANCOPHONES, 41, FRANCAIS, 4, FRAN-ÇAIS, 4, FRANÇAISE, 4, FRANCAISE, 3, FRANCO, 3), 480 references to ENGLISH and ANGLO* (ANGLO, 36, ANGLOPHONE, 32, ANGLOPHONES, 32, ANGLOS, 17) and only 53 references to ITALIAN/S. In other words, there is a much more concerted focus on French and English rather than Italian. The most frequent three-word clusters also indicate some of the dominant trends in the data (see Table 6).

The most frequent cluster (I DON[']T) indicates the personal and subjective nature of the discussions in this forum, with participants claiming they don't 'understand' (2), 'believe' (2), 'see' (6) and 'know' (7). Other clusters, such as 'it's not', 'it's a', 'I'm not', 'is not a' and 'there is no' reveal the argumentative nature of this participant forum.

The second-most frequent cluster is THE LANGUAGE NAZIS (39 occurrences) and the bigram LANGUAGE NAZI* is even more frequent (56 occurrences). Notably, 96% (54) of these instances occur in comments on the *National Post* article and 93% (50) of these instances can be attributed to a single user. The (perhaps) less contentious label 'language police' (51 occurrences) is used in a broader range of news commentary: the *Economist* (24 instances), the *Guardian* (20 instances), the *National Post* (5 instances) and the *Globe and Mail* (2 instances). In some instances, commentators critique journalists' use of this label; in Example 9, the commentator argues that the *Economist* journalist should have avoided using such as 'nasty slur'.

Example 9: Contestation of the journalists' use of the term 'language police'

DISCOURSE AND SOCIAL MEDIA

Table 6. Ten most frequent clusters in English commentary.

Cluster	Frequency
I DON T	40
THE LANGUAGE NAZIS	39
IT S NOT	30
THE FRENCH LANGUAGE	30
THE REST OF	30
THE LANGUAGE POLICE	26
IT S A	24
I M NOT	21
IN THE WORLD	21
OF THE WORLD	19

It's a fun round-up, but I'm slightly appalled that a publication like The *Economist* thinks it's acceptable to dub the OQLF as the 'language police' – a monicker coined and championed by the reactionary Quebecophobe right-wing press of the Rest of Canada. 'Language police' isn't a neutral description of the OQLF, it's a nasty slur.

However, other participants support the use of this term, explaining that the OQLF inspectors 'have been called [this] for decades' and '[f]rom a bilingual Anglophone living in Quebec, plain and simple; the OQLF is known as the language police'.

Other notable clusters, such as THE REST OF (30), IN THE WORLD (21), OF THE WORLD (19) and REST OF CANADA (13) suggest the extent to which the theme of internationalisation permeates this data-set. Subsets of the cluster, THE REST OF (30), which include THE REST OF CANADA (12), THE REST OF THE WORLD (7) and THE REST OF THE COUNTRY (2), suggest that Quebec is often explicitly contrasted against other national (Canadian) and international contexts. Many of these explicitly frame Quebec negatively in such comparisons, as in one comment on the *Globe and Mail,* which laments 'A pity Mordecai Richler is no longer around to describe such nonsense to the rest of the world'. Also, FRENCH collocates with QUEBEC (57), QUÉBÉCOIS (22), QUEBECERS (8), QUÉBÉCOIS (5) and QUÉBEC (5) but it collocates far less frequently with FRANCE (13), CANADIAN (11), ITALIAN (10), CANADA (10), CANADIANS (9) and GERMAN (6). Thus, French is discursively linked to the Quebec context and much less so to general Canadian and international contexts.

The most frequent cluster containing FRENCH is THE FRENCH LANGUAGE (30), which tends to be used to discuss policy and the rationale for French policy – that is, the need to 'defend', 'protect' and 'promote' French. Similarly, the bigram FRENCH IS shows that a focus on – or debate over – French language endangerment preoccupies a number of participants, who discuss whether French is 'safe', 'worth defending' and 'going the way of hundreds of other languages [towards a slow and steady demise]' (see Table 7).

The focus on the wider context of French language endangerment indicates the overall lack of consensus about the status and well-being of the French language.

The language most under discussion in the French commentary is the French language, followed by English and then Italian (FRANÇAIS, 78; ANGLAIS, 29; ITALIEN, 25). The low frequencies of references to English and Italian mean that few

DISCOURSE AND SOCIAL MEDIA

Table 7.   Selected concordance lines with FRENCH IS.

```
the major neighboring languages. French is safe in Switzerland because it i
lar. Who cares if you think that French is not worth defending? The only fa
 worse) need support to survive. French is going the way of hundreds of oth
y. How is it possible then, that french is endangered in Quebec. It boggles
ctant to step up when they thinkFrench is being threatened.) . That criter
end it is a sterile debate. Fact french is being protected, or english is d
it just strengthen the idea that French is at risk in Quebec. If (as that s
own. >> Much to Quebec's credit, French is alive and well there, even thoug
```

patterns emerge from the data (e.g. there are no ANGLAIS or ITALIEN clusters). Most references to *anglais/e* occur within discussions of speaking (*parler*), writing (*écrire*) and 'using' (*utilise/r*) English. Discussions of Italian, like in the articles, refer to words and terms and the menu containing Italian. French, however, is more topical in the commentary data. Discussions of French tend to express concern over the protection of French and its role in society. Many commentators express embarrassment over the Pastagate context and condemn the actions of the OQLF. For example, OQLF inspectors are in some cases labelled 'ayatollah[s]', 'guardians' (*gardien*), 'police' and 'zealots' (*zélotes*) *de la langue*, and one commentator in *Le Devoir* says 'good riddance' (*bon débarass*) to the exit of Louise Marchand. Nevertheless, many commentators argue that there is still a need to 'defend' (*défendre*) French and the 'protection of' (*protection de*) French is important. One comment on *Radio Canada* argues that French has 'clearly regressed [...] in Montreal' (*le français a nettement régressé [...] à Montréal*).

There are also commentators who use the platform to lament the decline of 'proper' French. The voicing of standard language ideologies occurred in both Canadian (e.g. *Radio Canada*) and international (e.g. *Nouvel Observateur*) news commentary. In Example 11, a commentator argues that more must be done to ensure the 'quality of French'.

Example 11 (*Radio Canada*)

... De plus, au lieu de donner des leçons aux autres, nous ferions mieux de nous occuper de la QUALITÉ du français, dans nos écoles, nos entreprises. À voir des courriels qui circulent parfois, à faute échelle hierarchique, truffés de fautes d'amateurs, et des générations qui ne savent plus comment écrire une phrase correctement, pour moi c'est celà, le plus alarmant!

[... Moreover, instead of giving lessons to others, we would be better off paying attention to the QUALITY of French in our schools, our businesses. Seeing emails that circulate sometimes, because of hierarchical scales, riddled with amateurish mistakes, and the generations that no longer know how to write a sentence correctly, for me that's more alarming!]

The same commentator goes on to argue that he would 'rather hear English or Russian' than witness speakers of those languages destroying the French language (*J'aime mieux entendre les gens parler anglais ou russe que les entendre démolir la langue comme ça*). In the *Nouvel Observateur,* several commentators contest the journalist's negative account of Pastagate and argue that more must be done to speak and write French well [e.g. *il faut bien parler et écrire le français* (French must be spoken and written well)].

5.3. Twitter findings

The final step in the analysis was to determine how the story was taken up and shared on Twitter. In English, it was found that the *Guardian* was the most retweeted, the *Economist*

DISCOURSE AND SOCIAL MEDIA

Table 8.   Most frequent hashtags in English corpus of retweets.

Hashtag	Frequency
#LANGUAGE	29
#QUEBEC	29
#PASTAGATE	22
#NEWS	16
#CANADA	8
#FRENCH	5
#COOKING	4
#OQLF	4
#PASTA	4
#QCPOLI	4
#ASSNAT	3
#BILL101	3
#CDNPOLI	3
#DMCRSS	3
#ITALIAN	3
#LINGUISTICS	3
#MONTREAL	3
#POLQC	3
#BILL14	2
#BLOGS	2

the second-most retweeted and *NPR* the third most retweeted article (247, 140 and 99 retweets, respectively). Notably, the Canadian publications are retweeted far less frequently than the international publications: the *Globe and Mail* article was retweeted only 31 times and the *National Post* article only 25 times (see Table 2).

The most frequently used hashtags (see Table 8) reveal that language issues (e.g. #LANGUAGE, #FRENCH, #ITALIAN, #LINGUISTICS) and geography (e.g. #QUEBEC, #CANADA, #MONTREAL) are the most frequent. Another trend is a focus on Quebec politics (e.g. #OQLF, #QCPOLI, #ASSNAT, #BILL101, #CDNPOLI, #POLQC, #BILL14).

In addition to hashtags, many readers also expressed reactions to the story on Twitter by posting micro-comments asking questions (e.g. 'Seriously?', 'How ridiculous can one be?'), making exclamations (e.g. 'That's embarrassing!'; ''Hilarious!'), using repeated punctuation (e.g. '!!!!!!', '?????????????????????????'), or combining these elements together (e.g. 'LOL!!:-)', 'Laugh or cry?!').

In French, the most frequently retweeted article is *La Presse,* followed by *Le Devoir* (44 and 21 retweets, respectively). Although these figures are lower than the English retweeting figures, notably, national publications have markedly higher retweeting figures than the international (French) publication (*Nouvel Observateur,* 10 retweets). Unlike the English Tweets, the most frequent hashtags in French tend not to be very revealing because they are not widely used: only 18% of *La Presse,* 23% of *Le Devoir*, 17% of *Radio Canada* and 20% of *Nouvel Observateur* retweets use hashtags. When hashtags are used, they mostly refer to Quebec politics (e.g. #ASSNAT, 6, #POLQC, 6, #MAROIS, 2, #QCPAYS, 2) or Quebec language politics more specifically (#OQLF, 8, #LOI101, 2, #OLF, 1). Although the *La Presse* retweets tend not to contain hashtags, they do contain the most freely worded commentary: 34% of retweets include some freely worded commentary. Readers' comments tend to be negative and express embarrassment (e.g. '[it's] lucky that ridicule doesn't kill'; *Une chance que le ridicule ne tue pas!*), argue that the OQLF lacked judgement and wasted public funds (*une absence totale de jugement et un gaspillage de fonds publics*), and comment that the entire affair is 'ridiculous' (*Tsé quand c'est ridicule ...*).

6. Conclusions

To summarise the various elements of this study, let us return to the research questions. The first question asked how languages were represented in articles, commentary and retweets. Findings showed that the English articles depict English as a humanised, international language that is necessary for business and French as a marginalised, overly policed language. In the French articles, there is little discussion of the English language, and most references to French pertained to the current and proposed changes to language policy in Quebec. English commentators sometimes objected to the interpretations of Quebec's language situation, but mostly there was a large degree of unanimity in negative representations of the Pastagate affair. While French commentators often expressed embarrassment over the actions of the OQLF, there still seemed to be a consensus that the French language needs to be protected – both from incursions from other languages and from a general linguistic decline from the 'standard'. In contrast, many English comments indicate a lack of consensus over the issue of French language endangerment.

The second question asked if representations of languages differed according to the country of origin. Findings revealed similarities across English language articles and indeed across English comments and retweets that suggest a uniformity of opinion; more specifically, these texts are largely unanimous in their negative representation of the affair and their focus on the international and business-related contexts. Also, articles published in the UK obtained the most reader comments and the most retweets; one American publication (*NPR*) also obtained more retweets than its Canadian counterparts. In contrast, while there appeared to be consensus in French Canadian publications, these differed from the publication from France, which thematised issues in keeping with the English articles. Furthermore, there appeared to be less consensus between the journalists and the readers, with the latter expressing embarrassment and negativity. In addition, French Canadian publications did not obtain large numbers of comments or retweets, but the *Nouvel Observateur* obtained even fewer of both. These findings and statistics suggest that the English language may have facilitated the creation of the 'moral panic' through the dissemination of the story to a wider, international audience and the concomitant marginalisation of representations that predominated in French language media.

Finally, the third research question asked if representations of languages differed according to the linguistic medium. As already indicated, the English language data were strongly cohesive in their representations of languages and the Pastagate affair more generally, and while these were somewhat similar to the article published in France, the French Canadian publications differed in that they did not focus on international contexts, business or negativity. French commentators also expressed more negativity than their journalistic counterparts and they aired concerns about the decline of 'standard' French, which was not an issue in French or English news articles. English articles were widely retweeted and hashtags tended to indicate a focus on language, geography and Quebec politics; freely worded commentary tended to be more creative and expressed disbelief and ridicule about the reports. French articles were much less retweeted and contained far fewer hashtags and commentary; nonetheless, there were indications of negativity dominating the 'sharing' of this news story.

Although these findings help demonstrate the language ideologies embedded in this 'moral panic', there are limitations to this study. Only a small number of articles were analysed and it is debatable if all of these publications were comparable in terms of their genres (e.g. news magazine vs. news blog vs. news article) and their access to different channels (e.g. radio, print and online versions) and audiences (e.g. circulation figures). Furthermore, methodologically there were challenges pertaining to the application of corpus and discourse methods to these different data types (articles, comments, tweets) and the meaning of patterns within these different genres (e.g. hashtags, verbatim retweeting); it has not been possible to address these challenges in the present paper. Nevertheless, the findings of this study suggest some of the emerging contexts facing language planners and policy-makers in a globalised and increasingly interconnected world.

This study has indicated that nation states' ability to institute language policies and protect language rights are perhaps being curtailed by an international audience whose understandings of current affairs are driven by English-dominated news and social media. Language policies exist in a globalised world in which discourses specific to linguistic cultures compete offline and online to represent the interests, values and power positions of respective communities. In this globalised world, the dominance of the English language facilitates ethnocentrism not only in terms of (English) language use, but also in terms of common-sense understandings about languages (i.e. language ideologies), which underpin other seemingly unrelated issues and arguably foster cross-cultural *mis*communication. Therefore, the protection of language rights is not simply a matter of linguistic provision, as the Standing Senate Committee has indicated (see Section 1); rather, such protection is contingent upon complex, dynamic and shifting language ideologies in a range of different contexts.

While 'discourse planning' (Lo Bianco 2005) could perhaps contribute to the stabilisation of language ideologies such that they could become more conducive to language policy-makers' aims and objectives, the rise of user-generated media and Web 2.0 pose important challenges to language planning even in its more traditional forms (Wright 2013). Within this context, language planners will need to take into account global perspectives and the linguistic norms and values of the international community even when planning at the local level in order to avoid backlash similar to that seen with reference to 'Pastagate'. This tenuous balance between the global and the local is crucial for the future of language policy and planning, especially as language issues are reported in news and social media. Without language policies, media can simply become channels for majority and market-driven trends (cf. Kelly-Holmes 2010) – a means of catering to and favouring groups with access to particular communication channels for specific linguistic communities. The 'barometer' effect of the media reveals the intensification of pressure exerted on minoritised groups to translate linguistic cultures into English and globalised, market-driven contexts. In terms of research on the cultural diversity of human discourses (Shi-xu 2015), the case of 'Pastagate' reminds us that we, as researchers, need to identify, characterise, explain, interpret, appraise and compare discourses with reference to the local and global contexts and markets in which they operate and circulate in order to better understand intercultural dialogue and debate and to advance real inclusivity in an increasingly interconnected world.

Disclosure statement

No potential conflict of interest was reported by the author.

Notes on contributor

Dr Rachelle Vessey is Lecturer in Applied Linguistics at Newcastle University (UK). She uses corpus linguistics and discourse analysis to analyse news and social media in order to demonstrate how 'common-sense' beliefs about language are related to broader social issues and hierarchies within minority groups, national groups and a globalised world. In particular, she focuses on the role of former colonial languages (English and French) and their role in countries such as Canada. She has published articles related to these areas in the journals *Language & Intercultural Communication*, *Discourse & Society*, *Corpora* and *Multilingua* and her monograph is forthcoming with Palgrave Macmillan.

References

Alexa. 2014. *The top 500 sites on the web*. http://www.alexa.com/topsites, accessed on 4 December 2014.
Audited Media. 2012. *Consolidated media report:* The Economist *(Worldwide) as of December 2012*. http://auditedmedia.com/media/212062/economist12.12.pdf.
Blommaert, J., ed. 1999. *Language ideological debates*. Berlin: Mouton de Gruyter.
Cameron, D. 1995. *Verbal hygiene*. London: Routledge.
Cohen, S. 1972. *Folk devils and moral panics: The creation of the mods and rockers*. Oxford: Martin Robertson.
Cotter, C. 2010. *News talk: Investigating the language of journalism*. Cambridge: Cambridge University Press.
Di Giacomo, S.M. 1999. Language ideological debates in an Olympic City: Barcelona 1992–1996. In *Language ideological debates*, ed. J. Blommaert, 105–142. Berlin: Mouton de Gruyter.
eBizMBA. 2014. *Top 15 most popular media websites*. http://www.ebizmba.com/articles/media-websites, accessed on 4 December 2014.
Fairclough, N. 2010. *Critical discourse analysis: The critical study of language*. Harlow: Longman.
Fowler, R. 1994. Hysterical style in the press. In *Media texts: Authors and readers*, ed. D. Graddol and O. Boyd-Barrett, 90–99. Clevedon: Multilingual Matters.
Halliday, M., and R. Hasan. 1976. *Cohesion in English*. London: Longman.
Heller, M. 1999. Heated language in a cold climate. In *Language ideological debates*, ed. J. Blommaert, 143–170. Berlin: Mouton de Gruyter.
Hult, F.M. 2010. Swedish television as a mechanism for language planning and policy. *Language Problems & Language Planning* 34, no.2: 158–181. doi:10.1075/lplp.34.2.04hul
Johnson, S. 1999. From linguistic molehills to social mountains? Introducing moral panics about language. Lancaster University Centre for Language in Social Life Working Papers Series 105. http://www.ling.lancs.ac.uk/pubs/clsl/clsl105.pdf, accessed on 4 December 2014.
Johnson, S., and A. Ensslin. 2007. Language in the media: Theory and practice. In *Language in the media: Representations, identities, ideologies*, ed. S. Johnson and A. Ensslin, 3–23. London: Continuum.
Johnson, S., and T.M. Milani. 2010. *Language ideologies and media discourse*. London: Continuum.
Kelly-Holmes, H. 2010. Rethinking the macro-micro relationship: Some insights from the marketing domain. *International Journal of the Sociology of Language* 202: 25–39.
Leppänen, S., and A. Häkkinen. 2012. Buffalaxed superdiversity: Representations of the other on YouTube. *Diversities* 14, no.2: 17–33.
Lo Bianco, J. 2005. Including discourse in language planning theory. In *Directions in applied linguistics*, ed. P. Bruthiaux, W. Atkinson, W. Eggington, and V. Ramanathan, 255–263. Clevedon: Multilingual Matters.
Marchi, A. 2013. *The Guardian on journalism*. A corpus-assisted discourse study of self-reflexivity. PhD diss., Lancaster University.
Mediaobs. 2014. *L'offre exclusive Mediaobs culture*. http://www.mediaobs.com/titre/nouvelobs_com, accessed on 4 December 2014.

DISCOURSE AND SOCIAL MEDIA

Newspapers Canada. 2013. *Daily newspaper circulation report*. http://www.newspaperscanada.ca/sites/default/files/2013%20Daily%20Newspapers%20Circulation%20Report%20FINAL.pdf accessed on 7 April 2015.

Raboy, M. 1991. Canadian broadcasting, Canadian nationhood: Two concepts, two solitudes and great expectations. *Electronic Journal of Communication* 1, no.2. http://www.cios.org/EJCPUBLIC/001/2/00123.HTML, accessed on 4 December 2014.

Schiffman, H. 2006. Language policy and linguistic culture. In *Introduction to language policy: Theory and method*, ed. T. Ricento, 111–125. Hoboken, NJ: Wiley-Blackwell.

Shi-xu. 2015. Cultural discourse studies. In *International encyclopedia of language and social interaction,* ed. K. Tracy, C. Ilie, and T. Sandel. Boston, MA: Wiley-Blackwell.

Stubbs, M. 2001.*Words and phrases: Corpus studies of lexical semantics*. Oxford: Blackwell.

Vessey, R. 2013. Challenges in cross-linguistic corpus-assisted discourse studies. *Corpora* 8, no.1: 1–26. doi:10.3366/cor.2013.0032

Woolard, K. 1998. Introduction: Language ideology as a field of inquiry. In *Language ideologies: Practice and theory*, ed. B. Schieffelin, K. Woolard, and P. Kroskrity, 3–50. Oxford: Oxford University Press.

Wright, S. 2013. Status planning. In *The encyclopedia of applied linguistics*, ed. C.A. Chapelle, 1–6. London: Blackwell.

Wyatt, N. 2013. Pastagate: Quebec to review language law violation policies after PR mess. *National Post*, February 26, online edition. http://news.nationalpost.com/2013/02/26/quebecs-pastagate-pr-nightmare-story-gets-60-times-more-coverage-outside-province-than-marois-investment-trip/, accessed on 4 December 2014.

Zappavigna, M. 2012. *Discourse of Twitter and social media: How we use language to create affiliation on the web*. London: Bloomsbury Publishing.

Index

@-character 53–4, 72

Abati, R. 81, 82
abstract concepts/metaphors 52–3
abstractions 38
action panel 93
action-oriented de/legitimisation 17–18, 19, 20–3, 28–9
actor-oriented de/legitimisation 17–18, 19, 20–3, 28–9
affect 66, 67, 73
Aikhomu, A. 81
air passenger, wrongly suspected 59, 62
AKP (Justice and Development Party) 33–4, 41, 43–4, 45
Al-Maliki, Nouri 20–1, 24, 25, 27–8
Al-Qaeda 68, 70
Al Shabaab 68, 69–70, 71; stance in tweets 74–85; terrorist acts and bombings 69–70; Westgate Shopping Mall attack 74, 75–6, 78–9, 83–4
algorithms 5
alignments 19, 23–5, 29
Allan, S. 90
altruism 18
anonymity 7–8
anti-government comments 40–2
anti-government pop video 32–48
antiterrorism discourse 52–3
Anundsen, A. 55–6, 59
Aral, S. 93
Arewa, Republic of 76
Atatürk, Mustafa Kemal 33, 41–2
attitude 73; attitudes on Twitter towards Norwegian terror alert 49–65
attitude markers 73, 80–1, 84, 85
authorisation 17–18, 20, 22, 26
Ayro, Aden Hashi 69

Bamberg, M. 18–19
banking scandal 45
Bjørnland, M.B. 55, 56, 62
black 97
blame 60–1, 62
bleeding 98–9

blinding 40, 41
Blommaert, J. 2
Boko Haram 67, 68–9, 70, 71–2; stance in tweets 74–85; terrorist acts and bombings 68–9
boosters 73, 78–80
Breivik, A.B. 49, 54
Buonanotte restaurant, Montreal 106, 111, 114, 115; see also 'Pastagate'
business 112
Buzan, B. 49, 50

Cameroon 68
Cammaerts, B. 53
Canada 105–6, 108; language policies 106–7, 114–15; 'Pastagate' 106, 108–20
Canadian Standing Senate Committee on Official Languages 105, 121
Cap, P. 16
çapulcu 42–3
Carpentier, N. 35
Castells, M. 2
certainty, levels of 56
Chad 68
Charmarkeh, H. 2
Charter of the French Language 106, 107, 115–16
Chovanec, J. 17
clarification 112–13
clickivism 6
collectivised pronouns 36–7
colour 96, 97–8
colour palette 97
comment-threads 19–29
communicative capitalism 4, 91
communities: imagined 27–8; sociopolitical 19, 25–8, 29
composition 98–9
computer-mediated discourse (CMD) 66–7
connectivity 6–7
control 111, 112, 113
corpus-assisted discourse analysis 110–11
Couldry, N. 6, 91
critical discourse analysis (CDA) 32–3
cross-cultural sharing 3–4

INDEX

Crystal, D. 72
cultural discourse studies 50
culture: cross-cultural sharing 3–4; relationship
  to information 91; social media, globalisation
  and 2–3

dating websites 7–8
De Cleen, B. 35
De Courcy, D. 112–13
De Zuniga, H.G. 3
Dean, J. 3–4, 5, 6, 9, 34, 91, 101–2
de-contextualised images 95, 96
deindividuation 19, 25–8, 29
de/legitimisation 15–31
demotic turn 8–9
design, visual *see* visual design
discourse approach 1–14
discursive psychology 50, 55–63
distancing 58
Doctor, K. 5
Downey, J. 4

Edwards, D. 55
Egyptian revolution 10
elite, self-serving 41, 42, 43
engagement 73
English language: dominance 121; language
  ideologies 105–23; representations of 114,
  115, 117–18, 120–1
Erdoğan, Recep Tayyip 33, 37, 39, 41, 42, 43
ethnic minorities 60–1, 62
evaluation 72–3; of action 17–18, 21
event attributions 93
event comments 93, 94
event focus 93, 94
event society 9
evidentiality 67, 73, 74–7
existential threat 51

Facebook 5, 8, 9, 53; *Futurity* Facebook post
  93–4; *Futurity* news page designed as
  Facebook post 100; pursuit of power in Iraqi
  political discourse 15–31
Fenton, N. 4
Floch, J.M. 97
fonts 98
format tying 24
forms of address, visual 88–104
Foucault, M. 51
francisation 116
French language: language ideologies 105–23;
  representations of 114, 117–18, 120–1
Frith, S. 35
Futurity 89, 91–102; Facebook post 93–4;
  home page 94–9; news pages 99–100

Gales, A. 70
gender 51–2, 57–8, 62

genre 92
genre-specific roles 23–4, 25
Gentleman, J. 71
Georgakopoulou, A. 41
Gezi park protests 33–4, 42
Gilbert, M. 60, 61
Gillmor, D. 53
globalisation 2–3, 102, 121
Godane, Ahmed Abdi (Abu Zubayr) 69
Gonzalez-Bailon, S. 71
Goodluck, J. 81, 82
Google 5
governance 51
graduation 73
Greek crisis 41
group identity 70–1, 82
Gunkel, A.H. 6
Gunkel, D.J. 6

Hall, S. 45
Hardt, M. 3–4
hashtags 53–4, 72; 'Pastagate' 110, 119;
  #terrortrussel tweets 54–5, 57–61
head-tail layout 99, 100
hedges 73, 77–8, 80
Hilbert, M. 3
home page 94–9
Humlegård, O.R. 55, 56, 57
Hyland, K. 66, 73, 77, 78, 81
hypermodal nucleus 99–100

ideal identities 7–8
identity 2–3; group identity 70–1, 82; online
  performance and the online-offline
  relationship 7–10; positioning analysis and
  political discourse 19, 25–8, 29
ideologies 68, 70–1; language ideologies
  105–23
images 94–6
imagined communities 27–8
in-group members, representation of 17–18,
  24–5, 81–2
indexing responsiveness 24
individualisation 37, 38
'Infidel' attitude marker 80, 84
information-culture relationship 91
international context 111–12, 113, 117, 120–1
Internet dating sites 7–8
Iraq 15–31
Islam 33, 41–2, 71, 75; *see also* Al Shabaab,
  Boko Haram, Muslims
Israel 43
Italian language 106, 114, 115, 117–18

Jihadism 71
Johnson, S. 3, 107
Journal of Multicultural Discourses 1–2
journalistic model of communication 90

INDEX

Julier, G. 91
Justice and Development Party (AKP) 33–4,
  41, 43–4, 45

Kareem, Fakhri 27
Kenya Westgate Shopping Mall attack 74,
  75–6, 78–9, 83–4

Laclau, E. 35
language 7, 9; linguistic features of tweets 62,
  72–3; specialist 4
language ideologies 105–23
language planning 121
'language police' 115, 116–17
language policies 106–7, 114–15, 121
legitimisation 16; see also de/legitimisation
liberal Muslims 71
Lievrouw, L.A. 88
Lim, M. 10
Lindgren, S. 34
lurkers 3

MacDonald, M.N. 52, 53, 60
Machin, D. 90, 91, 98
Mali 67, 68
Marchand, L. 106, 113, 118
marginalisation 112
marketisation 90
masculinity 51–2, 57–8, 62
material verb processes 38
media practices 6–7
migration 2
minority language 7
modality 56
moral panics 107–8, 120–1; see also 'Pastagate'
multimodal discourse analysis (MDA) 92–3
Murthy, D. 8–9
music 39; see also protest pop video
Muslims: blaming of 60–1, 62; liberal 71;
  Shiite 25–6, 28; Sunni 21, 25–6, 28; see also
  Islam
Myers, G. 4, 91

Nairobi Westgate Shopping Mall attack 74,
  75–6, 78–9, 83–4
naming 6, 41
nationalist discourses 41–2
navigational dimension 92, 94
negative identification 26
negativity 58; language ideologies in news and
  social media 111, 113, 114–15, 116–17, 118,
  120–1
Negri, A. 3–4
neo-liberalism 2, 45, 102
networks 52–3; networked society 6
news 5
news articles 108–16
news commentary 116–18

news media 105–23
news pages 99–100
Niger 68, 69
Nigeria 67, 68–9, 75, 76, 79, 82; university
  closures 79; see also Boko Haram
Norwegian terror alert 49–65

Obradovic, L. 51–2
Office québécois de la langue française
  (OQLF) 106, 111, 112–13, 115–16, 116–17,
  118, 120
offline-online relationship 7–10
Omokri, R. 81, 82
online-offline relationship 7–10
online performance 7–10
orange 97
out-group members, representation of 17–18,
  21, 22, 24–5, 81–2
overlapping 98–9

Page, R. 8
paralinguistic devices 66–7
parallel state 45
'Pastagate' 106, 108–20
peer surveillance 56, 58–60, 62
'people, the' 35
performance, online 7–10
Pfeiffer, S. 6
police, Norwegian 49, 54, 55–7
political communication 67–8
political discourse 15–31
political economy of social media 4–7
political fronts 19, 23–5, 29
political participation 9
Polzer, L. 90, 91, 98
pop music: protest pop video 32–48; resistance,
  popular politics and 35
populism 35
poses 37–8
positioning see stance
positioning analysis 18–29
Potter, J. 55
power 2; pursuit of in Iraqi political discourse
  15–31; security and 51
prediction 17
presence 67, 73
privatisation 33–4
profit 5
pro-government comments 42–4
pronouns 36–7
protest movements 9–10
protest pop video 32–48
proximisation 17
PST (Norwegian security police) 49, 54, 55–7,
  62
public, responsibilisation of 51, 56, 58–60, 62

Quebec 107, 112, 117; see also 'Pastagate'

127

INDEX

radicalist discourse 66–87
rationalisation 17–18
reading dimension 92, 94–9
recontextualisation 17
recruitment 71
repetition 58
representation of in-group/out-group members 17–18, 21, 22, 24–5, 81–2
representational practices 90–1
resistance 35, 70
responsibilisation 51, 56, 58–60, 62
retweeting 53–4, 71; 'Pastagate' 119–20
Reyes, A. 17–18
rhetorical questions 59
Ringo Jets, *The Spring of War* 36–45

safety 57
'scan and go' culture 5–6, 101
scepticism 3–4, 91
Schiffman, H. 106
Science 2.0 88
science communication 88–104; in Web 2.0 89–90
scifoposts 101
scripts 7, 36
securitisation 49–65; conceptualisation 51–2; securitising actors' communication 50, 55–8, 61–2
security police, Norwegian (PST) 49, 54, 55–7, 62
self-mention 73, 80, 81–2, 84–5
self-serving elite 41, 42, 43
Sharia law 68, 69, 71
Shi-xu 68
Shiite Muslims 25–6, 28
social capital 8
social media 53–4; and cross-cultural sharing 3–4; globalisation, culture and 2–3; perspectives on 34–5; in political communication 67–8; political economy of 4–7; Web 2.0, representational practices and 90–1
social media sharing tools 99–100
society of experience 9
sociopolitical communities 19, 25–8, 29
Somalia 67, 68, 69–70, 75–6, 82; *see also* Al Shabaab
specialist language 4
Spring of War, The (The Ringo Jets) 36–45
stance 66–87
Stenvall, M. 52–3
stock images 95, 96, 98
Street, J. 35
Sudan 67
Sunni Muslims 21, 25–6, 28
symbolic gaps 4
Syrians 60

terrorism: attitudes on Twitter towards the Norwegian terror alert 49–65; defining 52; radicalist discourse and stance in tweets 66–87
textual use of colour 97–8
Thatcher, M. 45
threatening communication 70
threats: existential 51; radicalist discourse 80, 82–5
'traitor' naming strategy 41
Tunisian Revolution 67
Turkey: Gezi park protests 33–4, 42; protest pop video 32–48
Twitter 8, 9–10, 53–4; attitudes towards the Norwegian terror alert 49–65; 'Pastagate' 110, 118–20; stance in radicalist discourse 66–87
'two solitudes' 107, 108

Uganda 70
United Kingdom (UK) 45
United States of America (USA) 43, 70; presidential election of 2008 9
unproven events 52

vagueness 52–3, 58, 61
Van Dijck, J. 6
Van Dijk, T. 81
Van Leeuwen, T. 7, 17–18, 36, 99
Vatikiotis, P. 34
VG 59, 62
visual design 89, 90–1; *Futurity* science mag 91–102
visual forms of address 88–104
Von Hippel, E. 34

Web 2.0 5, 88, 108; science communication in 89–90; social media and representational practices 90–1
web pages: *Futurity* home page 94–9; *Futurity* news page 99–100; two-dimensional model 92
Western lifestyle 69, 75, 78
Westgate Shopping Mall attack 74, 75–6, 78–9, 83–4
Wetherell, M. 55
white space 97
Wodak, R. 7, 36
women 51–2, 57–8, 62
Wordsmith 84

YouTube 5, 53; analysis of YouTube comments 39–45; Turkish protest pop video 32–48
Yusuf, Mohammed 68

Zappavigna, M. 72–3, 110
Zhao, S. 8
Žižek, S. 3, 6, 91